Spirituality, Corporate Culture, and American Business

Critiquing Religion: Discourse, Culture, Power

Series editor: Craig Martin

Critiquing Religion: Discourse, Culture, Power publishes works that historicize both religions and modern discourses on "religion" that treat it as a unique object of study. Using diverse methodologies and social theories, volumes in this series view religions and discourses on religion as commonplace rhetorics, authenticity narratives, or legitimating myths which function in the creation, maintenance, and contestation of social formations. Works in the series are on the cutting-edge of critical scholarship, regarding "religion" as just another cultural tool used to gerrymander social space and distribute power relations in the modern world. *Critiquing Religion: Discourse, Culture, Power* provides a unique home for reflexive, critical work in the field of religious studies.

Spirituality, Corporate Culture, and American Business

The Neoliberal Ethic and the Spirit of Global Capital

James Dennis LoRusso

BLOOMSBURY ACADEMIC
LONDON • NEW YORK • OXFORD • NEW DELHI • SYDNEY

BLOOMSBURY ACADEMIC
Bloomsbury Publishing Plc
50 Bedford Square, London, WC1B 3DP, UK
1385 Broadway, New York, NY 10018, USA

BLOOMSBURY, BLOOMSBURY ACADEMIC and the Diana logo are
trademarks of Bloomsbury Publishing Plc

First published in Great Britain 2017
Paperback edition first published 2018

Series design by Dani Leigh
Cover image © Yddet Maryann Bermeo / EyeEm / gettyimages.co.uk

A catalogue record for this book is available from the British Library.

ISBN: HB: 978-1-3500-0627-0
PB: 978-1-3500-8120-8
ePDF: 978-1-3500-0625-6
ePub: 978-1-3500-0626-3

Names: LoRusso, James Dennis, author.
Title: Spirituality, corporate culture and American business: the neoliberal
ethic and the spirit of global capital / James Dennis LoRusso.
Description: London, UK; New York, NY, USA: Bloomsbury Academic, an imprint
of Bloomsbury Publishing, Plc, [2017] | Series: Critiquing religion:
discourse, culture, power; 3 | Includes bibliographical references and index.
Identifiers: LCCN 2016039049| ISBN 9781350006270 (hb) |
ISBN 9781350006256 (epdf)
Subjects: LCSH: Religion in the workplace. | Corporate culture. |
Business–Religious aspects. | Management–Religious aspects. | Business
ethics. | Neoliberalism.
Classification: LCC BL65.W67 L67 2017 | DDC 201/.73—dc23

Series: Critiquing Religion: Discourse, Culture, Power

Typeset by Newgen Knowledge Works (P) Ltd., Chennai, India

To find out more about our authors and books visit
www.bloomsbury.com and sign up for our newsletters.

Contents

Acknowledgments

This book has benefitted greatly from the careful guidance and generous support of a number of individuals and organizations. I would like to begin by thanking series editor, Craig Martin, for his continued support of my scholarship over the years and for the opportunity to be a a an inaugural author for this new series on *Critiquing Religion: Discourse, Power, Culture.*

Also, I must recognize my long-time mentor, dear friend, and colleague, Dr. Louis A. Ruprecht, Jr., William Suttles Chair of Georgia State University. Lou, more than any other individual, has been integral to my development as a scholar over the last decade. He has been an ever-present sounding board for this project since its inception and continues to create opportunities for my professional development.

In addition, I would like to acknowledge the ongoing feedback I have received from Dr. Bobbi Patterson, who has offered helpful comments in transitioning my dissertation project into this publication. My dissertation advisor, Dr. Gary M. Laderman, chair of the Religion Department at Emory University, also deserves my sincerest gratitude for all he has done for my growth as a scholar.

I would especially like to include a thanks to several people affiliated with the Center for the Study of Religion at Princeton University on whose support I have greatly depended on for completing this book. First, I am most grateful Dr. Robert Wuthnow and all of my colleagues in the Religion and Public Life Seminar who took the time to offer very helpful feedback for individual chapters. Also, thanks to the participants in the American Religion Workshop in Princeton's Religion Department and, in particular, Dr. Judith Weisenfeld for inviting me to share my work with seminar.

To Dr. David Miller, the director of Princeton University's Faith and Work Initiative, I am ever grateful for all of the ongoing support and confidence that he has consistently imparted to me. David has been one my biggest cheerleaders over these last two years, and although we had many other competing projects in need of completion, he ensured that I have the free time and flexibility to complete this manuscript. So, for that, and countless other reasons, thank you, David.

Others in the academy that have helped along the way and deserve special mention are Andrew Durdin, Ben Brazil, Bethany Moreton, Christopher White, Dan Macnamara, Faith Ngunjiri, George Gonzalez, Lake Lambert, Michael Thate, Steven Tipton, and many more.

Also, I must also extend thanks to those that took the time to participate my research, including Matthew and Terces Engelhart and everyone at Gracias Madre with whom I spoke, Les Kaye and Kannon Do Zen Meditation Center, Judi Neal, Alan Lurie, Peter Roche, and Marc Miller.

On a personal note, I would like to thank my family, starting with my parents, Jim and Pat LoRusso, who have always given me their unconditional support throughout my many vocational lives. They have always encouraged me in all my endeavors (even when it may have been nothing more than a fool's errand) and continue to inspire me to excel. I also wish to offer special thanks to my brother, Steve, his wife, Takesia, and their two children, Taquilla and Alyssa, for being a source of true happiness in my life.

Finally, I dedicate this book to my life partner, my wife Rebecca, who has always created an environment in which my intellectual efforts could succeed. I am forever thankful for her willingness to embrace the often unpredictable realities of being married to an academic. Thank you for being my best friend and for laboring alongside me to make all of this possible.

Introduction

In November of 2011, I was invited to Fayetteville, Arkansas to present a short paper at the annual *International Faith and Spirit at Work* Conference sponsored by the Tyson Center for Faith and Spirituality in the Workplace at the University of Arkansas. The center, founded in 2006, is affiliated with the Sam M. Walton College of Business and aspires to be "a nexus for thought leaders to exchange views and encourage research projects around faith and spirituality in the workplace."[1] At the conference, I would be discussing some of previous ethnographic research on the corporate culture of Starbucks Coffee Company, which I had conducted several years earlier in completing a graduate thesis. The contrast between my departure from LaGuardia International Airport in Queens, New York and my arrival at Northwest Arkansas Regional Airport could not have been more striking. I left behind a cacophony of taxis and rushed passengers with baggage barely in tow for a modest, single-terminal building surrounded by wide-open cow pastures. Excited to finally discuss the intersection of spirituality and business with like-minded specialists, I anticipated the insights I might acquire, the new directions to which the intellectual exchanges would lead. Indeed, the conference would prove to be a pivotal point in my research, but not quite in the way I had imagined.

While I expected an interdisciplinary crowd and perhaps even some non-academics to be in attendance, I was unprepared (somewhat naively in hindsight) for the strong sense of advocacy that defined the conference. As we convened for the inaugural address that first evening, management scholars sat beside entrepreneurs and business leaders, as well as theologians and religious leaders. Involvement was truly international. A number of individuals travelled from Europe to take part, and I heard research from two individuals based in Australia. Yet, I found it mildly unsettling that, at a conference on religion, I encountered not a single individual scholar of religion. All the notable guests were public advocates of workplace spirituality, some of whom will be discussed in subsequent chapters. For instance, the Director of the Tyson Center and host of the conference was Judi Neal, who has been instrumental in making spirituality an accepted topic for management scholarship. Alan Lurie, an ordained Rabbi and New York real estate executive, was present to receive the first annual "International Faith and Spirit at Work Leadership Award." I soon realized that this amalgam of voices was coming together not to necessarily understand the role of faith and spirituality in the workplace but to celebrate it. The conference was event of collective effervescence, to reinforce a group identity around a shared discourse, a sense of common origin and future trajectory.

This ritual process began immediately on that first evening. David Wetton, an interfaith minister and founder of an online consulting service *Spirit in Work*, convened the conference with an "inspiration," reading several stanzas of a poem called "Blessing for a Leader."[2] As I soon learned, each day of the conference began and ended with a similar inspiration from a religious figure, marking off the space and time of conference events as exceptional, a Durkheimian sense of the sacred.

After this inspiration, our host Judi Neal took the stage to celebrate the year's honoree, Alan Lurie. On the projection screen, a photograph of a middle-aged white man appeared, and, Neal posed a question to the audience, "Do any of you know who Willis Harman is?" While a scattered number of hands went up across the room, the majority exhibited no movement. Pointing to the photo, Neal described how Harman, an engineer turned futures researcher, was her mentor and a pioneer of the "movement." He had, she claimed, "discovered human potential," as far back as the 1950s and was one of the earliest proponents of bringing faith and spirituality into the workplace. In fact, she continued, Harman was the inspiration for the award that Lurie was receiving. By introducing Harman, Neal was crafting a sense of history. She had named the movement's founder, who, although deceased, could now be brought to life as a symbol. Moreover, in accepting the award from Neal, Alan Lurie was also accepting the mantle of Harman's legacy, emphasizing the historical continuity between himself and the founder. Finally, as witnesses to this even, the audience likewise become a part of this history.

Following the awards ceremony, Neal offered her formal welcoming remarks to the audience. She expressed concern for the future of the world, citing the countless challenges facing humankind. "Business," she concluded, "is the way we can transform consciousness precisely because it is so powerful today." In this bold statement lies a central theme of this book, that the increasing business interest in spirituality is a reflection of its global dominance. The ideas, institutions, and individuals detailed in subsequent chapters all support the premise that business is the institution best suited to bring about a prosperous future for the world. In the context of the conference, Neal's bold declaration passed unassumingly, as if it were simply self-evident. The power of the statement lay hidden, just as the nexus of power behind the conference itself remained in the shadows.

The University of Arkansas is a particularly significant location for conference, situated in the city Fayetteville, only a few miles south of Springdale, Arkansas which boasts the headquarters of Tyson Foods, the world's largest food processing corporation as well as the primary underwriter for the aptly named Tyson Center. Just a few miles further north from Springdale lies Bentonville, where the corporate headquarters of the world's largest retailer, Wal-Mart, can be found. The fact that the university's business school, home of the Tyson Center, bears the Walton name hints at some of the deeper connections between corporate interest in spirituality and global business interests.

As historian Bethany Moreton has documented, businesses of the American Mid-South have played an influential role in bolstering business education in the region. An unprecedented gift of fifty million dollars from the Walton family to the University of Arkansas in 1998, for example, established the Sam Walton College of Business.[3] In *To Serve God and Wal-Mart* (2009), Moreton argues that regional business brought a commitment to "Christian free enterprise," an wiledy devotion to entrepreneurship couched in a regional evangelical populism.[4] Perhaps it is no surprise, therefore that, funding from Tyson Foods had made the center and the conference possible.

This connection between the conference and global business manifested in the parade of corporate leaders that delivered keynote addresses. Day one featured John Tyson, chairman of Tyson Foods, who spoke about his company's efforts to create a "faith-friendly" workplace through an extensive corporate chaplaincy program. He recounted an incident at one of their processing plants where a chaplain helped to resolve a dispute between management and several Muslim employees over daily prayer accommodations. For Tyson, the episode evidenced the positive effect of bringing faith onto the factory floor. However, he avoided any mention of the complicated spaces that chaplains have to negotiate as paid company employees who must at times consider the interests of workers. Tyson remarked that the chaplaincy program offers employees "a sense that they are being listened to," but this obscures the fact that these chaplains must always listen through a filter constrained by interests of the company. Such programs appeal to the cultural authority of religion in order to effectively reinforce the established power relations of the organization—another central theme of this book. The "sense" of dignity is not quite dignity realized.

While Tyson's speech was revealing, it was Don Soderquist's keynote address the next afternoon that most readily shaped the overall argument of this project. A retired Wal-Mart executive, Soderquist embodied Moreton's description of "Christian free enterprise." He described in his speech how Wal-Mart's "Judeo-Christian culture" accounted for its success and stressed that "Wal-Mart believes it has a responsibility to God to take care of the planet." Yet, when one audience member asked if Wal-Mart has helped or hindered the plight of the poor with its commitment to low-cost goods and services, especially in light of the "Occupy St." protests that had recently occurred, Soderquist responded with force:

> I have an obligation to provide the same opportunity to others, but not an obligation to provide wealth...Poverty is a mentality, a cycle. People can break out of this cycle, because everyone has a chance to make it. I don't know about this inequality deal, it's not right to take away and give to people who don't want to work...There's too much welfare already.

His remarks disarmed the audience, including myself. We exchanged looks of disbelief and whispered words of dismay at his attitude toward the poor. In the midst of this atmosphere of benevolent care, here was a successful business leader who exhibited great respect for his religious beliefs, but adamantly condemned state-sponsored redistribution as coercive, government overreach. As I pondered the importance of this episode, it occurred to me that he had exposed something crucial about this corporate interest in spirituality that typically remained concealed. The audience, and the movement more broadly, evince a rather liberal political orientation that obscures *its complicity with neoliberalism.*

Yet, when Soderquist reduced poverty to a mentality, a cycle from which one can freely escape, he sounded remarkably similar to Judi Neal who declared that world's problems could be solved with only a shift in "consciousness." At the heart of this entanglement of business and spirituality is common assumption that suffering is simply matter of perspective, that spiritual practice can correct, and business, under the guidance of spiritually attuned leaders and free of the constraints of the welfare state, can lead the way to this new order, in which individuals are truly free to pursue the good, and where human flourishing unfolds through the mechanisms of the global marketplace.

A new religious movement? A progressive business practice? Or capitalist appropriation?

The conference and its assorted mixture of participants speak to a much wider set of discussions taking place about the role of spirituality and business. For instance, the nonprofit Institute for Mindful Leadership offers a variety of course that instruct managers and business leaders in mindfulness practices.[5] The institute's executive director Janet Maturano, a former manager at General Mills, has provided this training for a number of major corporations, including Proctor & Gamble, Target, and the American Red Cross.[6] In fact, the World Economic Forum in Davos, Switzerland even featured one of her workshops, "Finding the Space to Lead," at their 2013 annual meeting.[7]

In the wake of the financial crisis of 2008, the World Economic Forum launched the Global Agenda Council on Faith and Values to address the ethical deficiencies that contributed to the collapse of financial institutions and housing markets.[8] Furthermore, annual meetings now invite representatives from religious and spiritual organizations. The Archbishop of Dublin, a founder of a New Mexico Buddhist Center, and Evangelical Christian minister Jim Wallis, were among the attendees of the 2011 Conference, while in January of 2014, actress Goldie Hawn opened the morning session with a guided meditation for approximately sixty participants.[9] The inclusion of religious dignitaries and spiritual practices on the agenda of Davos suggests that the Arkansas conference is part of a much larger trend.

Scholars who have documented the business turn to spirituality generally agree that this phenomenon originated sometime in the late 1980s or early 1990s and continued to grow into the new millennium.[10] However, they provide a wide range of explanations for its genesis and evolution. Scholars of management have proven particularly interested in the topic of what they often refer to as "workplace spirituality," arguing that business leaders and manager have an obligation to attend to the spiritual needs of their employees. As one business scholar articulated, the "psychological contract for work" since the late 1980s has irreversibly changed, encouraging individuals to depend less on the secure corporate career and draw resolve from within, "from their spirituality" to find meaning and purpose in their working lives.[11] Sociologist Douglas Hicks points to shifting social changes like new immigration patterns and the permeation of women and minorities into the workforce. The resulting demographic and cultural diversity has challenged businesses to respond by acknowledging the spiritual perspectives of employees.[12] Conversely, David Miller, the director of Princeton University's "Faith and Work Initiative," suggests that "tectonic changes to information technology, telecommunications, transportation, manufacturing, globalization, and political ideologies began to challenge old paradigms and fundamentally transform how we work and the society in which we live."[13] Religious scholar Lake Lambert emphasizes a Protestant origin for this "workplace spirituality," tracing current American attitudes about work to Puritan notions or work as "vocation" or "calling." His book *Spirituality Inc.* (2009) describes workplace spirituality as a new religious movement taking shape in American business.

Other scholars take a more critical approach than Lambert or Miller, citing business interest in spirituality a form of social control and exploitation of labor. In *Selling Spirituality* (2005), Jeremy Carrette and Richard King describe this trend as a corporate cooptation of religious practices, teachings by the capitalist marketplace. The authors maintain that in successfully commercializing "religion," businesses have pacified and depoliticize its content, resulting in a variety of sanitized "capitalist spiritualties." In short, King and Carrette depict this phenomenon as a predictable outcome of capitalist societies where religion is subject to the logic of the marketplace. Corporations in due course have adapted "spirituality" to increase productivity and reduce work-related distress in the pursuit of higher profits.[14]

These studies provide helpful insights about the history of spirituality in American business, yet they could easily be describing entirely different social phenomena. When, for instance, David Miller details the "faith and work movement," he discusses something that only marginally overlaps with what management scholars label "workplace spirituality." In *God at Work*, because he "focuses largely on the Christian dimension of the movement, with recognition of and reference to other religions and forms of spirituality in the movement," Miller assembles a history in which the key players, institutions, and assumptions about concepts like "faith" and "work" bear a decidedly Protestant, professional, white, and male bias. In privileging the voices of Protestant business elites, Miller consequently overlooks the potential insight from differences of class, gender, and culture.

Business researchers, on the other hand, are keenly interested in distinguishing "spirituality" from "religion." Ian Mitroff and Elizabeth Denton, for example, claim that "organizations and formal structures," characteristic of religion, "are not critical ingredients in spirituality," which for them represents a "universal and timeless" attribute of human experience.[15] Therefore, the growth of "workplace spirituality," they assert, should be seen as a positive development for business, a corporate embrace of a vital aspect of human life.

While Hicks and Lambert also prefer the "workplace spirituality," they each seek distinct goals. Lambert subsumes workplace spirituality within religion as itself "an important religious movement, shaped and being shaped by American business," bearing unique practices, beliefs, and identities.[16] On the other hand, Hicks views workplace spirituality less as a distinct religious movement, but as a kind of "civil religion" in which the corporation is sacred, the CEO a high priest, and middle managers serving as "corporate acolytes."[17] Because Hicks seeks to protect religious diversity in the workplace, he is less sympathetic than Lambert's more neutral assessment of workplace spirituality as emerging movement.

King and Carrette echo Hick's resistance to the "spiritualization" of corporate cultures. However, instead of "workplace spirituality," they favor the term "capitalist spiritualties" to stress the connection between this trend and an underlying neoliberal political ideology that have come to dominate globally in the wake of communism's decline at the end of the 1980s. They define "neoliberalism" ostensibly as an ideology that "puts profits before people, promotes privatization of public utilities, services, and resources, and in the process of eroding many of the civil liberties that were established under its forerunner—political liberalism."[18] While these capitalist spiritualties provide a release valve for work-induced stress, they obscure "increasingly oppressive and insecure job conditions" that individuals confront under neoliberal capitalism.

Are King and Carrette's "capitalist spiritualties" remotely similar to the lay-driven Christian "faith and work" movement described by David Miller? While these wide-ranging narratives enrich our collective knowledge about business and religion, they leave a great deal of room for further exploration. Is this even a single social movement or is it better defined as a collection of related but distinct trends? How important is "religion" and religious history to its development? Is it wholly positive, as some researchers indicate? And do critical accounts that reduce this phenomenon to a function of the marketplace adequately capture its dynamics?

Much of the scholarship relies on essentialist notions of "spirituality" or "religion." Mitroff and Denton, for example, assume the ontological reality of spirituality, as an objective quality capable of scientific measurement and evaluation. Likewise, Miller articulates "faith" as something ubiquitous and more inclusive than terms like "religion" or "spirituality." He equates "faith" with *Weltanschauung*—"worldview"—something that even the atheist or agnostic presumably possess. Thus, he merely substitutes one problematic classification for another, without at all muting the risk of misrepresentation. For whatever reason, the vast majority of scholarship on religion and spirituality in business fails to acknowledge the more critical theoretical perspectives of thinkers like Talal Asad who argue that concepts like "religion" are elements of discourse produced in and through historical, political, and social change.[19]

Of the scholars mentioned thus far, only King and Carrette recognize how essentialist definitions create "the impression that spirituality is somehow *really* divorced from other spheres of human life such as economics, culture, and politics."[20] Instead, they assess spirituality as a rhetorical tool, a discursive invention serving particular interests in society rather than as concept that points to some transhistorical reality. However, as much as *Selling Spirituality* resists reified definitions of religion and spirituality, the authors routinely treat ideas like "the market" or "corporate interests" as opaque, monolithic, and overdetermining social forces against which individuals stand defenseless. An oppressive capitalist social structure simply dictates to its hapless victims what to believe and how to act. Yet, as much as this theoretical frame illuminates the role of power in social relations, it inadequately allows for institutional structures like global markets and "big business" to be historically situated, human constructions.

The recent work of George Gonzalez introduces ethnography in order to deal with the lack of focus on human agency. In *Shape-Shifting Capital* (2015), Gonzalez uses extensive ethnographic research on practitioners of workplace spirituality to demonstrate how individuals are shaped by and continuing to shape broader ideological constructions. He aspires to "sustain a thoroughgoing ethnographic encounter with the ways in which going or shared ideas about 'spirituality' are reproduced according to the logic and time of lived practice and by the carnal existences of the persons" in his ethnographic research.[21] His is an important step in painting a more complete picture of how business and spirituality comingle through individual social relations. Yet, as much as *Shape-Shifting Capital* refocuses attention on lived experience, because its analysis resides at the level of language, metaphor, and discourse, its reference to ideologies can appear as abstractions, divorced from identifiable and particular historical events. This is not to say that Gonzalez fails to properly historicize the production of ideology; only that his histories are typically general and lack specificity, if only because his analytical interests lie elsewhere.

The entanglement of spirituality, corporate culture, and American business

A central intellectual aim of this book, then, is to provide a fresh perspective that builds on and challenges the existing body of scholarship on religion and spirituality in business. In recognizing that concepts like "spirituality" and even "work" are products of history and get mobilized for numerous reasons in countless contexts, I repeat Courtney Bender's assertion that we cannot study spirituality divorced from its specific social locations. "Extracting spirituality from the institutions where it is lived out distorts and mischaracterizes the phenomenon, and draws attention away from the conundrums it poses and the possibilities it allows."[22] Bender asks instead that we examine the various ways in which spirituality is *entangled* in social life, in history, and in discourse.

One of goal of this project, then, is to document some of the ways that "spirituality" has been enlisted in a wide range of business contexts over time. Remaining attention to how discourse unfolds in social life, I argue that this entanglement of spirituality, corporate culture, and American business is deeply implicated in the neoliberalization of the global political and economic systems over the last several decades. Thus, it suggests that more identifiable social formations such as the so-called workplace spirituality movement, corporate mindfulness programs, or the rise of "faith-friendly" companies like Tyson Foods indicate more gradual tectonic movements at the systemic level. What, on one hand, can be seen as a movement calling for the moral reform of business or, on the other hand, can be understood as simply another example of capitalist exploitation, also represents practical strategies, which draw on existing cultural resources to respond to and effect the structural realities associated with two mutually constitutive historical conditions: neoliberalism and global capitalism.

Conceptualizing neoliberalism and globalization

Naturally, introducing such ambiguous and, perhaps, overused terms like "neoliberalism" or "globalization" can be a path riddled with potholes. Indeed, to modify anything as "neoliberal" risks being as intellectually imprecise as labeling American football a "religion" or suggesting that Islam is inherently "violent." They often serve as convenient boogeyman for scholars looking to advance a polemic without overtly disclosing their intentions. Because these problematic terms are central to the arguments herein, I must clarify their explanatory role in this book.

Globalization and neoliberalism are interrelated concepts that contain ideological as well as practical ingredients. Nobel laureate Joseph Stiglitz defines globalization as "the closer integration of countries and peoples of the world, which has been brought about by the enormous reduction of costs of transportation and communication, and the breaking down of artificial flows of goods, services, capital knowledge, and (to a lesser extent) people across borders."[23] This expansion of capitalist production across a truly global scale coupled with improvements in technology has facilitated a "post-industrial" social order in the United States as manufacturing and extraction of natural resources get dispersed to cheaper labor markets or simply automated.

While Stiglitz's definition presents globalization as an organic process of technological progress and objective economic processes, Pierre Bourdieu calls attention to its political dimensions. Globalization, he writes, is also "the product of a policy implemented by a set of agents and institutions, and the result of the applications of rules deliberately created for specific ends, namely, trade liberalization (i.e., the elimination of all national regulations restricting companies and their investments)."[24] It is more than a descriptive term for a set of social facts; it is equally a prescriptive set of historically observable actions and goals designed to serve the interests of those who stand to benefit from their implementation and realization.

David Harvey suggests that neoliberalism too exhibits this dualism, both theoretical and concrete. On one hand, neoliberalism is "a theory of political economic practices that proposes that human wellbeing can best be advanced by liberating individual entrepreneurial freedoms and skills within an institutional framework characterized by strong private property rights, free markets, and free trade."[25] On the other hand, it is also a political project "to re-establish the conditions for capital accumulation and to restore the power of economic elites" lost to the welfare state and labor in the first half of the twentieth century.[26] In short, Harvey depicts neoliberalism both as an ideology *and* as a set of practices in order to advance the interests of business. While pundits may often emphasize neoliberalism as an ideology, Harvey suggests that its concrete aims—to serve business interests—has "in practice dominated" historically.[27] "The evidence suggests," he observes, "that when neoliberal principles clash with the need to restore or sustain elite power, then the principles are either abandoned or become so twisted as to be unrecognizable."[28] Consider, for instance, how suddenly fiscally conservative financial institutions embraced

Keynesian-inspired government bailouts in order to ensure their continued survival. Yet, as quickly as they accepted these funds, banks blamed the resultant debt crises in weaker states like Spain and Italy (with the notable exception of Greece, whose crisis indeed originated as public, rather than private, debt) on bloated welfare bureaucracies.

Rather than a steadily advancing process, neoliberalism has unfolded evenly and in stages in response to particular historical moments. As sociologist Jamie Peck asserts, "if there is an enduring logic to neoliberalization, it does not follow the pristine path of rolling market liberalization and competitive convergence; it is one of repeated, prosaic, and often botched efforts to *fix* markets, to build quasi-markets, and to repair market failures. Neoliberalization," he continues, "is not the antithesis of regulation, it is a self-contradictory form of regulation-in-denial."[29] Neoliberalism and globalization are, perhaps, different ways of describing the same overall long-term phenomenon. They each highlight different aspects of a comprehensive and expansive process of (re)asserting the hegemony of business elites. Moreover, they are not spectral boogeymen who can be discerned only in their wake. Neoliberalization and globalization can be definitively observed in those particular moments and spaces along the way when business successfully increased its authority.

I want to argue that "spirituality" has become entangled with business during the latter half of the twentieth century precisely because it has, at least in part, proved to be a useful strategy for bolstering the power of business elites. In addition, this arrangement has normalized new practices and modes of individual subjectivity that can survive, and perhaps thrive, under the conditions of global capitalism.

Structure and scope

In unpacking this argument, I am not proposing a conventional "religious history" of American business that traces how existing elements, themes, and trends of American wove their way into marketplace. Instead of framing religion(s) as causal factors, I generally treat religious resources as available forms of cultural capital that individuals and groups mobilize, mute, and reformulate in order to accomplish certain aims. Consequently, this book really provides a glimpse into how actors in the context of business have engaged in these practices and, in turn, upheld and/or changed the status quo. Each of the book's three sections approach the topic differently, and each chapter represents a particular vantage point from which we can observe the entanglement of business and spirituality.

Part One—The Changing Discourse of Business—traces and deconstructs the broad shifts in management discourse and public discussion about work, covering a broad period roughly between 1950 through the first years of the twenty-first century. Although not a strict chronology, the three chapters that comprise this section illustrate how various thinkers appealed to religious and spiritual resources in order to respond to various perceived crises. Chapter 1 documents how management and popular psychology converged in the post-war period to engage pervasive anxieties of collectivism and alienation in modern bureaucratic society to transform management discourse into a program of individual and social moral reform. These thinkers crafted a grammar that incorporates religious and spiritual language that would become the basis for future trends in management thought.

The next chapter begins with the turmoil of the late 1960s and early 1970s. I argue that the unraveling of the social, political, and economic strife was, in hindsight, an opportunity for business to bolster its cultural authority even further. New popular ideas about leadership, which mystified management and used religious language to redescribe business as an institution worthy of assuming global leadership, surpassing even nation-states. These structural shifts culminate in Chapter 3 with the emergence of organized and sustained form of management research dedicated to studying the role of "workplace spirituality." This trend began in response to important political and economic changes associated with the rollback of labor power and the regulatory apparatus under President Reagan. "Spirituality" proved an appealing idea for management thinkers struggling to makes sense of the new socioeconomic realities of the new neoliberal state.

Part Two—Religion and Spirituality in the New Economy—moves away from management thought to examine how the entanglement of spirituality and business literally facilitated and sustained the professional and private lives of successful businesspeople in the late twentieth century. Chapter 4 is framed around the high-tech industry, as it emerged on the U.S. West Coast after the Second World War. These firms were reorganizing the means of production to suit the particular demands of their industry, emphasizing a more decentralized, team-oriented work environment which afforded individuals greater autonomy as well as more responsibility for company goals. The entrepreneurs and engineers of Silicon Valley used spiritual beliefs and practices in order to cope and succeed under these conditions. Chapter 5, on other hand, illustrates how this attention to the "spiritual" in business is closely associated with advancing the capitalist power around the world. Specifically, it follows the evolution of "Conscious Capitalism," a business philosophy espoused by John Mackey, founder and CEO of Whole Foods Market. First articulated in the 1990s, Conscious Capitalism has blossomed into an organized movement of like-minded business elites who promote the idea that ethically attuned business owners are best equipped to address the depraved temporal and spiritual state of the world. Accordingly, under laissez-faire market conditions, these "conscious capitalists" will bring about an abundant future.

Finally, Part Three—Formations of Spiritual Labor—shifts from these more publically accessible examples or business interest in spirituality and looks closely at two localized contexts in which this entanglement occurs. In each case, the language of spirituality serves a number of purposes, but predictably always reasserts the authority of business elites, managers, and capital.

Part One

The Changing Discourse of Business

1

The Death and Resurrection of a Craftsman: Toward a New Mythology of Work

The man who makes an appearance in the business world, the man who creates
personal interest, is the man who gets ahead. Be liked and you'll never want. . .
—Willy Loman

In February 1949, Elia Kazan's production of a new play by Arthur Miller, *Death of A Salesman*, made its debut on Broadway. The play follows the long, agonizing demise of William "Willy" Loman, an aging salesman from Brooklyn, whose delusions of grandeur conceal the lackluster achievements of a mediocre life. The *New York Times*, in its review of the performance, offered high praise, stating that "Mr. Miller has looked with compassion into the hearts of some ordinary Americans and quietly transferred their hopes and anguish to the theatre."[1]

In the years after the Second World War, the white American middle and working classes had much about which to be hopeful. The United States, bustling with fresh confidence, emerged from the Second World War with the only intact economy in the industrialized world. No longer suffering the hopelessness of Depression, the markets boomed, and for the first time in memory, labor was in high demand during a time of peace. Cities exploded and massive public housing projects rose over the urban terrain with the promise that even the poorest would have a place to call home. A new "suburban" landscape grew with rows of uniformly constructed domiciles dotting the once rural pastures and forests surrounding the urban centers. The tempo of life for the burgeoning white middle class increased as these metropolitan areas built highways and public transportation infrastructure to move large numbers of men (and increasingly women) from the periphery to their jobs in the city each weekday. With real incomes on the rise yearly, families gained unprecedented access to a whole new range of consumer goods and services. Weekends could be set aside for leisure activities, with the exception of Sunday mornings, which naturally were reserved for the pews of the local Protestant church, as postwar participation in religious worship soared. Such was the picture of life of postwar middle America, or least the version that one could find saturating radio, cinema, and that newest, most profoundly transformative medium of television.

Idyllic narratives invariably conceal the contradictions inherent in any social or historical context. American society in the decades or so after the war was certainly no exception, with the rampant and still legal racial and gender discrimination, as well as the escalating antagonism with the Soviet Union. Playwrights like Arthur Miller proved to especially adept at exploring the incongruities between these cultural expectations and the lived experience of what the *New York Times* referred to as "ordinary Americans" Thus, if Spencer Tracy in *Father of the Bride* (1950) embodied the archetypal father of an affluent white America, then what were these "hopes and anguish" to which the tragedy of Willy Loman gave voice?

Foremost, *Death of a Salesman* expresses the anguish over the "death" of a certain kind of hope: the hope of a certain kind of self-reliant, rugged individual. Through the character of Willy Loman, Miller exposes the myth of the self-made man as utterly fraudulent. Despite Loman's constant exuberance and overflowing self-confidence, he lives an unexceptional life, carefully concealed from no one but himself. Perhaps Miller's genius was an ability to capture in the main protagonist the generic everyman, who by the mid-twentieth century seemed to be in danger of becoming no one in particular at all.

Furthermore, Miller emphasizes the vocational identity of Loman, thereby stressing that "work" plays a central role in the narrative. It is a story about the psychological dissonance between, on one hand, the devotion to an ethic of self-reliance, and, on the other hand, the experience of living in an advanced capitalist society where impersonal forces and organizations largely determine social conditions. As his wife Linda laments, "he works for a company for thirty-six years this March, opens up unheard-of-territories to their trademark, and now in his old age they take his salary away."[2] Loman, however, remains blind to his literal status as the "low man," and clings ever more tightly to a mythology of work that provides diminishing solace as time passes. Driven to mental breakdown, Willy, of course, will ultimately take his own life, the only act of self-determination left to him.

Miller's Pulitzer Prize–winning account of how the American Dream abandoned one man reflected wider anxieties that bureaucratic society, particularly evident in conformity of corporate culture, dehumanized and eviscerated individual agency, leaving only "organization men" in its wake. Critics like C. Wright Mills and William H. Whyte complained that the post–New Deal society of organizations no longer rewarded the creative efforts of individuals. William H. Whyte's *The Organization Man* (1956) took direct aim at the corporate life, suggesting that a new "Social Ethic" was gradually infecting society and would eventually undermine the "Protestant Ethic" responsible for American success. The Social Ethic upends individualism and repositions "man" as merely a "unit of society."[3] Whyte framed the problem of the so-called organization man as a moral crisis, of a "middle class who have left home spiritually as well as physically, to take the vows of organizational life."[4]

In *White Collar* (1951), Mills, offering a rather cynical analysis of industrial society, criticizes the large interwoven structures of bureaucratic society as a threat to individual freedom. With a melodramatic and nostalgic appeal to the nineteenth-century farmer, which made curiously makes mention of neither the systematic containment of Native American populations nor the role of slave labor in American economic prosperity, he warned that the independent individual of the past has been replaced by a new kind of subject who looks only to others for self-worth and cues for action. The craftsman, who was "free to work according to his own plan," free to develop "his own nature," and has been relegated to the dustbin of history in favor of the "white collar" worker.[5] "When work becomes just work," Mills wrote, "activity undertaken for reason of subsistence, the spirit which fired our nation to its present greatness had died to a spark."[6]

Yet, the rumors of the death of the craftsman proved in this case to greatly exaggerated. Amid these anxieties, business thinkers like Peter Drucker and Douglas McGregor, along with humanistic psychologist Abraham Maslow proposed to restore dignity to the individual while upholding the integrity of the organization by transforming modern management. In so doing, they transformed management from a "science" that treated individuals as mere factors of production into a moral discourse aimed and individual and social progress. Yet, as much as this new management discourse attempted to reassert respect for the individual worker, it was, from its inception, also a deeply ideological project to elevate the status of managers that would shape the direction of "corporate culture" in the future. Furthermore, these advocates performed a facelift on the work ethic for the postwar age of big business, mobilizing religious and spiritual language to link human labor to psychological theories about human flourishing.

Management as a moral enterprise

Management appeared as a distinct profession within business during the final decades of the nineteenth century and the early twentieth century. Figures like Frederick Winslow Taylor declared "scientific management" as the panacea for the social strife that had defined labor relations during the Gilded Age. According to Judith Merkle, the success of this new management science and other related innovations such as Henry Ford's moving assembly line upended more than conventional production methods. The drive for efficiency also transformed the way all organizations, private and public, operated across North America and Europe.[7] Corporations, government bureaucracies, and even religious denominations increasingly embraced the benefits of rationalization. Despite its positive results, such ordering left workers with less authority, made them greatly dependent on the new strata of expert planners, and fomented widespread fears of individual alienation. In response to these critiques, management thinkers, beginning in the late 1930s, moved away from this Taylorist orientation and drew increasingly on ideas from the behavioral sciences.[8] By the postwar years, leading management thinkers were devoting their efforts toward a greater understanding of how employee wellbeing contributed to overall productivity.[9]

Yet, like F. W. Taylor, who touted his principles of "scientific management" as a panacea for the social ills earlier in the century, the postwar generation of management theorists understood their ideas as more than simply business strategies for increased productivity and profit. They saw their work as a sociopolitical project to resist the slide toward bigger, more impersonal social organization everywhere and restore authority and dignity to the individual. To craft this vision of social reform, pioneering management thinkers like Peter Drucker and Douglas McGregor shifted the focus of managerial discourse away from its origins as a highly technical field centered on the proper allotment and rational assessment of duties. Rather, the new management would be a moral enterprise, promoting a capitalist social order that rolled back the welfare state and cast work as a virtuous and sacred activity.

Perhaps no figure in postwar American business played a more prominent role in changing the language of management than the Austrian-born author and educator Peter Drucker (1909–2005), whom *Forbes* has labeled the "founder of modern management."[10] According to popular tradition, his childhood home in Vienna served as incubator for the future business icon. The Drucker home reportedly played host to some of the most heroic figures of the so-called Austrian school of economic thought, including Ludwig Von Mises, Frederick

Hayek, and Joseph Schumpeter.[11] From an early age, Drucker encountered the basic ingredients of a conceptual universe that would eventually provide the foundation for neoliberalism.[12] Consequently, Drucker's ideas and management thought more broadly would reflect and reinforce this neoliberal worldview.

Like the Austrian economists, Drucker remained suspicious of statist attempts at economic planning and worried that the move toward collectivism during the first half of the twentieth century would undermine the foundations of modern liberal society. After immigrating permanently to the United States during the Second World War, he directed his efforts toward positioning management as a remedy for these threats. In his 1954 classic, *The Practice of Management*, he declares that management "expresses the basic beliefs of modern Western Civilization" and "will be decisive both to the United States and to the free world in the decades ahead."[13] At stake, according to Drucker, was nothing less than the survival of liberal democracy across the world, and it would be the managers who would lead the nation and its allies in the Cold War to eventual triumph. "Whether the formerly colonial and raw-material producing countries will succeed in developing their economies as free nations or will go Communist, depends to large extent on their ability to produce competent and responsible managers in a hurry."[14]

Effectively managing other people first required a proper understanding of human nature, and the new management presented itself as a corrective to older approaches premised on wrongheaded assumptions about the relationship that individuals have to their labor. According to Drucker, work was essentially a moral enterprise situated at the center of human life and which he imagined through the language of Christianity. He declared,

> Work was not, Genesis informs us, in man's original nature. But it was included soon after. "In the sweat of thy brow shalt thou eat thy bread" was both the Lord's punishment for Adam's fall and His gift and blessing to make bearable and meaningful man's life in his fallen state. Only the relationship to his Creator and that to his family antedate man's relationship to his work; only they are more fundamental. And together with them relationship to his work underlies all of man's life and achievements, his civil society, his arts, his history.[15]

All aspects of human life therefore reduce to these three relationships of man to God, to family, and to work. The institution of work separates human beings from the rest of God's creation because it is an expression of human freewill, of an inherent desire to "grow." Drucker, moreover, describes this growth as interior, as "always from within," and therefore accents the intrinsic, immaterial value of labor in lieu of its material fruits.[16]

If work represents a divine injunction for humans to become more than their base nature, Drucker also believed fervently that management must facilitate, rather than hinder, human growth. Counter to the prevailing wisdom, he professed that "people want to work." Without some kind of productive activity, "most people disintegrate morally and physically" and there management should "reach the worker's motivation and to enlist his participation, to mobilize the worker's desire to work."[17] In accordance with other social critics like Whyte and Mills, Drucker argued that organizations will thrive when they dignify rather than denigrate the individual, and involve him or her in creative process.

Drucker was neither alone in his call to restore dignity to the individual at work nor unique in articulating human labor through the language of Protestant Christianity. Douglas McGregor (1906–64), a contemporary of Drucker and professor at MIT Sloan School of Management, similarly sought to recast work as divinely ordained and its management as a virtuous pursuit. An engineer and psychologist by training, McGregor, perhaps even more than Drucker, stressed the subjective dimensions of good managerial practice. He vigorously attacked the prevailing wisdom, accusing firms of uncritically accepting a worn-out and ultimately incorrect assumptions about human attitudes toward work. While Drucker embraced the Genesis narrative about work, McGregor perceived it as the root of the problem. Because Adam and Eve were "banished from Eden into a world where they had to work for a living," conventional management thinking, he argued, incorrectly inferred that "the average human being has an inherent dislike of work and will avoid it if he can."[18] In fact, this notion —that human beings were disposed to idleness —however misguided, had served as an underpinning of society since the Biblical "Fall." The development and application of management too relied on this mistaken conception of human nature, and in the last years of his life, McGregor proposed a stark reassessment of business thought to correct this original sin.

In 1957, he introduced the major tenets of the theory during a convocation at MIT's school of Industrial Management and for which he continues to be widely known. At the heart of conventional management practice, McGregor claimed, lay a set of faulty presuppositions about humanity that he dubbed "Theory X." Theory X depicted "the average man" as "indolent," lacking "ambition," and holding disdain for personal "responsibility," and McGregor accused managers of approaching their employees as "gullible, not very bright, the ready dupe of the charlatan and the demagogue."[19] Accordingly, these lethargic would-be laborers required managers to direct their efforts. Workers, McGregor announced, "must therefore be persuaded, rewarded, punished, and controlled—their activities must be directed."[20] Like Whyte's "organization man" and Mills's "other-directed" individual, under current managerial regimes, workers remained passive, dependent on others, and without interiorly generated agency.

While he agreed with the tenor of Whyte's thesis, McGregor nonetheless saw *The Organization Man* as unduly critical of the so-called group phenomenon. Groups, McGregor felt, are necessary for organizing production and therefore unavoidable. "The real problem," he retorted directly to Whyte, "is that we have given so little attention to group behavior that management does not know enough about how to create the conditions for individual growth and integrity in the group situation."[21] Whereas Whyte had advocated that individuals reassert their importance within organizational life, McGregor was arguing the inverse that organizations, through effective management, must first establish the circumstances in which workers can flourish as individuals. The problem was not structural, an inherent flaw in "the organization," but rather an issue of moral character and strategy, of poorly managed organizations.

Against Theory X, McGregor offered a new portrayal of human nature, which he consequently labeled "Theory Y." This new paradigm for management envisioned people as naturally motivated, eager to assume responsibility, and willing to work toward corporate goals. "Management does not put them there. It is a responsibility of management to make it possible for people to recognize and develop these human characteristics for themselves."[22] Organizational success depended on the ability of companies to leverage the creative impulse that hitherto lay dormant within their employees.

Theory Y was not only a business strategy; McGregor presented it as a critique of the contemporary social order. "Under the conditions of modern industrial life," he charged, "the intellectual potentialities of the average human being are only partly utilized."[23] As much as the rationalization of social life has improved the efficiency and capacity of production, it leaves little room for individual initiative and creativity. Rather, in an era of mass consumption, individuals "are accustomed to being directed, manipulated, controlled in industrial organizations and to finding satisfaction for their social, egoistic, and self-fulfillment needs away from the job."[24]

In 1960, McGregor introduced his fully articulated vision of Theory Y with the publication of *The Human Side of Enterprise* (1960), just four years before the end of this life. It became the unorthodox work for which McGregor's otherwise conventional career as an educator was known, exerting a lasting influence on popular management thought in subsequent decades. Companies that sought his expertise to rehabilitate their production facilities along the lines of Theory Y reportedly experienced dramatic improvements in productivity.[25] Even in the early twentieth century, *The Human Side of Enterprise* frequently appears on short lists of influential management texts.

Beyond the domain of business, however, Theory Y signals a more general shift in American attitudes about work emerging during the postwar period. First, McGregor's indictment of consumer culture—that work remained utterly separate from the rest of life—suggested that work not only could be but, indeed, *should* act as a domain where one's social and psychological needs might be fulfilled. Furthermore, his ideas exemplify how management thought was experiencing a turn toward moral language concerned not only with "bottom line" but also the intrinsic value of work held for individual wellbeing and societal health. Acknowledging "the human side of enterprise will not only enhance substantially these materialistic achievements but will bring us one step closer to 'the good society.'" As McGregor asked his brethren in the private sector, "shall we get on with the job?"[26]

Work as a spiritual project

In crafting Theory Y, McGregor drew heavily on the work of his friend and associate Abraham Maslow, whose theory of human motivation would prove equally instrumental in shaping cultural attitudes toward work in the latter decades of the twentieth century. Abraham Maslow was born in Brooklyn, New York in 1908 to Russian Jewish Immigrants. He received a PhD in Psychology from the University of Wisconsin and dedicated his early professional years to the study of primate behavior. However, his days as a conventional psychology came to an abrupt end with the US entry to the Second World War. Years later, Maslow recalled in his diary the realization that would change his personal and professional life thereafter:

> One day, just after Pearl Harbor, I was driving home and my car was stopped by a poor pathetic parade. Boy Scouts and fat people and old uniforms and a flag and someone playing the flute off key. As I watched, the tears began to run down my face. I felt we didn't understand—not Hitler, nor the Germans, nor Stalin, nor the Communists. We didn't understand any of them. I felt that if we

could understand, then we could make progress. I had a vision of a peace table, with people sitting around it, talking about human nature and hatred and war and peace and brotherhood... It was at that moment that I realized that the rest of my life must be devoted to discovering a psychology for the peace table. That moment changed my whole life.[27]

In pursuing this "psychology for the peace table," he helped to develop an entirely new branch of psychological research, a "third force" that aspired to move beyond the failings of the two entrenched approaches for studying the mind—psychoanalysis and behavioral psychology. At the time, psychologists from both schools of thought focused on understanding mental illness and proposed various methods to help its victims to "adjust" to a normal life. Maslow, however, initiated a different line of inquiry: what is revealed if we consider not the *mentally ill* but rather the psychological contours of *healthy, even exceptional* individuals? How can we, he asked, address mental illness if we don't first understand it's complete absence? After all, "the study of crippled, stunted, immature, and unhealthy specimens can yield only a cripple psychology and a cripple philosophy."[28]

Eventually, Maslow outlined his new model for human behavior in 1943 with the publication of "A Theory of Human Motivation," a sober title for what would become a foundational text for the "human potential movement." While psychoanalysts generally maintained that unconscious "drives" determined much of human behavior, Maslow countered that individuals were fully equipped to know their interests and could, through deliberate efforts, achieve their full potential. If anything stood in the way of this inherent drive toward one's potential, he contended it was not Freud's so-called death drive outlined in *Civilization and Its Discontents*, but rather external, socially imposed constraints that hindered growth.[29]

Full human potential was possible only if all basic needs had already been met, and Maslow explained human activity in terms of this basic *hierarchy of needs*. As individuals fulfill their basic survival needs, they will naturally seek safety, then esteem, and finally, at the apex, individuals will strive for what Maslow dubbed *self-actualization*.

From its inception, this theory of the highest, or "actualized," self was intimately bound up with a particular ideology of human labor echoing Protestant notions of "calling." Maslow states that the self actualizes when one "is doing what he is fitted for. A musician must make music, an artist must paint, a poet must write, if he is to be ultimately happy."[30] Each individual therefore exhibits some innate propensity to engage in a certain kind of activity, to perform a certain type of work, the discovery and realization of which represents the ultimate purpose of all human life. Work appears here as self-evident, a ubiquitous aspect of human experience that transcends cultural and historical boundaries. Moreover, Maslow privileges the intrinsic rewards of work over its material benefits, and depicts the activity of work, regardless of context, as a moral good, insofar as it expresses the latent potential of an individual.

Maslow's theory not only psychologizes work, but it presents a mode of human subjectivity that upholds cultural norms, modes of production, and political perspectives favorable of Western capitalism. Robert Shaw and Karen Colimore argue that the idea of work as individual "self-actualization" supports a form of market liberalism while the *hierarchy of needs* tacitly accepts "the class stratification found within a capitalistic society."[31] The actualizing self reiterates capitalist norms because it translates business goals—productivity and growth—as qualities of the individual psyche. Work represents the apex of human action, and "to prevent [actualizing individuals] from working would be as cruel a punishment as could be imagined."[32] Consequently, efforts to lessen the necessity for work prove to be self-defeating because they will destroy the very foundation upon which human potential rests. This logic implicitly renders leftist policies, from Social Security to National Labor Relations, particularly suspect and idealizes a laissez-faire social order.

Although Maslow never plainly asserted a connection between his theories and market liberalism, he nonetheless enjoyed a close affinity with the private sector. On one hand, management thinkers found Maslow's ideas extremely relevant for corporate strategy, while Maslow himself championed business and understood the workplace as a primary site for self-actualization. In fact, he even actively conducted research in the corporate setting out of which he produced a fully developed management theory based on his ideas about human motivation.

Maslow's positive psychology directly influenced Douglas McGregor as he initially formulated "Theory Y." Effective management demanded a thorough grasp of human behavior, which Maslow, McGregor believed, had actively portrayed in his hierarchy of needs. He directly used Maslow's concepts to represent Theory Y as a management strategy uniquely appropriate to an affluent society such as postwar America capable of meeting the survival needs of its working people. The fact that American businesses largely provide for the basic sustenance and security of their workforce, McGregor argued, "has shifted the motivational emphasis to the social and egoistic needs. Unless there opportunities *at work* to satisfy these higher-level needs, people will be deprived."[33] Theory Y, in short, articulated a management strategy that prioritized specific tactics according to the psychological schema developed by Maslow. Firms that subsequently embraced Theory Y management principles effectively affirmed Maslow's humanistic psychological model as well.

The association between Theory Y management and Maslow become explicit in 1961, when Non-Linear Systems (NLS), a California-based aerospace firm that had already reorganized itself according to the principles of Drucker and McGregor, invited Maslow to observe and assess its operations.[34] Over the next few years, Maslow would visit one plant per week, collecting and analyzing a great deal of material on the inner workings of the company. While Maslow may have esteemed the company's president Andy Kay, who was responsible for introducing the new approach to management, as "a living example of the self-actualized man," he remained somewhat critical of their blind acceptance of these new principles, confessing privately in his diary that "they're being taken as gospel truth, without any reliability, validity."[35]

The years of close observation and critical examination at NLS yielded Maslow's own competing model of management, fully articulated as *Eupsychian Management* (1965). Here Maslow overtly connects self-actualization to work and in the process reformulates labor as a practice of great intrinsic value. Work, under the right conditions, literally comes to be the means though which individual potential is realized, and happiness is achieved.[36] For those exceptional, self-actualizing individuals, "work actually becomes part of the self, part of the individual's definition of himself." Maslow characterized this program as a project that would ultimately reform more than individual experience of work but also effect broader social change. The "proper management of the work lives of human beings, of the way in which they earn their living, can improve them and improve the world and in this sense be a utopian and revolutionary technique."[37]

Even as Maslow saw the possibilities of an enlightened management to transform individuals and society alike, he also maintained an ongoing interest in religious experience. Remaining true to his rebellious disposition, he took issue with entrenched scholarly perspectives that depicted religion as either a relic of the premodern period, as secularization theories declared, or, as Freud (1927) suggested, an "illusion" intended to sustain order in society. Maslow instead viewed religion, and specifically religious experience, with promise, as evidence of an overlooked, yet vital, ingredient of human nature. In the last decade of his life, Maslow turned increasingly to religion as a topic of study and in the process would help to reshape the American religious landscape.

During the same years he was conducting research at NLS, Maslow published his first book focused exclusively on religion, entitled *Religions, Values, and Peak-Experiences* (1964), in which he would effectively redescribe religion through the language of psychology. He remained confident that humanistic psychology held the key to unlocking the hidden purpose of religion and could rehabilitate its somewhat tarnished image as superstition. The humanistic psychologist, he asserted, as the guide for "a positive, naturalistic faith, a 'common faith' as John Dewey called it, a 'humanistic faith' as Erich Fromm called it."[38]

Turning to a tradition of liberal religious thought in North America extending back to William James, Maslow privileged individual experience as the authentic center of all religious life. "The very beginning," he argued, "the intrinsic core, the essence, the universal nucleus of every known religion…has been the private, lonely, personal illumination, revelation, or ecstasy of some acutely sensitive prophet or seer."[39] While reductionist, Maslow does not dismiss organized religion outright, but rather suggests that institutions, traditions, and specific doctrines serve as carriers of these original, essentially psychological events. Traditions subsequently emerge as strategies for sustaining the memory of these experiences and conveying, however imperfectly, their content to others.

Historically, societies had deemed these experiences as supernatural events, as divine revelation or prophecy. However, Maslow states that "mystery, ambiguity, illogic, contradiction, mystic and transcendent experiences may now be considered to lie well within the realm of nature."[40] Humanistic psychology, and specifically his theories, could not only explain these events but also harness their transformative potential. He referred to them as "peak-experiences," and to them Maslow ascribed a number of attributes that could easily have been lifted directly from the pages of James's *Varieties of Religious Experience*. Peak-experiences revealed the universe as whole; they transcended ego; they conveyed esoteric knowledge and imbued life with meaning. The peak-experience represented the pinnacle of self-actualization, when the individual has reached her full potential. "In peak-experiences," he wrote, "there is a tendency to move more closely to a perfect identity, or uniqueness, or the idiosyncrasy of the person or to his real self, to have become a real person."[41] By association, then, those individuals that tradition has dubbed prophets, seers, and oracles are simply the fortunate few who have achieved the highest level of psychological health.

Religions, Values, and Peak-Experiences announced that psychology had inherited the mantle of traditional religion and would carry its truths forward into the future. As other scholars have already noted, humanistic psychology and Maslow specifically helped to reshape American attitudes toward religion and spirituality during the latter half of the twentieth century. Maslow popularized his ideas about human potential and peak-experiences at places like the Esalen Institute, one of the early epicenters of this new "spirituality" that would become so prevalent in subsequent decades. As historian Eugene Taylor notes, "in the 1970s, humanistic psychology graduated to transpersonal psychology," serving as the basis for a whole range of new social formations, from encounter groups to the New Age, and played an important part in constructing a new salient identity: "spiritual, but not religious."[42]

While some scholars acknowledge Maslow's impact on American spirituality and others document his penchant for the business world, rarely, if ever, have these two domains of Maslow's work been considered together. Yet, I want to suggest that the linkages between these two seemingly disparate threads remain vital for understanding how American attitudes toward work have shifted in recent decades. Both work and religious experience, according to Maslow, have important roles to play for healthy human development. On one hand, work, when performed under proper conditions (i.e., according to Maslow's management principles) facilitates self-actualization, which constitutes the most advanced psychological state for individuals. On the other hand, peak-experiences, formerly deemed "religious," represent the pinnacle of self-actualization. Taken together, these propositions establish an intriguing possibility—not only that work can be intrinsically rewarding but that it should be understood as an inherently spiritual activity.

If Peter Drucker and Douglas McGregor reformulated popular management theory as a moral discourse, Maslow was engaged in a similar project. For him, work was not only a moral virtue, it was the central activity for human development and program for spiritual enlightenment. He understood humans as hardwired to fulfill needs, and, albeit temporarily, labor satiated these needs, for food and shelter, for friends and family, and finally for self-esteem and actualization. The climb to the apex of human flourishing required more than sheer will; it needed the appropriate conditions and guidance. In contemporary society, Maslow imagined managers, following his eupsychian program, as the ones who would guide individuals in the workplace toward self-actualization and, ultimately, toward the promise of gnosis through the peak-experience.

Conclusion

In the postwar period, thinkers like Peter Drucker and Douglas McGregor decidedly altered the terms of discussion around the proper function of business management. They saw themselves as reacting against outdated business wisdom which for decades had purportedly depicted management as "getting things done through other people."[43] Such views, they believed, radically misrepresented human nature, and the positive impact of work on individual life and on society more broadly. Moreover, these tired approaches dehumanized workers, removing their ability to make independent decisions regarding production, and assuming they cared little for organizational goals and desired only material rewards in the form of wages and other tangible benefits. In other words, little attention was given to the experience of work, even though industrial psychology had long established the relationship between satisfaction and productivity.

Drucker and McGregor were representative of broader efforts to reformulate the foundations of business thought. While acknowledging the benefits of rationalized production, they equally recognized the social and psychological repercussions of "scientific" approaches like Taylorism. According to them, effective management required more than proper planning, organization, and supervision; management, as Drucker would famously declare decades later, "is what tradition used to call a liberal art."[44] It demanded from employers respect for the psychosocial needs of their employees and recognition of the intrinsic value of human labor. In sum, they reimagined management as a moral pursuit and freely enlisted religious language to advance these reforms.

The rehumanization of management was representative of broader efforts to reformulate the ethical norms of postwar American capitalism. Drucker and McGregor joined a chorus of social critics who discerned a conflict between the virtues of liberal society and the conditions of social life under the post–New Deal welfare state. While critics such as C. Wright Mills and William Whyte decried the ascendance of corporate entities as the death knell of the free, self-reliant individual, others like Ayn Rand directed their animus toward rapid expansion of the state, insisting that business and entrepreneurs were the last bastion of such liberty. The new management in some sense split difference because it implicated all organizations, whether public or private, and instead proposed a strategy for the self-reliant individual to thrive *within* organizations.

Beyond management, understanding the conditions necessary for human flourishing was also a chief concern for positive psychologists like Abraham Maslow. Indeed, McGregor drew upon Maslow's theories of human motivation while Maslow envisioned management as a technique for realizing human potential. Along the way, they accomplished more than simply reorienting intellectual discussion among business theorists and humanistic psychologists. They also reconceptualized work as an intrinsically reward-ing activity that even exhibited a spiritual dimension. Of course, this was not entirely novel, as the Protestant notions of *vocation* and *calling* had long shaped modern ideas about work. However, this new vision of work departed from previous iterations of the work ethic because it carried the additional cultural authority of the behavioral sciences. Through Maslow's work on human development, the discourse on religious experience was brought into contact with human labor. He situated work not only as important for sur-vival but as the central activity of human life. Through work the path was laid open to realize one's potential, to "actualize" the inborn unique capacity of each individual.

While management was reinvented as a moralizing discourse and humanistic psychology helped to redefine work, the social turmoil of the 1960s and early 1970s provided the perfect opportunity for these emerging disciplines to elevate their status even further and insert themselves in larger debates about social, political, and economic reform.

2

A New Business for Business

While thinkers like Peter Drucker and Douglas McGregor had certainly drawn attention to the "human side of enterprise" by the end of the 1960s, many leaders in business and economics continued to cling to the conventional wisdom that business should solely focus on factors of production. "The business of business is business," declared the long-time president of General Motors Alfred P. Sloan in a speech reportedly in 1964.[1] Such clichés paint business as a hard-nosed, competitive, and frequently unforgiving activity. The statement conjures images of the ambitious businessman, driven by pure self-interest, and singularly focused on the securing of profits without consideration of any broader impact. Moreover, to confine business to its own profit-driven aims imagines a social order in which each sphere of human activity is rationally ordered and autonomous. Business is distinct from government; work opposes free time and leisure; and religion intermingles with neither politics nor the economic. Echoing Weber, each sphere operates according to its own self-regulating logics, ethics, and structures, all of which ultimately act concertedly in the unfolding of modern societies.

Novel theories of management that advocated treating workers as multi-faceted individuals rather than impersonal factors of production resist these conventional social divisions and therefore pose a challenge to the views of business leaders like Sloan. What, after all, obliges a company to concern itself with the psychological health of employees? What interest does an employer have in assisting individuals in pursuing their personal career (or extra-vocational) goals? Are not other social institutions—schools, families, churches—designed for precisely these concerns? Is not employment simply a contractually agreed upon exchange of labor for wages and benefits? While industrial psychology had certainly uncovered a correlation between job satisfaction and productivity, to some, like Nobel Prize-winning economist Milton Friedman, the notion that business assume any responsibility beyond its immediate profit-seeking goals remained patently absurd. In a 1970 editorial for *The New York Times Magazine* discussing the "social responsibility of business," he argued that "the manager is the agent of the individuals who own the corporation or establish the eleemosynary institution, and his primary responsibility is to them."[2]

At the time, Friedman was responding to a rising popular tide of anti-establishment sentiment and disillusionment with traditional institutional arrangements. Much of this opposition was directed squarely at the corporate world and at the very foundations of the market economy. Friedman's was a classic defense of economic liberalism, that businesses existed to serve investors and stockholders—the formal owners of the means of production—-and the expectation that they do otherwise would be violation of the ethical norms of business.

Yet, other defenders of the status quo took a different tact to confront the social strife during those years. They saw in the unrest an opportunity to retool management philosophies as solutions to these social ills, effectively expanding the role of management thought in shaping society more broadly. This elevated cultural authority of managerialism reflected the growing tendency for business perspectives to set the terms of public discourse, including American attitudes toward work. It even manifested in an increased willingness for business thinkers and reformers to speak authoritatively about religion and spiritual matters, enlisting traditionally religious resources in the service of capitalist goals.

Management: America's elixir

In 1968, a year that student protests exploded across the West, Peter Drucker wrote of a sense that "something" profound "*is* going on," that profound changes were taking place that would require fresh, untried solutions.[3] A year later he published *The Age of Discontinuity* (1969), a work of remarkably different tone than that of *The Practice of Management* fifteen years earlier. Whereas Drucker had long argued for management as a vital piece of any larger reform initiative, *The Age of Discontinuity* elaborated a sweeping set of solutions to what Drucker understood as an unprecedented breakdown of the social order. A long period of social, political, and economic "continuity" extending back into the nineteenth century was rapidly coming to its end, and a new consensus around new values, ideas, and institutions would inevitably replace it. "The young everywhere," he declared, "are indeed rejecting *all* institutions with equal hostility."[4] However, it was not business institutions but bloated government on which Drucker placed the blame for hindering the march into this new era. He labeled government as "fat and flabby rather than powerful; that it costs a great deal but does not achieve much."[5] Instead, he advocated for a process of "reprivatization," of dismantling the state apparatus and allocating some of welfare functions to nongovernmental organizations. Because "it is predominantly an organ of innovation," business, he proclaimed, would be "particularly appropriate for reprivatization."[6]

While he sought to extend the authority of business, Drucker also suggested that, in this period of so-called discontinuity, his principles of effective management would play a crucial role. The emerging economic order would require new kinds of workers with new skills. The new economy would be a "knowledge" economy and require more "entrepreneurial" thinking and practice. Yet, this was not a return to a pre-corporate society of independent entrepreneurs, it would be a society where entrepreneurship would "be exercised in and through a managerial, and usually a fairly large and complex, organization."[7] All in all, Drucker was developing a vision of society in which his particular philosophy of management would thrive and in which business would serve as the dominant institution of society.

Drucker was not alone in seizing the social strife to bolster the cultural authority of management and business. Against the backdrop of a perceived social breakdown, some would even invoke religious rhetoric to retool management as a kind of sacred discipline. In addition, during this period of upheaval, the idea that work should serve as form of self-improvement, something Maslow and others had articulated in years earlier, would gain public ascendency. As this chapter will illustrate, the social tensions that permeated American society during the late 1960s and early 1970s not only produced new expectations about work and forged novel conceptions of religion or (to use a term that gained traction at this time) "spirituality," but also reformulated the way that Americans understood the relationship between the two. Yet, this was not some metaphysical shift in consciousness or moral sensibility, but rather resulted from attempts to advance the cultural authority of business and management at a time when capitalism was facing a perceived existential threat.

Servant-leadership

While Peter Drucker was heralding the Age of Discontinuity, another well-known management expert was embarking on a speaking tour of college campuses in an effort to discourage youth from rebellion and inspire their leaders to improve upon the status quo. In the process, Robert Greenleaf (1904–90) would craft a philosophy known as "servant-leadership," which over the years has attained near iconic status in management circles and beyond. For him, "servant-leadership" encompassed much more than business management; it represented a way of life inextricable from his Quaker convictions and what he called the "Judeo-Christian" moral tradition. In many ways, he reiterated management as a sacred practice that set the stage for others who would later develop an explicit "spirituality" for management.

A native of Terre Haute, Indiana, Greenleaf would leave behind his rural Midwestern beginnings for a career spanning nearly four decades at one of the largest corporations in North America as the head of its corporate training initiatives. From 1926 until his retirement in 1964, Greenleaf participated in developing and implementing the training and development programs for American Telephone and Telegraph (AT&T), which at the time held a government-authorized monopoly on telephone service throughout the United States.[8] Although he was celebrated during his career in the business world as a leading figure in corporate training, it would be his vocation later in life as a speaker, writer, and proponent of a management philosophy he designated "servant-leadership" for which he would be most revered. Peter Drucker reportedly hailed him as "the wisest man I ever met." Yet, although their worlds and ideas overlapped, Drucker nonetheless distinguished himself from Greenleaf in important ways. "Our aims were quite different," he recalled in a foreword to a collection of Greenleaf's writings. "Bob was always out to change the individual, to make him into a different person. I was interested in making people *do* the right things." Drucker saw himself as the pragmatist to the moralist Greenleaf. Unlike Greenleaf, he admitted, "I know that I am not effective as a preacher, I am effective as a teacher, and the two are very different things."[9]

Like his contemporaries—Drucker and McGregor—Greenleaf believed that effective management must go beyond efficiency and consider the human element in productive processes. In a 1958 address to the Ann Arbor Bureau of Industrial Relations, he called for managers to "take into account the best of our experiences, the soundest of ethical ideals, the spiritual nature of a man as it relates to his capacity to venture and assume responsibility in the face of uncertainty."[10] Management was not merely a technical discipline but a moral philosophy that recognized individuals as essentially spiritual beings, some of whom possessed a unique, broader vision. Unlike the typical worker, the manager could recognize the spiritual nature of work, the higher purpose it served.

"The issue," he told the audience, "has never been more clearly stated than in the old story of two stone-masons; when asked about their work, one replied, 'I'm setting stone,' the other, 'I'm building a cathedral.'"[11] Work represented more than the literal act of laboring; it was an expression of human nature and management, he argued, was the strategy that linked the individual's need to work with organizational goals.

Greenleaf spoke of a "business-dominated society" as unprecedented in human history, and therefore businesses generally as well as managers in particular are uniquely charged "with shaping the character of our society than any other force."[12] Under this social order, work and career yield more than the material benefits of economic security. He argued that they are pedagogical, that businesses should recognize their role in shaping individuals in profound ways. Businesses could "help young people resolve their questions and get them started on a sound course of development" if companies "surround them with a strong and compelling idealistic concept of a business that helps them find an adequate sense of purpose, and get their own directions set as part of the enterprise."[13] As a director for training and development, Greenleaf was encouraging businesses to assume responsibility for and authority over the most intimate aspects of individual life.

Upon his retirement from AT&T after thirty-eight years, Greenleaf founded the Center for Applied Ethics, where he would serve as a full-time consultant on leadership to a number of organizations, from private firms to major universities. While he had made a name for himself in the management world as an authoritative voice on corporate training, his later years as an independent consultant, and notably as a prolific author, would prove to be his most influential. In 1968, Greenleaf delivered a series of lectures at Dartmouth on "Leadership and the Individual," over the course of which he would outline the basic ideas that eventually develop into servant-leadership. It is significant to note that Greenleaf designed these lectures not as a model for effective business management but rather as a response to the student protests spreading through college and university campuses across the United States at the time. He framed the civil strife as a "crisis of leadership," because "so many people who concerned about the state of the world, or some part of it, and have the opportunity and perhaps the obligation to lead are perplexed and unsure about what to do."[14] While the stakes—the direction of American society—may have seemed much higher than the profit-seeking goals of private enterprise, he nonetheless believed that the same principles of effective leadership that had proved useful to businesses could heal deep wounds in society.

Though sympathetic with the grievances of the protestors, he characterized their repudiation of basic social institutions as misguided. "Not only do some of our best young people reject the Establishment and its ways, but they also believe that when the present order of society is destroyed (which they hope is soon because they don't want to live in it as it is), the more ideal society they hope to see replace it will not have leaders as we know them."[15] The "anti-leaders," he argued, had fundamentally misunderstood how social change demands not the abolition of authority altogether but merely its effective use. To be sure, Greenleaf agreed with his younger contemporaries that some fundamental assumptions required critical reexamination, but tearing down the institutions in which new values might flourish would prove an utter failure.

Greenleaf understood institutions, be they government, business, or universities, as essentially neutral social structures. "Individuals," he told the audience, "are the foundation of the social order," and, countering the indignant students, he maintained that injustice stemmed not from "the system" itself but from its misuse.[16] The problem, it seemed to Greenleaf, was one of culture, of the declining influence of Christian virtues. He lamented thus:

> The value system of the Western World that has been building since Moses brought the tablets down the mountain some three thousand years ago has been pretty badly shattered and, I believe, irretrievable so within the lifetime of the youngest person here. I assume that it will not be reconstructed as it was. It will be replaced, by something better (Robert Greenleaf, "The Crisis of Leadership).[17]

The fervent anti-institutionalism, Greenleaf feared, threatened to undermine some of the basic tenets of modern society, specifically citing "such important assumptions as the Protestant work ethic, traditional morals, our views on property, and many others."[18] If the crisis was cultural, then Greenleaf makes clear that it was a crisis precisely because it endangers the institutions of American capitalism: free labor and private property. What society needed was not the destruction of the established capitalist-democratic order, but rather for better leaders to step forward and right the direction of existing institutions.

As a young adult, Greenleaf became involved in the Society of Friends, an affiliation that he would maintain for the remainder of his life. Quaker teachings and what he called the "Judeo-Christian" tradition played an important role in how he would articulate a response to this perceived crisis of leadership among American youth. "How," he pondered, "did our society get to be so bureaucratic?" He refers to Exodus 13, in which Jethro, whom he labels the "first management consultant of record," advises his son-in-law, Moses, to enlist the help others in adjudicating Israelite affairs.[19] "Every student of management knows this story," he presumed, "and knows that this is the first statement of the hierarchical principle of organization."[20] While Greenleaf does locate the origin of social hierarchy in biblical narrative, he suggests, however, that the story is not a justification but rather a veiled criticism of bad leadership. He reminded his audience that in the end "the Lord sacked Moses," and therefore "could it be," Greenleaf asked, "the Lord's real criticism of Moses that led to the substitution of another leader was that Moses had taken this stupid advice from Jethro and that the unfortunate bureaucratic consequences were already evident in the tribes of Israel?"[21] "The long-term result, of course, for the Western world and ultimately the whole world, is that the world has been stuck with a lousy organization theory for three thousand years."[22]

Just as he had looked to sacred texts to diagnosis the problem, he also invoked the example of Quakers, specifically the life of John Woolman (1720–72), an eighteenth-century itinerant Quaker preacher, as an ideal example of leadership. Woolman, said Greenleaf, was "the model of the great and gentle persuader," exhibiting the quietism valued so highly among the Society of Friends.[23] In 1754, he published *Some Considerations on the Keeping of Negroes*, in which he accused his contemporaries of hypocrisy and of failing to recognize their Christian obligation to love all of humanity.[24] Woolman worked tirelessly in his remaining years, visiting Friends's meetinghouses across North America, to convince his fellow Quakers to voluntarily abandon chattel slavery. Partially through his efforts, Quakers were some of the earliest vocal supporters of abolition in North America.

Greenleaf celebrated Woolman for his generally passive or pacifist approach to advocacy. Implicitly attacking student activists and supporters of nonviolent resistance, Greenleaf stressed that Woolman "never did a protest, nor did he go to jail or found movement."[25] Instead, he relied solely on his skills of persuasion and the reasonableness of his audience. Similarly, Americans in Greenleaf's day needed leaders of this ilk, who could inspire individuals to change, to embrace new ethical foundation upon which to build the future. Only voluntary change, not coerced, could establish lasting change and lead society beyond its current conflicts.

Woolman may have been an ideal leader, but, for Greenleaf, no one personified leadership more completely than Jesus. Referencing the story from the Gospel of John in which Jesus disrupts a mob intent on stoning a woman accused of adultery, Greenleaf presents Jesus to the Dartmouth audience as "a man, like you and me, with extraordinary prophetic insight of the kind we all have some of…He is a leader, as I see it, in the fullest meaning of the term." Jesus intervenes and remains willing to stand against the consensus of the crowd, because that consensus is wrong. Greenleaf stopped short of asserting the divinity of Jesus, instead referring to him as a man possessed of extraordinary gifts and whose biography serves as a model to which all leaders should aspire.

In refracting Christian theology and the image of Jesus through the lens of business, Greenleaf was not altogether new. Decades earlier, former advertising executive Bruce Barton authored *The Man Nobody Knows* (1925), in which he represents the Christian savior as the "founder of modern business," a strong and driven individual who "picked up twelve humble men and created an organization that won the world."[26] Earlier still, Russell Conwell, the founder of Temple University, had traveled the country to bring the singular message that one's Christian duty was "to get rich."[27] Audiences would hear Conwell's famous speech namely 'Acres of Diamonds' over 6,000 times during the late nineteenth and early twentieth century.

Yet, this was neither the "muscular" Christianity of Conwell or Barton nor the effeminate, weak Jesus against which they were arguing. Rather, Greenleaf articulated a humanistic Jesus, a messiah of human potential armed not with sheer will and a self-reliant disposition but acting out of a profound humility and moral durability. While Barton's Jesus is a master of delegation, of "getting things done," Greenleaf portrays him as someone who provides moral clarity, as someone who leads not by virtue of his position in the organization but as one whose character invited emulation.

Leaders therefore do not necessarily hold formal authority; leadership emerges from within the person. Leaders are exceptional individuals who possess extraordinary abilities, which defy rational explanation. They can "know the unknowable and foresee the unforeseeable";[28] they rely on intuition and harness their creativity through contemplative practice, achieving "an altered state of consciousness" to "toss up a new insight, a hunch—a leap of thought into the unknown."[29] Leaders possess *spirit*, an ineffable quality that Greenleaf can only explain as mysterious:

> There is, in my theology, a mystery before which I simply stand in awe. At the threshold of the mystery, I ask no questions and seek no explanations. I simply bow before the mystery, and what it wants to say to me comes as gently as doves as I achieve the quiet. Spirit is behind the threshold of the mystery. I don't know what it is, even though occasionally I get intimations about it, but I do have a

belief about what it *does*. When a leader has it, it builds *trust*; it builds trust not only between leader and follower but also between followers.[30]

This rhetoric of "spirit" mystifies leadership and deifies leaders, imbuing them with secret knowledge and charisma which ultimately obscures the larger socio-political milieu to which it is tethered. For example, Greenleaf looked beyond his Quaker community or Christian concepts. He engaged religion liberally and pragmatically, garnering the intellectual resources from any number of traditions as long as they proved illustrative. "My decision," he announced, "was to regard all scriptures of all religions as great stories of the human spirit and take them for the insight they yield on that basis."[31] Greenleaf defined leadership as an essentially human trait, which transcended and preceded any cultural or religious boundaries. In fact, all prominent religious figures exhibited these leadership qualities to some degree, and individuals therefore should embrace their legacy. "Modern man as a leader," he argued, "must somehow effect a marriage between his Protestant-ethic conscience, which grows out of the Judeo-Christian tradition, and philosophical detachment about which the legend of the compassionate Buddha has much more to say."[32] In other words, for Greenleaf the ideal leader is a religious syncretist, but implicitly he privileges a leader who is male, white, Protestant, and bourgeois. Thus, while presented as an agent of transformation, "he" is nothing more than a reflection of the status quo.

Nevertheless, even if his prescriptions did not exactly upend the status quo, they did offer a fresh way of discussing these entrenched norms. If McGregor and Drucker had presented management as a moral activity, Greenleaf removed the bindings which had restricted to modern organizations and re-presented it as a concrete identity under the banner "leadership." Leaders emerged in all times and places according to a familiar schema, regardless of whether they ever assumed formal reigns of authority. Indeed, Greenleaf argued that, more often than not, the most authentic leaders were those, like John Woolman, who led quietly, unpretentiously, and devoid of all outward indications of power.

Two years after the Dartmouth lectures, Robert Greenleaf finally committed his thoughts to print when he published a short essay, "The Servant as Leader" (1970), summing up his philosophy. Although it received only modest attention among popular management circles, the tract eventually gained a devoted following and spawned an entire genre of management discourse based on one, seemingly simple notion: that "the servant-leader is servant first."[33] In short, leadership and service are different aspects of the same virtue. "Servant-leadership," as he dubbed the concept, was not only a method for exercising authority, for it also indicated a particular kind of subject: a selfless figure, the gentle persuader he had previously articulated.

Although "The Servant as Leader" reiterated much of his earlier lectures, it more aggressively asserted the mysterious, exceptional attributes of servant-leaders. First, the servant-leader enlists both reason and esoteric, intuitive ways of knowing to assess problems and articulate solutions. She relies on *intuition*, "a feel for patterns... based on what has happened previously," as a supplement, not a replacement of, reasoning and empirical evidence to make decisions.[34] These hunches help the servant-leader to have *foresight*, the ability to anticipate and therefore shape events as they unfold. In addition, leaders are imbued with a special *awareness and perception* to which the rest of us are not privy, leaving them "unusually sharply awake and reasonably disturbed."[35] In short, they possess "a sense for the unknowable," and it is these individuals that must assume the mantle of leadership and in whom the remainder must place their faith if society is to thrive.

In order to animate his description of servant-leadership, Greenleaf turns to German novelist Herman Hesse (1877–1962), whom he declares a "prophet." Specifically, Greenleaf focuses on Leo, one of the central characters in Hesse's 1932 novella *Journey to the East*, as a Christ-like figure who embodies the traits of the servant-leader. Throughout the story, Leo plays to role of the lowly servant, only later to be revealed as the secret leader, quietly influencing the main protagonist, known only as "H.H." Leo leads from behind the scenes where he can avoid the formal trappings of authority, relying instead on quiet persuasion and influence, like John Woolman, to shepherd others on journeys of self-discovery.

"The Servant as Leader" established a new, more intimate way of talking about management and birthed an entire generation of thinkers who would emulate this approach. He described management as a way of being in the world, but not necessarily of it. Instead of chief executives like Alfred P. Sloan or the captains of industry like Henry Ford or J. D. Rockefeller, the exemplars of servant-leadership were the pious and prophetic; teachings drawn from an eclectic reservoir of religious and spiritual traditions, ancient and contemporary, provided the grammar through which servant-leadership would be passed to legions of those increasingly categorized as "management" across the post-industrial, post-Fordist economic terrain of American society. This new managerialism, then, must be understood as complicit in these tectonic shifts taking place in the United States. From this perspective, we can appreciate the significance of servant-leadership in two ways. First, it serves as a useful example of how the language of management was bound up with the larger cultural changes occurring at the time.

Servant-leadership echoed the anti-establishment sentiments of young, afflu-ent, white Americans that were driving the New Left. The "Servant as Leader" reminded readers of the potential for individuals, through rather than in spite of institutions, to transform society. Greenleaf's Quaker piety resonated with the anti-war movements' commitment to pacifism. Moreover, Greenleaf shared with the countercultural youth a penchant for spiritual eclecticism. Along with his self-proclaimed "Judeo-Christian" heritage, he embraced the perennialism of Aldous Huxley (not to mention his interest in the psychotropic inducement of altered states of consciousness) and the mysticism of Herman Hesse.

Yet, even as servant-leadership aligned with cultural reformers at the time, it also reveals how the language of management was escaping the confines of the private sector. Greenleaf openly declared that "leadership" applied not only to workplace but to all domains of life. Leadership signified much more than a management technique; it denoted the disposition of exceptional people, of "leaders" who could emerge and thrive in any institutional context—be they corporations, universities, churches, or government. Rather than dismantling the social order, Greenleaf urged servant-leaders to grab the ship's wheel and correct its course.

If the language of management was becoming ubiquitous, it illustrated how business wielded a new cultural authority during the 1970s, and to a certain extent "The Servant as Leader" was an exercise in mythmaking. When he sig-nificantly revised the original 1970 essay a few years later for more general audi-ences, Greenleaf transformed a critique of youth rebellion into a template for a managerial tour de force. Instead of profiling student leaders and touting higher education as the most crucial institution for the future, Greenleaf placed his confidence definitively in the business world. "A hopeful sign of the times," he proclaimed, "in the sector of society where it seems least likely—highly competi-tive business—is that people-building institutions are holding their own while they struggle successfully in the marketplace."[36]

The specific changes that Greenleaf made to servant-leadership in this period effectively transformed a critique of youth anti-institutionalism into a template for a managerial revolution. The significance of these changes profoundly altered the way that audiences would receive the idea of servant-leadership because they obscured the essentially conservative foundation of the philosophy. What would masquerade as a radically new leadership philosophy for business remained nonetheless a defense of the status quo, of the existing social structure. In the original 1970 edition, for instance, he overtly criticized student radicalism and praised student leaders (including former Wellesley student body president

Hillary Rodham) who chose to work within the legitimate university hierarchy. He characterized the university as "the most troubled, the most fragile" institution, but argued that it "must become the institution-building model" for the rest of society. Servant-leaders, unlike radical dissenters, accomplish change while simultaneously upholding the integrity of society, because they respect the necessity of order. "There must be some order," wrote Greenleaf, "because we know for certain that the great majority of people will choose some kind of order over chaos even if it is delivered by a brutal nonservant and even if, in the process, they lose much of their freedom."[37]

With the publication of the first book, the bestselling *Servant Leadership: A Journey into the Nature of Legitimate Power and Greatness* (1977), servant-leadership would become a phenomenon of popular management literature, moving far beyond its largely forgotten origins as a response to student radicalism. Numerous companies have implemented training programs explicitly based on his ideas. The Center for Applied Ethics that he founded in 1964 is now the Robert Greenleaf Center for Servant Leadership, headquartered in Atlanta, which not only publishes Greenleaf's writings, but also hosts an annual conference and provides several leadership certification programs for business professionals. One can even enroll in online courses at Greenleaf University, a not-for-profit university founded in 1989 that offers advanced degrees in Management Leadership.[38]

As much as Greenleaf originated a novel management philosophy, he was, in many ways, merely extending earlier contributions of Drucker, McGregor, and others who articulated management as a transformative moral discipline. Like these others, Greenleaf wove together religion and business in ways that elevated the cultural authority of management. Servant-leadership, however, represents only one example of how the cultural authority of management and business were shifting in the early 1970s. In fact, even the general attitudes that Americans held toward work were beginning to reflect the managerial emphasis on the human side of enterprise.

Work in America

On 6 September 1971, President Richard M. Nixon delivered his annual Labor Day address. Like countless other Labor Day speeches, the president discussed the contribution of the work ethic to American prosperity. "The work ethic," he stated, "is engrained in the American character" and accounts for "why a poor nation of 3 million people, over the course of two centuries, lifted itself into the position of the most powerful and respected leader of the free world today."[39] Yet, amid the turmoil of the early 1970s, Nixon warned of a work ethic "under attack" by voices that condemned materialism, ambition and urging "members of disadvantaged groups…to take the welfare road rather than the road of hard work, self-reliance, and self-respect."[40] Admitting that the "work ethic in America is undergoing some changes," Nixon urged business, government, and organized labor to come together and "give the individual worker more responsibility—more of the feeling that his opinion counts."[41] Echoing the earlier concerns of Drucker and McGregor, Nixon declared that "we must always remember that the most important part of the quality of life is the quality of work. And the new need for job satisfaction is the key to the quality of work."[42]

In the wake of President Nixon's Labor Day speech, the federal Department of Health, Education, and Welfare took actions to respond to his concerns. On 29 December, Elliot Richardson, then-Secretary of the Department, formally organized a task force to assess the state of "work in America." Headed by a young Anthropologist James O'Toole, the team would spend the next year working with scholars and formal experts to evaluate ideas and make recommendations about how the public and private sectors might move the nation out of its current social and economic quandary. Coming at a time of significant social change, the final report, published in 1973 as *Work in America: Report of a Special Task Force to the Secretary of Health, Education and Welfare* in 1973, illustrates how general perspectives about work were being transformed.

By the early 1970s, problems ran much deeper than social unrest and campus protest. These problems, to which individuals like Robert Greenleaf had devoted so much energy to solve, were inextricable from broader structural pressures. The effects of capitalist expansion were beginning to strain the postwar systems. National borders were becoming insignificant to the scale and scope of production, trade, communication, and finance. These trends weakened the nation-state itself, while simultaneously increasing the relative power and influence of large private interests. In short, although the United States held onto its dominant position in the emerging global economy, it no longer exercised unquestioned hegemony. The situation had become inordinately more complicated as transnational private institutions began to rival nations as competing political and economic forces with which states had to reckon.

Of course, globalization was not a novel phenomenon, but it was during this particular period of the twentieth century when market expansion rendered conventional macroeconomic principles utterly ineffective. The time-tested

Keynesian economic policies, the accepted wisdom since the New Deal, seemed only to exacerbate the problems. When a ninety-day freeze on wages and prices in August 1971, for instance, failed to stem the tide of inflation, President Nixon began to experiment with less common approaches, culminating with the removal of the dollar from the Gold Standard, a move that essentially marked the final blow to the post–Second World War monetary system known commonly as "Bretton Woods."[43] Moving forward, the legitimacy of the dollar would rest on its status as legal tender alone, and exchange rates, no longer fixed to gold, would be allowed to fluctuate, a change that introduced new volatility into what hitherto had been a relatively stable and predictable international fiscal structure.

With the advantage of hindsight, we can see how these decisions radically altered the dynamics of the entire international financial system. In context, however, they may have represented a sensible option to the practical challenges of the times. By the end of the 1960s, with public debt mounting over the conflict in Southeast Asia, and with eager and able buyers in the fully recovered national economies of Western Europe and Japan, the U.S. government had largely depleted its share of the world's gold supply. Thus, by 1971, the so-called Gold Standard was nothing more than a convenient fiction that no longer could be effectively maintained. The new system of floating exchange rates and fiat currencies, which relied on the logic of market forces to determine prices, would be the new fiction, requiring its own unique set of policies, as yet undefined, through which governments could manage areas of economic distress.

If the intention of these new arrangements had been to reestablish some measure of control over macroeconomic forces, they proved utterly ineffective, at least in the short-term, and only seemed to further demonstrate the irrelevance of the "national" economy in the face of more complex global power relations. The OPEC crisis of 1973 awakened many Americans to a factor of life, of just how deeply the United States was beholden to the global marketplace. Media reports of "gasoline fever" gripping the nation emphasized how individual lives separated by oceans and vast continents were now inextricable.[44] No longer could North Americans expect their economic partners to simply acquiesce to their interests, for the "political" in political economy had been definitively reasserted.

Despite these tremors, we can look back to this time as a period when a new transnational arrangement was taking shape. The establishment of the world's first electronic stock market in 1971, the "over-the-counter" exchange now known as NASDAQ, signaled the initial steps of high finance on its march toward its current dominance in the global economy. Another powerful player in this emergent milieu, the high-tech industry, which we will explore in a later chapter, was providing the underlying connective glue upon which this new transnational capitalism could thrive.

In the midst of these sweeping changes, many entrenched cultural norms and practices appeared dysfunctional, and the *Work in America* study represents an attempt to reassess some of these fundamental assumptions about production. While the report gestures to these macroeconomic and political forces reshaping society, what is perhaps most interesting about *Work in America* is that the authors place the blame for these problems squarely on productivity. In turn, they echoed Nixon's assertion linking "quality of work" with "job satisfaction" and explained declining productivity as a function of individual attitudes about work. *Work in America* effectively redescribes complex political and socioeconomic problems as pathological in nature. The problem, the report claimed, stemmed from two converging factors. On one hand, it was consequence of work in advanced industrial society itself, which typically consisted of "dull repetitive, seemingly meaningless tasks" that undermined American individualism and ingenuity, that "offer little challenge or autonomy."[45] On the other hand, this apathy toward work was something new, an unintended consequence of the recent gains by all segments of postwar American society. Citing the rising status of women, minorities, and "a general increase" in "educational and economic status" of working people, *Work in America* argued "that work has not changed fast enough to keep up with the rapid and widespread changed in worker attitudes, aspirations, and values."[46]

If increased political equality and economic affluence were implicated as the sources of worker distress, rolling back such gains would prove to be no reasonable solution. Instead, O'Toole and his team looked to the addressing the incongruity between, on one hand, the expectations that Americans had about their work, and on the other hand, their lived experience as workers. They appealed to Maslow's theory of human motivation to explain this disjunction. "The very success of industry and organized labor in meeting the basic needs of workers has unintentionally spurred demands for esteemable and fulfilling jobs."[47] Under these changed conditions, established strategies, such as higher wages or shortened workweeks, designed to address what the report dubs "extrinsic factors"—"inadequate pay, incompetent supervision, or dirty working conditions"—were no longer adequate for a labor force that took such measures for granted. "High pay alone will not lead to a job (or life) satisfaction," they claimed. Rather, work, its design and culture, must be reconfigured to tackle the "intrinsic factors"—"achievement, accomplishment, responsibility, and chal-lenging work."[48]

Work in America systemically outlined a robust set of recommendations that would provide for greater worker participation in decision-making, increased autonomy and flexibility, and necessarily prove beneficial to business. The work-place, the educational system, and governmental policy toward industry and labor all required revamping to sustain a healthy and satisfied workforce. In keeping with the spirit of the times, their ideas were quite audacious in scope. They pitched ideas like mandatory sabbaticals for employees every seven years, government-funded retraining programs for redundant workers, and overhaul-ing schools to be less rigid and afford greater freedom to children as they prepare for the new labor market. The report made all of this palatable for businesses by suggesting that "the redesign of work" would presumably "lower such busi-ness costs as absenteeism, tardiness, turnover labor disputes, sabotage, and poor quality."[49]

Yet, as much as the report was a list of plausible strategies, it also documents how the cultural meanings attached to work were changing. The report idealized work, as something more than a necessary factor of production; it simultane-ously satisfies deep psychological needs and extends outward to the social. Work, it asserted, "responds to something profound and basic in human nature" that also "produces something of value for other people."[50] People yearned for mean-ingful, intrinsically rewarding work, "to become masters of their immediate environments and to feel that their work and they themselves are important."[51]

Like Greenleaf, the authors of *Work in America* framed their ideas as an elixir to current social strife. Just as servant-leadership had been critical of dissent while acknowledging the validity of their grievances, the report sought a bal-anced perspective between radicals striving to upend established institutions and conservatives for whom any concession to the opposition was tantamount to defeat. The authors rejected the latter's position that campus unrest con-stituted a "revolt against work" itself. Rather, they countered that the genera-tional protest against the status quo was not "a shift away from valuing work *per se*...but as a shift away from their willingness to take on meaningless work in authoritarian settings that offers only extrinsic rewards."[52] Rather than an attack on the free enterprise system, the counterculture had initiated an attack against the bureaucratic, corporatist capitalism that had come to define postwar indus-trial America. It was, if anything, an embodiment of capitalism's core principles. "Today's youth," they declared, "believe in independence, freedom, and risk—in short, they may have the entrepreneurial spirit of early capitalism...On the other hand, their parents share a managerial ethic that reflects the need for security, order, and dependence that is born of hard times."[53] Just as businesses once had made concessions to a generation of workers during the Depression Era in order to stave off social unrest, a new generation of youth was calling out for corporate America to significance to the individual, to remake work into a meaningful experience, to tend to the immaterial needs of their flock.

In tying the "do-it-yourself" ethos of counterculture to a capitalist nostalgia for earlier days, *Work in America* helped to make the counterculture safe for American capitalism. It acknowledged and reformulated the demands of protestors for existing institutions. Indeed, nearly a decade earlier, reform of work had been an integral component at the genesis of the student movements. Those portions of the Port Huron Statement that discuss work foreshadowed the concepts later developed in *Work in America*. "Work," according to this founding declaration of the Students for a Democratic Society (SDS), "should involve incentives worthier than money or survival; it should be educative, not stultifying; creative, not mechanical; selfdirect, not manipulated, encouraging independence; a respect for others, a sense of dignity and a willingness to accept social responsibility."[54] The fact that *Work in America* lent credence to this critique about work demonstrates how, by the early 1970s, these concerns had entered the mainstream public discourse. Yet the report turned these concerns on their head, redeploying a vehement leftist condemnation of capitalism as its defense. Young Americans simply desired a return to a purer capitalism, to the kind of rugged individualism afforded their ancestors before the rise of bureaucracy and "organization men." They worried that "the American Dream is rapidly becoming myth, and disappearing with it is the possibility of realizing the character traits of independence and autonomy by going into business for oneself."[55] As we will see in later chapters, this is precisely what some baby boomers would do, striking out to found new kinds of businesses infused with these countercultural libertarian values.

As much as *Work in America* was a defense of capitalism, it equally boasts a historical narrative about work that upholds an implicit white, middle-class Protestantism. Starting with the Ancient Greeks and the Hebrews who presumably viewed work negatively, the report traces how various historical eras imagined work differently. In the tradition of Weber, all of this changes with Luther and Calvin during the Reformation when "work became the only way of serving God." Predictably, this in turn "became the foundation for what we call the Protestant ethic" and modern capitalism.[56] *Work in America* represents this particular Protestant inflection of history as universal in order to establish work as "a basic or central institution."[57] Because the report positions work at the center of human life, any reformation of work or the workplace would necessarily impact the social order more broadly. In restoring the intrinsic value of work, the authors foresaw a chance to indirectly strengthen other central (also bourgeois and Protestant) institutions such as family, community, and schools.[58]

As much as *Work in America* appeared to be a bold reimagining of society, it remains ultimately conservative, leaving existing institutions and entrenched social structures largely intact. As we might expect from a government report, the liberal democratic state retains a prominent role yet only insofar as it ensures the preeminence of the market economy. The social structure of the American economy (i.e., capitalism) is simply taken as self-evident and the welfare state presented as a problem. In fact, the report's primary observation—that people desire meaningful work—actually undergirds a veiled critique of the welfare state. "Providing decent work opportunities for lower-class men," the authors note, "would contribute to family stability by enabling women to anticipate marriage to a steadily employed and self-respecting man. We conclude that the key to reducing familial dependency on the government lies in the opportunity for the central provider to work full time at a living wage."[59] Such statements reveal how the this seemingly novel philosophy of work simply valorizes the idyllic picture of the bourgeois nuclear family with the husband/father as breadwinner and the wife/mother as domestic caregiver. If, and only if, businesses would take the necessary steps to provide "decent" work, the inherent failings of the welfare state can be overcome and the stability of the social order be assured.

If anything, *Work in America* situates the market on an equal footing with the state, and asks businesses to assume their proper role as purveyors of the social good. "If work is become a lever for actions, the responsibilities of employers, for example, would have to be greatly changed; they would no longer be considered as essentially producers of goods and services, but as actors who affect, and who in turn are affected by, the major institutions in society."[60] What was needed, the authors declared, was a "humanistic capitalism" that could acknowledge the relationship between economic production and the broader health of society.[61]

Willis Harman and humanistic capitalism

"Humanistic capitalism" was the brainchild of Willis Harman (1918–97), a futures researcher at the quasi-private Stanford Research Institute, who had brought his ideas to the Department of Health, Education, and Welfare in 1971, around the same time that it was beginning to take an interest in the workplace. His ideas about the direction of society not only played an important role in shaping the *Work in America* report but proved to be an important contribution to the discursive entanglement of "work," "religion," and "business."

Although originally an engineer by training, Harman had joined the faculty at Stanford University in 1952, where most of his research efforts focused on vacuum tubes, the technology behind the television, which was rapidly transforming American society.[62] As we will discuss in later chapters, to be an engineer at Stanford during the postwar period was to be at the crossroads of a number of significant trends. The corridor between Stanford and San Jose would soon become known by the moniker "Silicon Valley," bringing together a trifecta of government, academia, and the private sector, where lucrative government contracts and grants underwrote intellectual research and new forms of enterprise.

In addition to this flurry of research and development, Northern California was also home to an experimental hotbed for all things "spiritual." The Bay Area was home to a number of burgeoning spiritual communities and Harman was not immune these cultural forces. It was at this junction of spiritual eclecticism, on one hand, and cutting-edge scientific research, on the other, where his life would make a dramatic course change. In the process, he helped to reinvent the way Americans imagined their working lives.

Harman initially began to turn away from engineering in 1954, after an eccentric law professor named Harry Rathbun invited him to attend a week-long retreat in the hills above San Jose. Known as the "Sequoia Seminars" for surrounding flora, these periodic retreats were a chance for educated middle-class professionals to step away from their highly technical workaday lives and explore the creative, emotional, and intuitive parts of themselves. Popular business author Art Kleiner describes these gatherings as a "sort of secular church," where "members studied scripture and spoke of Jesus Christ as a teacher, but they also studied Jungian psychology and mysticism."[63]

In fact, the Sequoia Seminars were much more than an informal group of eccentrics. The husband and wife team of Harry and Emilia Rathbun saw themselves as leaders of a religious community. They had been avid followers of a Canadian religious scholar, Henry Sharman (1865–1953), who had retired to Northern California during the mid-1930s where he subsequently began mentoring a core group of Stanford faculty. The Rathbuns assumed leadership of the group in 1946 and reformulated it as the Sequoia Seminars. While formally centered on the teachings of Jesus, in practice these retreats drew upon a wide range of philosophical and religious perspectives, blending psychology, scientific rationalism, and non-Western "spiritual" practices.

According to Harman, his initial encounter with the Sequoia Seminar was, in his words, "upending." He recalled years later,

> It hit below the belt. I was aware of thinking about value issues and so on, but on the last day I started to report to the group what I felt and I burst into tears. I wasn't sad. They might have been tears of joy, except that I didn't know what I was joyful about either. I had no intellectual comprehension.[64]

After this encounter, Harman became a regular participant at Sequoia and fed his newfound curiosity for the "non-rational" aspects of human consciousness. He immersed himself in the study of the world's religious traditions, looking for clues to the hidden potential of the human minds. In particular, Harman was drawn to the ideas of Aldous Huxley and other Perennial philosophers who declared that all religions pointed to a common "mystical" reality.

During the years that followed, he moved away from engineering and began delving into the study of altered states of consciousness, a topic he approached with an engineer's penchant for precision and empirical testing. What mattered most to Harman was not whether so-called mystical experiences possessed some objective truth but rather how they might benefit individuals and society. How could these experiences improve psychological health? And, with a better understanding, could they serve as tools for creating a better world?

In pursuit of this new line of research, Harman probed some of the more controversial areas of cognitive research at the time. He visited the Society for Psychical Research, for instance, where RosalindHeywood had been investigating the paranormal since the late 1930s.[65] Closer to home, Harman reached out to people like Myron Stolaroff, who was conducting some of the earliest scientific studies into psychedelics. Soon, Harman and others were reportedly experimenting regularly with mescaline and LSD.[66] Like his better-known contemporary at Harvard Timothy Leary, he remained convinced that, when administered carefully, LSD could not only combat mental illness but open up humanity to new avenues of growth. In one study published in 1963, he claimed that these substances "give promise of being of immense aid in the exploration of other states of consciousness, in coming to new realizations of the nature of Self and of the potentialities of man."[67] While he expressed more caution than others like Leary, who at the time was testing the effects of LSD on prison inmates in Concord, Massachusetts, he nonetheless felt that altered forms of consciousness could unlock latent human potential, facilitate new ways of thinking that promised to alleviate some of the most pressing social, economic, and political issues of the day.[68] Ultimately, the use of psychedelics in formal scientific studies become increasingly questionable through the 1960s, and Congress finally imposed a ban in 1968.[69]

Perhaps in response to this growing unpopularity of psychedelic research, Harman left the university in 1967 to take a position with the Stanford Research Institute (SRI), a private research organization founded by university trustees after the Second World War to conduct interdisciplinary research across a wide range of subjects.[70] At SRI, Harman would not only continue his consciousness studies unimpeded but would help to establish "futures studies," a burgeoning field of study dedicated to developing models that could predict the possible "futures" of society.

Futures research suited Harman quite well because it presented the perfect opportunity to synthesize his interest in consciousness with his technical expertise. On one hand, futures research maps complex social systems, like social systems, and yet, on the other hand, Harman relied on a theory of society that privileged culture and values over structure. "Every society," he stated, "forms around some basic paradigm, some tacitly assumed set of fundamental beliefs about man, society, the universe, and the source of authority."[71] In sum, Harman argued that society can be best explained by its "worldview."

The worldview of American society at the end of the 1960s was rife with problems, according to Harman. He shared the sentiments of Greenleaf and Drucker that the conventional social order was breaking down. Yet resisted their fears that without proper leadership, society would descend into barbarism. Instead, he viewed these changes positively, as the inevitable growing pains of a society undergoing an evolution in consciousness. From time to time, he argued, such shifts had occurred throughout history. For instance, Harman explained the transition from the European Middle Ages to modernity as "a shift from a worldview of oneness, connectedness, wholeness, to a worldview characterized by *separateness*—separateness of mind from matter, observer from observed, man from nature, 'fundamental particles' and even persons from one another."[72]

Although the modern worldview introduced many benefits, according to Harman this only came at a high cost: modern rationalism divided life into discrete, rationally ordered domains. Reminiscent of Weber's "iron cage," each of these spheres (work family, religion, etc.) now functioned according to its own internal logic, yielding a schizophrenic lived experience. In particular, he cited "religion" and "work" as two domains where this unnatural separation was most acutely felt. In the medieval world, Harman stated, religion pervaded all aspects of life. "The world was enchanted, infused with spirit, permeated with mean-ing. The medieval individual felt at home in nature; the universe was alive and imbued with purpose."[73] The shift to modernity therefore was nothing less than the confinement of religion, a dramatic desacralization of politics, philosophy, and economy.

The confinement of religion, however, produced an inherent contradiction for industrial society. Also echoing Weber, Harman attributed the emergence of the market economy to the Protestant ethic. Because the work ethic provided modern individuals with meaning and purpose, not only had the increasing secularization of society eventually undermined the moral imperative to pro-duce, but industrialization was rendering the material basis for labor increas-ingly irrelevant. In an advanced global marketplace marked by high technology, the Protestant work ethic failed to account for individual experience.[74] Some individuals are simply left out (unemployment); others are forced to take what-ever narrow, menial, or hyper-specialized job they can find just to survive; only a fortunate few will achieve work that is truly rewarding. In short, Harman was suggesting that the modern worldview, like the earlier Medieval worldview, had reached its inevitable conclusion because it could no longer adequately cohere society.

While the picture seems bleak, Harman remained optimistic about the future. He fervently believed that humanity could overcome its problems, but solutions have would have to be unconventional, tapping into the realm of consciousness rather than seeking structural reform. We only needed to get out of the way and allow the emerging "transindustrial" society to replace the dying modern world. While not a return to the "oneness" of the medi-eval consciousness, this transindustrial society rejects the "separateness" of modernity in favor of "wholeness."

> Work, play, and learning would coalesce. The search for understanding that is science, the quest for wholeness that is psychotherapy, the reach for relationship that is religion, and the unfolding of potentialities that is education would be reunited, somewhat as they were in Ancient Greece and in Europe during the Middle Ages.[75]

The program for the future that Harman created and eventually pitched to the task force that produced *Work in America* he dubbed "Humanistic Capitalism." It entailed a completely new imagining of American culture that could estab-lish a sustainable future in this "transindustrial" age. First, he asserted the necessity of an "ecological ethic" that recognized the limits and environmental consequences of mass production. Second, and more importantly for our purposes, Harman advocated for an ethic of "self-realization" to replace the outmoded Protestant ethic. Clearly influenced by the popularity of Maslow's theory of self-actualization, Harman suggested that this self-realization makes sense for advanced industrial societies, like the United States, which require only a fraction of the labor force to be engaged in actual work to meet the basic survival needs of the whole society but nonetheless where work is still the source of individual self-worth. Under such conditions, "*employment is primarily the activity of self-development*, and secondarily the production of goods and services."[76] Society must therefore come to discern "work" as human right, as the area designated for human flourishing rather than merely a means to material rewards. "With these attitude changes," he argued, "there would be a redesigning of the workplace to invest work with more meaning."[77]

He anticipated that the release of "religion" from its modern confinement would provide the cultural resources required for meaningful work. He observed everywhere the "multifold signs of a respiritualization of Western society" that will imbue each and every aspect of life, including work, with new significance.[78] He was unwavering in his conviction that the "perennial wisdom" of the world's religious traditions would achieve a new dominant epistemic authority over cultural life in the transindustrial age. Through alternate forms of consciousness, individuals would cultivate intuitive, subtle ways of knowing that had been familiar to the ancients but nearly lost with the modern emphasis on rationality.

Of course, because the intrinsic value of some jobs was not obvious, "humanistic capitalism" would require businesses and the state to articulate some "meaningful 'central project' to give purpose to relatively routine work."[79] Just as the race to the moon had galvanized American society around developing space technology, a central mission ties each individual's contribution indirectly to greater purpose.

This mixture of new economic and ecological ethics, a renewed confidence in revealed or intuitive knowledge, along with organizations committed to the greater good, comprised the major components of Harman's "humanistic capitalism" when he approached the Office of Education in 1971. Even though Harman's ideas would prove to be important for the composition of *Work in America*, neither his ideas nor the O'Toole's report gained much support in the administration. According to one Harman's colleagues, his program was considered "so far out and touchy-feely and irrelevant."[80] The Office of Education, it seemed, was more concerned with immediate, short-term solutions to the disarray on colleges campuses at the time than experimenting with long-term unconventional programs for social change. Despite the lukewarm response, the completion of the *Work in America* study and Harman's influence on it does signal how even the state was willing to rethink the purpose of work. The public discussion of work was moving away from a materialist perspective and toward an emphasis on the *experience* of work itself. Entrenched views of work as a purely economic activity were losing ground and thinkers like Harman certain aided this process.

In light of the government's less enthusiastic reception, Harman and his colleagues at SRI turned away from the public sector and began to think of other ways to promote their ideas. In the years to come, he would make a home in the world of nonprofit research and, like Robert Greenleaf, would find in the business world a sympathetic ear for his programs. Over time, Harman came to view business, rather than the state, as the domain of society best equipped to lead humanity into the transindustrial age. From 1975 until his death over twenty years later, he served as the Director for the Institute of Noetic Sciences (IONS), a research organization dedicated to the study of "consciousness and healing, extending human capacities, and emerging worldviews."[81]

IONS had been founded in 1973 by the eccentric former Apollo 14 Astronaut Edgar Mitchell (1930–2016). According to Mitchell, in an oft-repeated account, while returning from his lunar mission, he experienced an epiphany that transformed his life:

> Seeing our planet from space was an event with some of the qualities traditionally ascribed to religious experience. It triggered a deep insight into the nature of existence—the sort of insight that radically changes the inner person. My thinking—indeed, my consciousness—was altered profoundly. I came to feel a moral responsibility to pass on the transformative experience of seeing Earth from the larger perspective.[82]

He subsequently started IONS as a way to bring together like-minded researchers who could pursue unorthodox projects. Its board of directors reflects this commitment to flouting convention, featuring an eclectic mix of traditional scholars like social psychologist Mica Estrada, progressive-minded activists such as Harriet Crosby, and leaders from the corporate world, including the founder of the successful men's clothier The Men's Wearhouse, George Zimmer. Moreover, an emphasis on "spirituality" is readily apparent throughout IONS. For instance, IONS partners with a number of overtly spiritual organizations such as the Esalen Institute, and Deepak Chopra's Chopra Center. Under

Harman's leadership, the institute served as a point of convergence for academic research, business, and spirituality.

While serving as the director of IONS, Harman cofounded the World Business Academy (WBA) in 1987, an organization through which he aspired to bring "humanistic capitalism" to a broader audience, more explicitly to bring "humanistic capitalism" out of the theoretical and into the mingled spirituality and business. Its mission is "to inspire business to assume responsibility for the whole of society and assist those in business who share our values."[83] Like IONS, the academy boasts a cast of business leaders, academics, and spiritual leaders. Academy fellows such as Deepak Chopra are featured alongside clinical psychiatrist Diane V. Cirincione, or Blaine Bartlett, founder of the leader consulting group Avatar Resources. WBA works on a number of initiatives, such as advocating the closure of the Diablo Canyon Nuclear Plant in California, which embody Harman's ecological ethic and seek the transformation of social consciousness through better business practices.[84]

The point is that, over time, Harman increasingly came to see business the institution primarily responsible for shaping the future of society, and dedicated his time to forming institutions that could further this goal. "The modern business corporation," he wrote in 1988, "is probably the most adaptive institution humankind has ever devised."[85] Global Corporations, not nation-states, would provide the great "central project" through which individuals find "a strong and deep sense of purposefulness and a vision of the future."[86] Moreover, the corporate environment would "emphasize growth and empowerment of the individual as the key to corporate success," linking corporate profitability to individual self-development.[87] Corporate leadership presumably would bring about a new epistemology, one that recognized the forgotten "perennial wisdom" present in the mystical core of all religions. "The revolution is already happening," he claimed,

> it involved both a new kind of businessperson and a restructuring of business as we have known it. Large Corporations are downsizing and dematerializing before our eyes. In many cases the organizational fragments and discarded persons create new paradigm entities with a new set of operative values and a new sense of the true mission of business.[88]

In many ways, Harman's description of this unfolding new age was quite accurate. When he wrote these words in the late 1980s, the postwar welfare state was rapidly losing ground to economic liberalization. Business had assumed unprecedented cultural authority as organized labor waned and the health of society came to be indistinguishable in public discourse from the health of "markets." A neoliberal consensus was emerging that placed the logic (and therefore the interests) of global capitalism beyond criticism, as simply the order of things. Indeed, only in the context of neoliberalization do Harman's prescriptions make sense. If, as he states, "the business of business must shift to playing a creative role in developing a sustainable culture on this planet," it is only because business already holds a hegemonic position in the global pecking order.

While Greenleaf enjoys a broad following in the business community, Harman's influence has proven to be more modest and targeted. Yet, both participated in reshaping business thought and blazed the trail for others who would even more explicitly link business to the religious and the spiritual. Their efforts had thoroughly inscribed "management" and "leadership" as much more than business professions; their work helped to remake managers into agents of moral wisdom who performed a vital service for society. As business scholars and managers began to open advocate for "workplace spirituality" in the late 1990s, they would remember Harman and Greenleaf as pioneers of what they understood as a bona fide movement.

3

Management, Spirituality, and Religion: Theology and Spiritual Practice in Neoliberal Society

Every summer, at the annual conference for the Academy of Management (AOM), scholars and practitioners from a wide range of fields, such as Human Resources or Organizational Behavior, gather to network and share ideas about management and organizations. While these aforementioned fields regularly boast several thousand members, a modest subset of AOM members take part in academic panels and workshops sponsored by the "Management, Spirituality, and Religion" Interest Group (MSR). According to its statement of purpose, MSR examines "how spirituality and religion can influence organizational dynamics and affect management outcomes."[1]

The scope of topics at these MSR panels range from empirically focused studies of religious expression in the workplace to more abstract explorations of the idea of "evil" in organizational cultures. Its members espouse a mixture of more "disinterested" scholarly research on religion and those that directly endorse or participate in practices deemed religious or spiritual. At the 2014 annual meeting in Philadelphia, for example, MSR sponsored early-morning meditation sessions, blurring the distinction between religious study and religious practice. Moreover, the group hosts an annual retreat each year in tandem with the AOM meeting where attendees can "explore practices from a variety of sacred, spiritual, and psychological traditions based on the interests of participants."[2] "Not only are we home to many of the world's leading academics, scholars, and researchers in this area," the group's website reads, "but our members include like-minded students, practitioners, thought-leaders, business professionals, public servants, consultants, and many others."[3]

To some degree, this blurred line between insiders and outsiders reflects the trajectory of management scholarship more broadly, which at once combines the disinterested study of organizations with the development and testing of various managerial strategies—observer and practitioner are equally welcome. AOM itself is a hybrid organization, an extension of social science and of industry, from which its professional standards and assumptions are never wholly divorced. Thus, for MSR to embrace religion and spirituality both as a topic of inquiry and as an instrument of practice simply aligns with the overall trajectory of management research.

Since the group's official inception in 2002, MSR has functioned as one of the epicenters of overt engagement of the business community with spirituality, which, according to scholars and advocates, seems to have emerged sometime between the late 1980s and early 1990s. In *God at Work: The History and Promise of the Faith and Work Movement*, author David Miller, the director of Princeton University's "Faith and Work Initiative" (FWI), argues that current interest in the integration of faith and work began around 1985.[4] Similarly Lake Lambert observes in *Spirituality Inc.* (2009) that "the 1990s witnessed an explosion in popular books about workplace spirituality, and in a few cases, the spirituality in business books were themselves written by established academics."[5] Management professor Jerry Biberman, the inaugural chair of the MSR interest group, writes that the relationship between spirituality and work is "as old as time" and that recent developments merely indicate a "renewed interest" in an important topic that has been too long ignored in modern society.[6] While the overt interest with the intersection of spirituality and work may have gained traction during the last decade of the twentieth century, it is important to note that it was the offspring of older trends in management discourse, as discussed in previous chapters. However, the emergence at the end of the millennium of a distinct subfield of management scholars dedicated to the study of "workplace spirituality," as it is often dubbed, does signal that something was happening.

Its advocates attribute this surge of business interest in religion and spirituality to a number of factors. However, as this chapter explores, the history of workplace spirituality, as it has been narrated, is largely the invention of its advocates and therefore is designed to serve their particular aims. Rather, these histories are themselves rhetorical constructions, an essential ingredient in discursive repertoire on workplace spirituality, which arose in response to the socioeconomic changes taking place in the late twentieth century. Contextualizing this discourse, its ideas, and its authorizing narratives reveals its intimate and inextricable relationship to neoliberal reasoning.

The neoliberal workplace

If the postwar economic order had begun to show fissures during the late 1960s and the early 1970s with the breakdown of Bretton Woods and increasingly global scope of production and consumption, it was during the 1980s and early 1990s when the postwar concord between industry, labor, and government that had made relatively stable and secure careers possible started to undergo dramatic structural changes. The election of Ronald Reagan to the U.S. presidency in the fall of 1980 exacerbated the demise of Keynesian economics that had gradually occurred over the previous decade and inaugurated new thinking that emphasized economic liberalization, a libertarian aversion (at least in the ideological sense) to state interference in the marketplace, and a commitment to policies favorable to the owners and investors of capital. Somewhat anachronistically, we might recognize these changes as the initial ascendency of neoliberal political economy.

Shortly after assuming office in 1981, Reagan demonstrated his mettle when, facing down striking Air Traffic Controllers, he chose to fire over 11,000 workers rather than consider their grievances. In the wake of the failed strike, organized labor, which since the New Deal had relied on some measure of government-endowed legitimacy to operate, found itself overnight without the government-endowed legitimacy it had enjoyed since the passage of the National Labor Relations Act in 1935. Although this instance concerned only public-sector employees, it undoubtedly encouraged labor leaders to be more accommodating when dealing with employers.

Reagan's anti-unionism coincided with other changes that were transforming the structure of work during this period. The Revenue Act of 1978, initially intended to limit access of executives to deferred income plans, inadvertently paved the way for the creation of the 401k retirement savings plan, which employers prefer because, unlike pensions, they shift the assumed risk of the plan from employer to the individual employee. Between 1979, when the first employer adopted a 401k option, and 1990, nearly twenty million individuals enrolled.[7] Further, the portable nature of the 401k diminished the prospect and the incentive for lifetime employment with a single firm. While greater mobility might decrease one's dependence a single employer, it also meant greater economic uncertainty for workers.

The proliferation of corporate strategies to maximize efficiency also impacted the structure of work. "Downsizing," "mergers and acquisitions," and "outsourcing" emerged as household terms. Companies reorganized, often opting to subcontract with other, smaller firms to fulfill needs previously accomplished internally. Salaries and wages, in the interest of productivity, once largely tethered to seniority, were instead associated with elaborate performance evaluations. Each of these strategic trends placed greater control over jobs into the hands of company authorities.

These direct changes to the nature of employment coincided with reforms at the macroeconomic level that would undermine economic security. Trade liberalization, culminating in the passage of the North American Free Trade Agreement (NAFTA) in 1994 and the formation of the World Trade Organization (WTO) a year later, eased the ability of capital investment and production to seek cheaper labor markets. Whether unionized or not, workforces faced a distinct disadvantage over their employers in an environment where threats of layoffs, offshoring, and downsizing could be more easily be carried out. All of these converging changes rendered work for many Americans more tenuous, unpredictable, and yielding less fruits.

Given the rising uncertainty and insecurity many Americans now confronted at work, it is perhaps unremarkable that management philosophies celebrating autonomy, entrepreneurship, and flatter hierarchies proved wildly popular. International bestsellers such *In Search of Excellence* (1982) by Thomas Peters and Robert Watermann and Steven Covey's *Seven Habits of Highly Effective People* (1989) defined cutting-edge of management thought during the 1980s. Working within the moralistic tradition of Drucker and Greenleaf, popular management thinkers asserted a vision of corporate authority as decentered and where managers expend their efforts not on control but primarily on articulating the firm's mission and upholding a core set of values. These blueprints of effective corporate culture work because they redescribe the very sources of employee distress as virtues. When Peters and Watermann, for example, suggest that "innovative companies are especially adroit at continually responding to change of any sort in their environments," they implicitly endorse the position that companies should have much greater discretion to pursue profitability.[8] Likewise, calls for increased employee autonomy positively reframe the loss of job security and career predictability facing workers. Moreover, the celebration of flattened hierarchies and meritocracy effectively mask the very real ways that power has shifted upward to management (and increasingly to major stockholders) and away from employees, whether organized or not. It is against this backdrop of rapidly changing conditions of society generally, and of workplace culture specifically, that we should examine the discourse about spirituality in the workplace that matured over the 1990s into first decade of the new millennium.

Inventing a spirituality for the workplace

By most accounts, business interest in spirituality and religion began to dramatically increase throughout the last decade of the twentieth century, culminating in some kind of distinct social movement. However, while perhaps chronologically accurate, these historical narratives prove to be little more than tautologies that merely serve the ideological aims of their authors. In fact, articulating a history for the movement contributed to its own invention. The very scholars that reported some variation of the claim that "there has been a dramatic upsurge in interest in spirituality among those who study, teach, and write about business management" were the ones expressing interest in the topic.[9] Unfortunately, the explosion of research over the course of the 1990s culminating in the formation of MSR in the first years of the millennium constitutes the bulk of available evidence that we have to substantiate attestations of this growing interest and therefore such histories are largely self-referential. However, by approaching these narratives as rhetorical, as performing some kind of ideological work, they offer clues from which we can begin to place them in the wider context of a socioeconomic change and the growing cultural authority of management discourse.

The economic liberalization of the Reagan era served as the foil against which workplace spirituality was constructed. Some business scholars explicitly cite the anxieties and distresses arising from corporate restructuring, globalization of production, and the more general shift away from manufacturing jobs as the reasons for the turn to spirituality at work. For instance, in one oft-cited study, Donde Ashmos and Dennis Duchon observe that "many believe that the downsizing, reengineering and layoffs of the past decade have turned the American workplace into an environment where workers are demoralized."[10] Coupled with the embrace of "philosophies such as Zen Buddhism and Confucianism" and other factors, these changes have piqued corporate interest in spirituality.[11] Judi Neal similarly opines that "downsizing and other turbulent changes that organizations have been going through over the past decade" have left working people "scared and feeling devalued and dehumanized."[12]

Although these scholars acknowledge these changes as a source of distress, they present these trends as inevitable and natural, rather than the product of historically situated interests. Downsizing, outsourcing, and offshoring merely represent corporate survival strategies as "markets become more competitive and technology more advanced," as one scholar stated in 1999.[13] Against the backdrop of these immutable forces and their necessary products, scholars like Judi Neal et al. (1999) suggest that the only option is for market actors to become more responsive by embracing market-based logic to solve problems. In her call for management researchers to embrace "spiritual perspectives," she writes:

> Individual transformation is needed because managers and leaders must be proactive leaders, open to change, and flexible enough to adapt to constantly shifting demands from their organizations. Organizations must transform because of the shift to the global marketplace, increased competitiveness, and the rapid acceleration of change. Societal transformation must occur because of environmental degradation, shifts in economic power, inequalities in distribution of wealth, and unsolved social problems such as discrimination and illiteracy.[14]

In Neal's depiction of the social order, individuals, organizations, and even societies are reduced to agents in a market environment. The global market inevitably creates problems with which societies must deal; the problem for individuals and organizations alike stems not from these market forces but rather from the unwillingness of agents to embrace the logic of global capitalism by "transforming" themselves according to the shifting demands of the marketplace. As we will discuss later, Neal, of course, will propose a spiritual solution to this dilemma.

The consequences of economic liberalization to individual workers, in turn, are presented as ontologically unavoidable and beyond critique. In *God at Work* (2007), David Miller, the director of Princeton University's Faith and Work Initiative, concedes that "the merger mania" of the 1980s "had a significant human cost" and that "stock market crash of 1987 caused further dislocation to blue- and white-collar workers alike."[15] However, Miller sees these changes as irrevocable and apolitical. "The old covenant between employer and employee," he concludes, "with expectations of loyalty and lifelong employment, was forever over."[16] The point is that while scholars like Neal and Miller may have acknowledged the consequences of economic liberalization, they nonetheless define them as processes that transcend human institutions, as existential realities with which we must contend. Furthermore, in order to deal with these "inevitable" globalizing conditions, business scholars crafted narratives promoting the integration of work and spirituality.

Some of these narratives are personal; they often convey a sense of loss, a perception that one's work is unrewarding, which subsequently gets resolved through some engagement with religion, spirituality, the sacred, and the like. In one of the earliest volumes on the topic titled *Spirit at Work: Discovering the Spirituality in Leadership* (1994), editor Jay Conger, at the time Associate Professor of Organizational Behavior at McGill University, follows this pattern. He introduces the volume by recounting his personal journey of spiritual growth through work. Conger maintains that, at some point in the late 1980s, he had concluded that an almost impassible chasm had opened between his professional life and his spiritual life. While "home can nourish my spirit through intimacy," he asserts, work "more often feels like a separate activity."[17] This sense of bifurcation apparently extended to his misgivings about organized religion as well. As a baby boomer, Conger admits that he drifted away from the religion of his upbringing and embraced a looser, less authoritarian brand of spiritual seeking. Yet, after turning to so-called eastern spirituality through the teachings of Ram Dass and texts such as the *Bhagavad Gita*, he continued to crave more structure akin to the church of his youth. Because work represented his primary community outside the home, he felt that perhaps work could be a place of spiritual sustenance.[18]

In 1992, Conger decides to organize what he dubbed a "small gathering of people interested in management and spirituality to begin wrestling with the possible intersections of these two seemingly disparate world."[19] Although expecting only modest turnout, he was surprised at the enthusiastic response. "It was like a secret society," he remembers, "where suddenly you discover half of your acquaintances are members."[20] Ultimately, the conversation initiated at the conference was the impetus to produce the 1994 volume in which he writes this narrative.

Many years later, David Miller repeats this approach in his discussion of the so-called faith and work movement. After sixteen years in international finance, Miller abruptly left in 1995 for "seminary to study theology and see what it had to do with the business world and the people in the workplace."[21] He recalls writing a letter to "some four hundred executive contacts and business acquaintances around the world" declaring his intention to change careers:

> Expecting mostly snickering and derisive responses, I was stunned to receive back more than 150 faxes, letters, and phone calls. What surprised me even more was that my letter seemed to strike a deep chord with the recipients. Despite external measures of career and financial success many of these executives were

feeling a deep emptiness and a disconnect from the beliefs, people, and things they valued most in life.[22]

Like Conger, Miller uses personal history to construct a rhetorical problem and its subsequent resolution. They each establish the separation of "work" and "spirituality" or (in Miller's case) "faith" as *unnatural*, and thereafter seek a remedy. In the process, Miller and Conger "discover" that others share their suffering, suggesting that the problem is actually cultural or societal rather than personal, all of which leads them to see the need for a movement that can (re)integrate these two domains of human life.

The idea that modern society coerces individuals to unnaturally separate their work from their spiritual or religious life runs throughout the literature and is repeatedly used to justify work/spirit integration. "Work," writes one author in 1997, "is being rediscovered as a source of spiritual growth and connection to others."[23] Gilbert Fairholm introduces his extensive study on quantitative spirituality and work in his book *Capturing the Heart of Leadership* (1997) by declaring that "business is business precisely because people bring their whole self, their spiritual self with them to work, not because they leave it at home."[24] The growing corporate interest in spirituality, according to this line of argument, is a corrective measure, an acknowledgment by business leaders that organizations must nurture the spiritual side of their employees.

While proponents see their message as novel, it merely recycles a long-established convention in management discourse, concerned with treating employees as distinct from other factors of production. From this perspective, workplace spirituality resembles McGregor's "Human Side of Enterprise," Maslow's "Eupsychian Management," or Willis Harman's "Humanistic Capitalism." Consequently, the role of managers in these "spiritually" attuned work environments appear similar, if not quite identical to, Greenleaf's servant-leaders. Although these thinkers emphasize "spirituality," they are nonetheless mobilizing rhetorical strategies and participating in a well-entrenched discursive tradition in business circles.

Neoliberal theology

As Lake Lambert observes, the business turn toward to the "spiritual" is basically "a matter of semantics as certain benefits have been repackaged and reinterpreted as being part of an employee's and employer's spiritual identity."[25]

However, interest in spirituality in the workplace cannot simply be reduced to a language game. The introduction of spirituality into management discourse transformed it into something altogether unique. As much as it extended popular managerial perspectives, workplace spirituality introduced new ways of conceiving work, business, and society within the context of the late twentieth century. It represents what Doreen Massey dubs a "vocabulary of the economy," a conceptual framework for describing the social world that reinforces neoliberal values. The language of spirituality serves "as a powerful means by which new subjectivities are constructed and enforced," configuring market processes as metaphysical and individual choice as a spiritual act.[26]

Because the discourse on workplace spirituality assumes the veracity of a spiritual dimension to human life in order to make broader claims about the nature of individuals and society, it could itself be characterized as a theological exercise. A closer look at three prominent examples from the literature demonstrates how these thinkers are negotiating normative ideas about individual selves, work, and spirituality. While masquerading as objective descriptions of the real, these examples illustrate how workplace spirituality actually performs ideological work. It provides an account of reality that makes sense of the prevailing conditions of workday life under neoliberalism.

One of the contributors to Jay Conger's early edited volume *Spirit at Work* (1994) was a sociologist turned Quaker named Parker Palmer. Like Greenleaf, Palmer narrates his life as complex entanglement of religious and professional life. As a young adult, he briefly pursued graduate studies in theology, enrolling for a year at Union Theological Seminary, before abruptly changing direction to obtain a PhD in Sociology from the University of California at Berkeley in 1970. Palmer claims that he always felt that American society, with its strict delineation between the sacred and profane worlds and rigidly define professional spheres, offered him no home. Through this struggles, he eventually carved out space for himself as a teacher on the topic of "vocation."[27]

Understood properly, the concept of "vocation" differs from "work" according to Palmer. Work is a response to a need, an "action driven by external necessity or demand,"[28] Vocation arises from within and expresses the inner, pure self, uncorrupted by culture. In his contribution to Conger's volume, a short essay entitled "Leading from Within," Palmer argues that one's vocation emerges from the interior and too often people allow the external conditions of the world to dictate their actions in life. Leadership, accordingly, requires a spiritual journey that "moves inward and downward, not outward and upward towards abstraction."[29]

Echoing earlier thinkers like Greenleaf and Drucker, he employs religious rhetoric to emphasize the moral or ethical dimensions of leadership, but Palmer also agrees with Harman's assessment that spirituality is something more elementary, as a subtle and oft-overlooked core of all experience. "The spiritual traditions are primarily about *reality*," and this reality, for Palmer, emanates from the individual subject.[30] He writes that the essential message of spirituality can be understood in the depth-psychological concept of *projection*. "Consciousness," he states, "precedes being, and consciousness can help deform, or reform, our world."[31] Leadership, therefore, begins in the mind with a conscious choice to see the world as it should be seen.

The self about which Palmer writes is radically individualistic and experiences freedom as an *a priori* condition of its existence, rather than the product of external social conditions. Individuals realize their freedom through "a process of contemplation by which we penetrate the illusion of enslavement and claim our own inner liberty."[32] Palmer imagines the self as real, as a bounded object located in, yet wholly separate from, the physical world. External factors, though they may obscure this authentic self, cannot corrupt its distinctive "inborn talents."[33]

Palmer's conception of the self is not rigid and unchanging, but a loose, flexible self. Practical spirituality, Palmer argues, allows the individual, first, access to this authentic self, and, second, to establish a harmony between it and the external world. Knowledge of one's true self imparts knowledge of one's "rightful place in the scheme of things, its rightful relation to the prince, the people, the tree, and the task at hand."[34] In short, the social order, its hierarchy of status, and as Palmer will suggest, one's work in the world, all acquire significance through a cultivated, spiritual awareness of the authentic self.

Ultimately, Palmer uses "spirituality," "self," and "vocation" in his writings to promote a program of *individual* rather than *social* change. However, he maintains that within these transformations at the individual level lie the seeds of societal healing. Healthy, spiritually astute selves persist in an interdependent relationship with the community, and "people who know that they are embedded in an eternal community are both freed and empowered to become who they are born to be."[35] Palmer's project, therefore, resists structural reform and rather offers autonomous individuals a path to reconnect with others (e.g., society) within the existing social order. Spirituality allows one to understand her true calling, which in turn represents how participates in this "eternal community."[36]

Palmer views spirituality as a way for individuals to overcome a perceived distance between "work," a socially defined act of survival, and "vocation," an inborn set of dispositions and talents unique to and constitutive of personhood. Spirituality accounts for and collapses this apparent chasm between, on one hand, an expectation of individual autonomy and, on the other, the social constraints imposed on this expectation by redefining freedom as an inner private state, achieved not through sociopolitical struggle but through interiorly generated liberation.

In the midst of an increasingly unpredictable global economy, Palmer's theology of work offers a program for psychic survival. It eliminates (or more accurately masks) a paradox of neoliberal capitalism stemming from two dueling forms of authority. While economic liberalism celebrates the individual as sovereign, it simultaneously exalts the market as a regnant ordering principle. The insecurity stemming from the conditions of the neoliberal workplace, Palmer suggests, are unconnected to individual freedom. A spirituality of work reassures individuals that, despite a dwindling welfare state and the rollback of favorable labor conditions, they remain the masters over their own lives, and that their inner, psychological "freedom" is far superior than any security that can be externally procured.

Parker Palmer follows in the footsteps of other management thinkers who discuss work as a moral act. For him the secret of a fulfilling working life remains unquantifiable and defies empirical measurements. Other management thinkers, however, have asserted that spirituality in the workplace *could* be empirically captured and rationally analyzed. Ian Mitroff and Elizabeth Denton conducted one of the first and most influential systematic studies of workplace spirituality in the late 1990s. Rather than explore the philosophical intricacies of work, spirituality, and self, Mitroff and Denton made them the dependent variables of their empirical research in order to explain the relationship between each. Their complete study, *A Spiritual Audit of Corporate America* (1999), established many of the parameters that have become central to ongoing research in this area and serves as a prime example of how workplace spirituality proffers a kind of neoliberal theology.

A Spiritual Audit profiles the results of an extensive qualitative and quantitative study conducted over a wide range of businesses. Mitroff and Denton complemented numerous in-depth interviews with senior executives with survey data from a mailed questionnaire targeting over two thousand human resources executives regarding the role of "meaning and purpose in the workplace."[37] In their analysis, the authors conclude that the contemporary workplace suffers a critical lack of spirituality and that, under current market conditions, "no organization can survive long without spirituality and soul."[38]

More precisely, they are suggesting spirituality as an effective business strategy to corporate leadership.

Mitroff and Denton attribute this presumed spiritual deficit of most firms to modern rationalism. Spirituality and work have become disassociated from one another in the contemporary world, a state of affairs that "goes against the grain of deep human needs and puts an intolerable burden on individuals."[39] While this separation may have allowed safe social spaces in which individuals could manage their spiritual lives privately, Mitroff and Denton argue that "at our current stage of human development, we face a new challenge. We have gone too far in separating the key elements."[40] Modern society has become overly rationalized and fractured. Casting the problem in dire terms, they warn that "unless organizations become more spiritual, the fragmentation and ambivalence felt by individuals cannot be repaired."[41]

Beneath this argument lies a particular model of the individual subject. Mitroff and Denton define the "soul" as "the deepest essence of what it means to be human" and "that which ties together and integrates all of the separate and various parts of a person."[42] The soul—the spiritual component of an individual— is the *sine qua non* of personhood. On the basis of this model of subjectivity, Mitroff and Denton see the modern world as an existential threat to the soul because it incarcerates spirituality within the religious domain. This proves no less truthful in the modern secular organization where expressions of religious and spiritual life are, at least informally, stigmatized. Naturally, they argue that "spiritual" organizations gain a competitive advantage over more conventional firms precisely because they align with the natural constitution of persons.

In their analysis, they propose a five-part typology of this organizational spirituality:

1. *Religious-based organizations* (religiously affiliated organizations, like Catholic charities, Mormon-based business firms, etc.)
2. *Evolutionary organizations* (firms, like the YMCA, which originate as religious but shift to a more ecumenical position)
3. *Recovering organizations* (organizations that adopt the 12-step principles of Alcoholics Anonymous)
4. *Socially responsible organizations* (firms whose leaders aspire to strong spiritual principles, e.g., Ben and Jerry's)
5. *Values-based organizations* (founders or heads subscribe to general philosophical principles but not explicitly identified as either religious or spiritual)[43]

Mitroff and Denton make a subtle, yet significant move here with this taxonomy. Not only do they recognize that organizations can exhibit "spirituality," but this "organizational spirituality" constitutes an inherent aspect of all firms, whether explicitly claimed or not. Spirituality refers to an objective condition of individual as well as organizational structure.

If spirituality represents an objective quality, Mitroff and Denton set out to define and measure it with scientific precision. Relying on the self-reports of their survey participants, they propose that "spirituality" should be understood (1) as highly personal and informal, (2) as distinct from religion, not formal or organized but perennial and trans-denominational, (3) as the source of ultimate meaning and purpose in life, and (4) as an "inexhaustible source of faith and will power."[44] Armed with this definition or spirituality, they proceed to develop a scale for determining how well a given organization expresses or suppresses these qualities. In effect, Mitroff and Denton treat spirituality as a categorically distinct yet normally occurring phenomenon of organizational behavior.

Mitroff and Denton complement this reified notion of spirituality with understandings of "work" and "workplace" that reflect and advance the material interests of businesses. For example, their research demonstrates that individuals privilege the intrinsic rewards of work over any material benefits. Interviewees desired in their jobs "the ability to realize my full potential as a person," while "making money" ranked much lower. To explain these counterintuitive results, Mitroff and Denton appeal to Maslow's hierarchy of needs, stating that the basic survival needs have been achieved and humans ultimately desire "self-actualization" in life.[45]

Maslow's model, however, can only account for these results insofar as they confirm the biases inherent in the research design itself. First, because the authors organized their interviews around one overarching question—what gives people meaning in their work— and they already presume the workplace to be a site where humans seek meaning in their lives. When Mitroff and Denton admittedly ask "what gives you the *most meaning and purpose* in your job," they merely prime respondents from the beginning to consider work and meaning-making as interconnected.[46] Moreover, the questionnaire associates meaning with "basic values" and, finally, with the role of "religion" and "spirituality" in the lives of participants.[47] Thus, while Mitroff and Denton aspire to a degree of objectivity, in some sense they are actively constructing the relationship between work and spirituality for respondents.

Prescription masquerades as description in other aspects of the study as well. While Mitroff and Denton claim to report general attitudes about spirituality and organizational culture, their target demographic is decidedly narrow. The study represents what are strictly the perspectives of business elites such as corporate executives and HR professionals as if they were the attitudes of the labor market more generally. After all, the fact that individuals may rank "a sense of purpose" over fiscal security may simply reflect the relative affluent status of the participants (a point, which interestingly enough, would also affirm Maslow's theory). The degree to which the aggregate opinions of HR professionals, whose job functions are concerned with employee morale, accurately speak on behalf of line-workers in a processing plant, part-time retail workers, or call center operators is highly questionable, given their socioeconomic advantages. Defining all forms of "work" in terms of elite perspectives serves to only reinforce prevailing neoliberal social order in which business interests appear and the common good.

The publication of *A Spirit Audit of Corporate America* proved to be a significant moment in the study of workplace spirituality. It laid the conceptual groundwork for a number of subsequent quantitative investigations and helped to legitimize the study of spirituality for empirically inclined fields such as organizational behavior. Other researchers adopted or adapted their taxonomy of organizational spirituality for their own ends and in the process further entrenched workplace spirituality in management discourse.[48]

While MSR members may remember *A Spiritual Audit* as a foundational text in their subfield, other business scholars have certainly played an equally, if not more, crucial role in popularizing workplace spirituality. Perhaps no individual has demonstrated a longer, more prolific, and singularly comprehensive contribution than Organizational Behavior scholar Judith (Judi) A. Neal. Since the early 1990s, not only has Neal authored numerous scholarly articles, books, and edited volumes on the subject, she has been at the forefront of the institution-building activities that have established MSR as a permanent fixture in the academy. Even scholars of religion have acknowledged her role as "one of the leading scholars of workplace spirituality."[49] In their respective treatments of the MSR group, Lake Lambert and David Miller both stress Neal's essential role in its establishment at the turn of the millennium.[50] While she certainly deserves credit for legitimizing spirituality and religion as topics worthy of study for business researchers, Neal, her scholarship, like those of her peers, more closely resembles a form of neoliberal theology of work rather than an attempt to analyze and theorize about religion and spirituality as human phenomenon that impact the workplace.

After earning her PhD in Organizational Behavior (OB) from Yale in the early 1980s, Judi Neal spent time in the private sector, where for five years she managed organizational development and training for the high-tech research firm Honeywell.[51] She remembers her time at Honeywell positively, and enjoyed the "very progressive self-managing teams" at the Joilet Army Ammunition Plant in Illinois primarily because "Honeywell would let us experiment with all the leading-edge management programs before implementing them at other facilities."[52] Neal, therefore, remembers her early days as an industry professional as a time when she was given the freedom and autonomy to develop and execute programs were breaking new ground.

Yet, as she will tell the story, her innocent devotion to the company was shattered when she discovered that management was intentionally altering faulty data in its reports to its client, the U.S. military. Neal claims that it was in light of this troubling decision when she made a difficult decision to become a whistleblower and contact Honeywell's ethics hotline. The ensuing backlash from management, she recollects, enveloped her career in uncertainty, from which she found solace in the writings of New Age author Shakti Gawain. Best known as the author of the bestselling *Creative Visualization: Use the Power of Your Imagination to Create What You Want in Life* (1978), Gawain combines religious, philosophical, and popular psychological concepts to teach "the principle that whatever you put out into the universe will be reflected back to you," the so-called Law of Radiation and Attraction.[53] Neal recalls how a particular chapter in Gawain's *Living in the Light* (1985) taught her that "we create our own lives and that everything that happens to us is a reflection of what we need to learn."[54] This insight led her to conclude that the ethical failings of Honeywell merely reflected her own moral deficit. Out of a desire for "people to like me," she states, "I told [management] what they wanted to hear" even after she became aware of the problems, which in turn she believes only prolonged the faulty reporting. From this point, Neal declares that she committed herself to "live in alignment with my core values and to always speak my truth, no matter what the repercussions might be."

She would eventually leave Honeywell, a change to which Neal credits her actions as a whistleblower, but she used this opportunity to bring her insights as a trainer back into the classroom as a faculty member at the University of New Haven teaching courses in management. According to her website, it was during this period at New Haven, in 1992, when "she made spirituality in the workplace a central focus of her research" and reportedly set out to remedy an ethically deficient management culture.[55]

By the last years of 1990s, Neal had become a leading advocate for the transformative capacities of "spirituality" for individuals, organizations, and society.

She had founded the *International Association for Spirit at Work* and was aggressively moving to make spirituality an accepted topic for business research. In a 1997 article for the *Journal of Management Education*, for example, she argued for the incorporation of spirituality into the curriculum of management programs in business schools, listing a variety of resources for "manager and organizational faculty who wish to teach from a more spiritual perspective."[56] Spirituality, she believed, is more than a passing fad or merely a form of self-help; it promises more than any other aspect of human life to be "a driving force" for social reform.[57]

Judi Neal has tirelessly promoted and sought to institutionalize workplace spirituality in the business community. Through a like-minded colleague, John Renesch, she became acquainted with the work of Willis Harman, whom she retroactively characterizes as a "pioneer of workplace spirituality," even though Harman himself may never have self-identified in precisely this manner. Beginning in 2001, Renesch and Neal created the International Spirit at Work Award (originally known as the Willis Harman Spirit at Work Award), bestowed each year on a different leader in the movement. Both Neal and Renesch imagine workplace spirituality as the legacy of Harman's work, and the award honors "Willis Harman's vision of business as the primary institution for helping to bring about a positive and health 'Global Mind Change.' "[58]

From 2009 to the summer of 2013, Neal served as the inaugural director of the Tyson Center for Faith and Spirituality in the Workplace, housed in the Sam Walton Business School at the University of Arkansas. She has used the visibility of this research center, a rarity among public educational institutions, as a platform to promulgate spirituality in business education. Each year, the Tyson Center hosts an annual "Wisdom at Work" conference, where advocates of spirit/work integration can exchange ideas, and strategies for the movement's future.

Neal left her post as the head of the Tyson Center to work full time at her consulting firm *Edgewalkers International*, dedicated to "supporting individuals and organizations that feel called to be on the leading edge."[59] She founded the firm in 2006 to coincide with the publication of her latest book, *Edgewalkers: People and Organizations That Take Risks, Build New Bridges, and Break New Ground* (Praeger Press, 2006). In *Edgewalkers*, Neal articulates her fully mature vision for social reform, and synthesizes an amalgam of McGregor's human-focused management, Greenleaf's mystified servant-leadership, Willis Harman's confidence in the transformative power of business, and Gawain's New Age spirituality. The world, she declares, is undergoing a fundamental paradigm shift from an older materialist age to one grounded in "spirit."[60] In this unfolding, "Edgewalkers," a kind of new "Global Human Being" for a global age who "walk between worlds," "between the visible and invisible," who can cross cultures, move seamlessly between paradigms, and straddle competing perspectives will lead human- kind toward a new prosperity.[61] Although they do not abandon rationality and empiricism, they move beyond them, augmenting rational knowledge with, as Neal states, a "gut-level, shamanic, intuitive" epistemic mode.[62] In short, the Edgewalker is in touch with the essentially spiritual nature of being human.

These Edgewalkers, presumably, will lead humankind through a transitional phase, and help us to overcome our most pressing global problems. Neal antici- pates that these new global citizens will address global inequality, environmen- tal destruction, racial and ethnic strife, because they correctly understand that these problems ultimately originate in our collective consciousness. Essentially, the Edgewalker thesis represents Neal's defense of and prognosis for global capi- talism. The fruits of globalization and economic liberalization—among them "time poverty," "less predictability," and rapid global communications, and an "increase in cross-cultural business and relationships"—will be solved not by the conventional national and international policy measures but through the organic unfolding of a new way of thinking and acting.[63] While these trends may have created "workplaces that can be described as uncertain, chaotic, and difficult," she writes, "they have contributed to the emergence of new kind of leader."[64]

Who are these emergent human beings? As she documents at length in *Edgewalkers*, they are not professors, priests, or politicians. Rather, they are business leaders, innovative entrepreneurs, the "corporate shamans who walk into the invisible world and bring back wisdom and guidance for their organi- zations."[65] Drawing from her New Age toolkit, Neal explains that Edgewalkers understand themselves as cocreators of reality, who remain attentive to their "own inner calling," "envision a desired future," and can "enlist both the physical world and the spiritual world in order to make the future a reality."[66] The fearless, risk-taking, and bold-thinking leaders of successful firms, she argues, are the ones paving the path to this new, more spiritually anchored future.

Yet, because she describes the appearance of Edgewalkers as metaphysical shift in consciousness, Neal successfully redescribes the status quo of global capitalism as a transformative process. The Edgewalkers are globally conscious, multi-culturally literate, leaders not merely because they have tapped into some latent shamanistic potential but because they are all, in her examples, global business elites who, in a neoliberal context, operate transnationally and transcul- turally. It is their advantageous structural positioning as leaders of powerful organizations, too, that lends cultural authority to their words and advice. In locating the source of individual, organizational, and social transformation in these corporate leaders, she is simultaneously reinforcing the neoliberal conviction that business is and should remain the most powerful institution in a globalized economy.

The point is that Neal, like her colleagues in MSR and elsewhere, has, over the years, crafted and refined a genre of management discourse that uses the rhetoric of spirituality in ways that purport to not only upend but also strengthen the entrenched neoliberal social order. The very socioeconomic conditions to which workplace spirituality rose in response—downsizing, globalization, deregulation, and so on—are the same conditions that it ultimately perpetuates. Through a process of mystification—of business and of business leadership—it erases the socioeconomic and historical processes out of which these changes have taken shape. While these scholars represent workplace spirituality and related trends as a return to more proper holistic social order, they participate in a process of forgetting, of writing a revisionist history that renders the conditions of work under neoliberal policies not only inevitable but desirable. Workplace spirituality informs individuals to experience the increasingly hegemony of global capitalism not as volatile and disenfranchising but as dynamic and empowering. Of course, for those global business elites whom Neal celebrates, the market *is* dynamic and empowering, but for the vast majority of working people, life remains more complicated.

Rather than disinterested research, workplace spirituality should be more properly characterized as ideological and practical reinforcement of neoliberal reasoning, or even akin to a neoliberal theology and praxis. To posit, for instance, that "spirituality" signifies a distinct mode of human experience overlooks the truly complex ways that such terms are embraced, resisted, and contested. Just as scholars of religion argue that "there is no such thing as a specifically *religious* social formation," the same can be said of "spirituality."[67] From a strictly empirical perspective, it is hard to pinpoint the specifically "spiritual" qualities of either work, management, or business. When Mitroff, Denton, or Neal discuss "spirituality" as a measurable phenomenon or as a characteristic of some emergent human being for a New Age, they expose their own ideological (or even theological) commitments about the nature of reality, of selves, souls, and spirits.

Essentially, the individuals highlighted in this chapter approach "spirituality" as advocates and practitioners of their own eclectic beliefs. The *study* of and the *practice* of spirituality in the workplace have arisen together and remain inextricable from history. In crafting their response to economic liberalization, thinkers like Conger, Neal, and Miller simply drew on and therefore transformed the discursive world of business in which they were nurtured. They were influenced by the legacy of Greenleaf, McGregor, and Maslow, all of whom had helped to remake management into a moralistic discipline culturally entangled with "religious" and "spiritual" concerns. If anything, the growth business interest in religion and spirituality, culminating in its current manifestations in groups like MSR, has been a long, complex historical development that has unfolded only gradually in response to various perceived problems and opportunities, be they fears of creeping postwar collectivism, youth rebellion, or economic neo-liberalization. At each juncture, management thinkers have responded to these perceived crises as opportunities to advance the scope and relevance of management, of business, and in turn have participated in the evolution of a neoliberal capitalist social order.

Religion and spirituality, in the instances outlined here, are not merely the moral resources that advocates of corporate spirituality claim of them. They represent powerful rhetorical and practical tools that shape and have shaped broader socioeconomic and cultural changes. The holistic drive to integrate spirituality into management and work is the cultural representation of its inverse. It is not religion and spirituality that have been reintroduced into workplace cultures, rather it is the expanded authority of business that has afforded management the opportunity to speak definitively about matters deemed religious or spiritual.

Part Two

Religion and Spirituality in the New Economy

4

Zen and the Art of Microprocessing: Liberating the Entrepreneurial Spirit in Silicon Valley

Beginning in 2012, Google began offering a free course on meditation to its employees called "Search Inside Yourself." Titled after a book of the same name by the course's instructor Chade-Meng Tan, it is "designed to teach emotional intelligence through meditation, a practical real-world meditation you take with you wherever you go," according to an article in *Forbes*.[1] The program, along with a variety of other unique features of Google's workplace culture, contributed to *Forbes* naming the company as the "best company to work for" in 2013. Google provides its workforce of nearly 35,000 with a variety of amenities, entertainment programs, and opportunities unavailable in the vast majority of American businesses. According to the magazine, "the Internet juggernaut takes the Best Companies crown for the fourth time, and not just for the 100,000 hours of subsidized massages it doled out in 2012. New this year are three wellness centers and a seven-acre sports complex, which includes a roller hockey rink; courts for basketball, bocce, and shuffle ball; and horseshoe pits."[2]

Certainly, only Google's considerable profits could facilitate such an unusual array of employee benefits, and achieving a high rank on this annual listing garners significant prestige for a firm. However, being the "best company to work for" also points to broader expectations regarding what constitutes the ideal workplace in American culture. Google offers a work environment where ideas of "work" and "play" mingle, where stress can be balanced with a relaxing massage, and even where mediation can nullify the rapid pace of each workday.

The image of the model workplace looked very different a half a century earlier. Companies such as General Motors and IBM represented the paragon of

American free enterprise. These brands signified stability, efficiency, and conformity. Work was work, and leisure took place outside its borders. The idea that a business should be concerned with the daily *experience* of its workforce represents a relatively recent form of public discourse.

The shift in the public discussion around work evidenced in the ideas of Willis Harman, Robert Greenleaf, and subsequently among advocates of workplace spirituality was not limited only to academic circles and official government studies. Rather, it was something occurring along much broader strokes of American life. The transition of the United States to what Daniel Bell terms a "post-industrial society" meant that manufacturing no longer dictated the pulse of the economy, while service-oriented jobs and newer industries like high technology were becoming more important.

Out of these new industries would emerge ideas about work that differed starkly from the Protestant work ethic that had legitimized earlier industrial societies of the nineteenth and early twentieth centuries. The centralized bureaucratic organizations of the welfare state no longer held sway over the order of things. Indeed, some of the pioneers of these business ventures were what Robert Wuthnow refers to as "spiritual seekers," who cultivated a spirituality of the inner self and understood their careers as extensions of eclectic spiritual disciplines. In the process, they not only helped to establish new standards for business in a post-industrial society, but also changed how Americans think about the workplace.

This chapter focuses specifically on the high-tech industry that arose in Northern California. The Bay Area was not only the birthplace of advanced computing industry; it had also served as a hotbed for new forms of spiritual seeking, particularly around Asian religious traditions, since the 1950s.

First, I demonstrate how this curious mixture of eclectic culture of spiritual seeking and high-tech business shaped the life of Steve Jobs, cofounder of Apple Computer, during his formative adult years. For Jobs—a self-identified Zen Buddhist—and according to many of his closest associates, work represented a forum in which to apply his spiritual practices, and business was a moral venture.

Next, I examine the life of Les Kaye, an ordained Zen priest who spent over thirty years as engineer for IBM in Silicon Valley. Years before the 'hippies' took over the Bay Area during the late 1960s, he was one of many young professionals interested in non-Western religious traditions. Like Jobs, Kaye understood his workplace as the "practice place" for his spiritual activities. In fact, over the years, he has been an outspoken advocate for thinking of work as a spiritual activity.

The lives of these two pioneers of the high-tech world illustrate how two seemingly incommensurable corners of American culture, spiritual seeking and the computer industry, actually grew up alongside and among one another as one discourse entangling both. As the computer industry matured and gained prominence, it became a model not only for a new kind of business, but also for American attitudes toward work and spirituality in a post-industrial society.

The seeker entrepreneur: Steve Jobs

As a child, Steve Jobs became skeptical of the institutionalized religion of his parents. According to his biographer Walter Isaacson, he was raised Lutheran and his parents took Jobs regularly to church until he was thirteen, when an article in *Life* magazine featuring the suffering of children in Nigeria shook his faith in a God that could allow such tragedy. After confronting the minister over the issue, Jobs made a decision to leave the church.[3]

Like many of his generation, Jobs saw the church as too disconnected from the world around him. It preferred abstract belief over practice, doctrine over practice, and the institution over the human being. "The juice goes out of Christianity," he told Isaacson, "when it becomes too based on faith rather than on living like Jesus or seeing the world as Jesus saw it."[4] Instead, Jobs adopted a form of suspicious perennialism. "I think different religions are different doors to the same house. Sometimes I think the house exists, and sometimes I don't. It's the great mystery."[5]

Job's aversion to institutional religion echoes what Robert Wuthnow identifies as a cultural shift from dwelling within a religious tradition to a mentality of spiritual seeking. He suggests that "people have been losing faith in a metaphysic that can make them feel at home in the universe and that they increasingly negotiate among competing glimpses of the sacred, seeking partial knowledge and practical wisdom."[6] Wuthnow provides a remarkably simple rubric: that during "settled times" individuals form stable religious communities, while "unsettled times" force them to contest prevailing traditions and work out new relationships with the sacred. Indeed, he even argues that the shift to a post-industrial paradigm, might be one way to understand the contemporary penchant for spiritual seeking.[7]

Yet, Wuthnow's explanation under-appreciates the strong tradition of individualism indicative of American culture. Spiritual seeking is nothing new to American culture, a point he readily admits, but its practice in the latter half of the twentieth century exhibits a distinctive quality. What remains unsettling, for Jobs, is not merely the shift to a new "post-industrial" cultural frame but, more specifically, the inability of religious institutions that acquired the characteristics of bureaucratic society to adequately account for and enrich the lives of real individuals. The church seems foreign and distant to individual experience, and more concerned with promoting itself than empowering its adherents. The disappointing episode with the minister taught Jobs that institutional Christianity prefers conformity to doctrine over individual thought, and trust in the institution over self-reliance. In a culture grounded firmly in the moral value of an independent, autonomous, individual, Jobs had to look beyond institutions, to personal experience, for the answers to spiritual concerns.

Jobs would embark on this journey to find his own answers during his brief time at Reed College. Even though he dropped out after only six months, Reed would leave an indelible imprint on Jobs's identity. He emerged from the experience as an active spiritual seeker interested in business.

Located in southeast Portland, Reed lay in the crosshairs of the countercultural milieu during the early 1970s. Here, Jobs encountered an atmosphere marked by experimentation, eclecticism, and openness. "There was a constant flow of people stopping by, from Timothy Leary and Richard Snyder," he recalled in an interview for *Playboy* in the early 1980s. "There was a constant flow of people questioning about the truth of life."[8]

Jobs quickly became immersed in a range of activities, experimenting with psychedelics and sex, but also with various forms of "Eastern" spirituality. Along with a tightly knit group of friends, he regularly attended a local Hare Krishna temple and vociferously digested the standard array of countercultural texts on personal and spiritual fulfillment. In particular, *Be Here Now*, Richard Alpert's (aka Ram Dass) seminal text on yoga, meditation, and spiritual practice, dramatically impacted his perspective on living. "It was profound," he would later say. "It transformed me and many of my friends."[9]

To be a young, middle-class college student trying on unfamiliar spiritual practices and views was nothing exceptional in 1972. Indeed, since the late 1960s, university campuses had functioned as hotbeds for the counterculture. Many Scholars typically have viewed the counterculture as a politicized movement against prevailing norms born out of postwar affluence.[10] Yet, Peter Braunstein and Michael William Doyle argue that such clean definitions overlook the ambiguous and disjointed nature of the phenomena normally encompassed in the term.

> The term "counterculture" falsely reifies what should never properly be construed as a social movement. It was an inherently unstable collection of attitudes, tendencies, postures, gestures, "lifestyles," ideals, visions, hedonistic pleasures, moralisms, negations, and affirmations.[11]

The disjointed quality of the counterculture was apparent to Steve Jobs while he was at Reed. Whereas groups like the SDS (Students for a Democratic Society) and events such as those at Kent State often color the counterculture as utterly political, for Jobs, it was decisively anti-political and personal. "None of the really bright people I knew in college went into politics. They all sensed that, in terms of making a change in the world, politics wasn't the place to be in the late Sixties and Seventies." Instead, he makes a curious observation about his associates. "All of them are in business now—which is funny, because they were the same people who trekked off to India or who tried in one way or another to find some sort of truth about life."[12]

One friend in particular, Robert Friedland, served as Jobs's spiritual mentor during his time at Reed. Friedland landed at Reed College after a short stint in federal prison for possession of 24,000 tablets of LSD while attending a small liberal arts school in Maine. When they first met, both Jobs and Friedland were interested in Eastern religious practices, but, according to Jobs, Friedland in short order "turned me on to a different level of consciousness."[13] "The thing that struck me," Jobs states, "was his intensity. Whatever he was interested in he would generally carry to an irrational extreme."[14]

Friedland's obsessive level of spiritual seeking, in fact, took him to India, in search of a guru. Walter Isaacson writes that Friedland, after hearing Ram Dass speak in Boston, decided to seek out Dass's teacher, Neem Karoli Baba, in the summer of 1973.[15] Upon his return, Friedland seemed changed, Jobs remembers. He had taken a new name and "walked around in sandals and flowing Indian robes."[16] It was Friedland's example that motivated Jobs, the following year, to embark on his now legendary trip to India in search of his own guru.

In addition, and perhaps more significantly for Jobs's career path, Friedland mixed his interest in spirituality with remarkable work ethic. During the course of their association, Friedland established a commune at a farm outside of Portland over which he held stewardship. Here, Jobs and others brought their search for enlightenment to fruition through the hard labor of the organic cider business. Friedland never lost his business acumen, and he went on eventually to become the Chief Executive Officer for Ivanhoe Mines, a major player in the global mining industry.

Jobs acquired from his mentor a set of skills particularly suited to the business world. Daniel Kottke, a mutual friend of Friedland and Jobs at Reed, recalls that "Robert (Friedland) was very much an outgoing, charismatic guy, a real salesman. When I first met Steve he was shy and self-effacing, a very private guy. I think Robert taught him a lot about selling, about coming out of his shell, of opening up and taking charge of a situation."[17] Thus, Jobs's brief friendship with Friedland gave him the building blocks upon which he would later erect his iconic career. He cultivated a strong commitment to spiritual seeking that was inherently linked to the practice of work from a mentor who gave Jobs the skills he would need to found and lead a successful company in the emerging post-industrial economy.

All in all, for Jobs, the spiritual discourse of the early 1970s shares cultural space with business. Reflecting on his college years, Jobs told *Playboy*, "that was a time when every college student in this country read *Be Here Now* and *Diet for a Small Planet*—there were about ten books. You'd be hard pressed to find those books on too many college campuses today. I'm not saying it's better or worse; it's just different—very different. *In Search of Excellence* [the book about business practices] has taken the place of *Be Here Now*."[18] This statement is illustrative of the discursive linkage Jobs constructs between business and spirituality.

First, he situates Dass's popular work on spiritual practice alongside *Diet for a Small Planet*, Francis Lappe's major critique of industrialized food production. While the former focuses on spiritual practice and the latter on the virtues of vegetarianism, both provide alternatives to prevailing "Western" modes of thought. Placing these two works together, Jobs acknowledges each as a part of single discourse; alternative forms of spirituality and new modes of production represent different dimensions of the same discussion; eclectic spiritual seeking is also about a new way of doing business.

Moreover, although he characterizes *In Search of Excellence* as starkly different from the popular texts of his youth, Jobs nonetheless understands each as functionally parallel. *In Search of Excellence*, like *Be Here Now* and *Diet*, remains staunchly anti-establishment, encouraging a decentralized, people-centered, and values-focused form of business organization.[19] What is most interesting about Jobs's remark is that, although he admits the culture has changed, the book that most clearly stands in for the radical texts to which he was exposed during his college years is a book about management. Statements such as these, there-fore, indicate that, for Jobs, spirituality is inextricably bound together with work and business.

Spiritual bricolage

Jobs's spiritual seeking remained intensely private and was directed almost exclu-sively toward self-development rather than any broad social transformation. Yet, entangling spirituality, with ideas about work and business, his spiritual prac-tices echoed the kind of radically subjective worldviews that were reformulating the public discussion around work and business at the time. Thus, when Steve Jobs brought his eclectic spirituality into his entrepreneurial activities, they shaped not only the particular aspects of his leadership but also contributed to the culture of Apple Computers.

His spiritual experiences as a young adult molded his worldview and his entrepreneurial activities. During his pilgrimage to India at the age of nineteen, Jobs acquired a robust appreciation for the difference between South Asian and "Western" knowledge systems.

> Coming back to America was, for me, much more of a culture shock than going to India. The people in the Indian countryside don't use their intellect like we do, they use their intuition instead, and their intuition is far more developed than in the rest of the world. Intuition is a very powerful thing, more powerful than intellect, in my opinion. That's had a big impact on my work.
>
> Western rational thought is not an innate human characteristic; it is learned and is the great achievement of Western civilization. In the villages of India, they never learned it. They learned something else, which is in some ways just as valuable but in other ways not. That's the power of intuition and experiential wisdom.
>
> Coming back after seven months in Indian villages, I saw the craziness of the Western World as well as its capacity for rational thought. If you just sit and observe, you will see how restless your mind is. If you try to calm it, it only makes it worse, but over time it does calm, and when it does, there' room to hear more subtle things—that's when your intuition starts to blossom and you start to see things more clearly and be in the present more.[20]

This alternative epistemology based on "intuition" appealed to Jobs because it could mitigate the psychological stresses of Western life. While he celebrated Western rationality, "intuition" constituted a more fundamental way of knowing and experiencing the world, and this, as he admits, would profoundly shape his approach to work.

Yet, Jobs easily equates his experiences of South Asian Hindu practice with the teachings found in Zen. The previous passage continues:

> Zen has been a deep influence in my life ever since. At one point I was thinking about going to Japan and trying to get into the Eihei-ji monastery, but my spiritual advisor urged me to stay here. He said there is nothing over there that isn't here, and he was correct. I learned the truth of the Zen saying that if you are willing to travel around to the world to meet a teacher, one will appear next door.[21]

Leaving commentary about Jobs's syncretism aside momentarily, I suggest that he was ascribed to each of these traditions a respect for intuitive, nonrational forms of thought. Furthermore, this passage reveals his deep sense that relying on intuition and cultivating a calm, passive awareness will affect one's experience. In other words, Jobs, like Harman, articulates a form of radical subjectivity in which the power to mold reality lies within one's ability to achieve the proper mental state.

The "Reality Distortion Field"

Jobs augmented his interest in spirituality with other disciplines, including therapy. As the research of Maslow and others attest, spirituality increasingly was becoming a relevant topic for psychologists, and many spiritual seekers looked into to novel approaches to empowering the self or overcoming insecurities. For instance, Jobs partook in Primal Scream Therapy, a widely popular form of regressive therapy that garnered the participation of such prominent figures as John Lennon and James Earl Jones during the 1970s. Created by psychologist Arthur Janov, author of *The Primal Scream*, this method posited that deep-seated pain resulted from childhood trauma, in Jobs's case, his adoption. While Jobs found it somewhat ineffective and overly simplistic, his associates reported that "he was in a different place. He had a very abrasive personality, but there was a peace about him for a while. His confidence improved and his feelings of inadequacy were reduced."[22] Together with his experiences in India and regular practice of Zen meditation, therapies like Primal Scream helped Jobs to deal with his persistent anxieties and bolstered his sense of self-reliance.

As an entrepreneur, he incorporated what he learned into his leadership style, a trend not lost on his colleagues. Jobs deliberately cultivated practices such as staring without blinking while conversing with others, believing that he could bend the will of others to his own. As one friend remembered, "He would stare into their fucking eyeballs, ask some question, and would want a response without the other person averting their eyes."[23]

His employees at Apple began to refer to Jobs's charisma as "the reality distortion field." Bud Tribble, an early Apple associate, claimed that "in his presence, reality is malleable. He can convince anyone of practically anything. It wears off when he's not around, but it makes it hard to have realistic schedules."[24] During the development of the MacIntosh, Jobs regularly refused to accept reasonable timelines or apparent technological limitations and pushed his teams to achieve seemingly superhuman feats. This undoubtedly accounts for some of Apple's success, but it more significantly points to how Jobs's spiritual practices remained an integral component of his approach to business.

At the core of Jobs's spirituality was a conviction that the human will transcended society. For him, a calm, focused mind could actually overwhelm external reality and will the outcome of events in spite of any apparent limits. Social conventions and rules failed to apply to the enlightened individual, and Steve Jobs perceived himself as one of the elect. Andy Hertzfeld, one of the Mac developers, summarized Jobs's exceptional self-image: "He thinks there are a few people who are special—people like Einstein and Gandhi and the gurus he met in India—and he's one of them…Once he even hinted to me that he was enlightened."[25]

This self-perception implied that conventions and rules failed to apply to him, that society only imposed illusory limits on the individual. Walter Isaacson, his biographer, notes, "if reality did not comport with his will, he would ignore it…Even in small everyday rebellions, such as a not putting a license plate on his car and parking it in handicapped spaces, he acted as if he were not subject to the strictures around him."[26] Even governmental authority, thus, could not legitimately lay claim on the spiritually enlightened individual.

Overall, Jobs's spirituality embodied an anti-authoritarian, libertarian ethos. Western industrial society, due to its extreme form of rationality and desire for order, threatens the integrity of the autonomous self. Because the individual stands at the center of his cosmology, it perverted the natural order of things. Through his spiritual practice, Jobs learned to conquer lingering anxieties over his adoption and lack of confidence, and, thus, he was able to restore the unity of his self.

Jobs saw his career as a conduit for his spirituality, and the spiritually attuned entrepreneur represented the heroic figure in this drama. Business was more to

Jobs than the pursuit of wealth and power, it epitomized a great moral struggle with implications for all of humanity. "If, for some reason," he stated, "we make some giant and IBM wins, my personal feeling is that we are going to enter some sort of computer Dark Ages for about twenty years. Once IBM gains control of a market sector, they almost always stop innovation."[27] He routinely countered prevailing economic logic in his business decisions, preferring product quality at the expense of affordability for the mass market or worrying over the aesthetics of the assembly line on which these products might be constructed.

Apple, of course, would eventually attain iconic status, and Steve Jobs's "reality distortion field" would be source of tech industry gossip around the water cooler. Jobs wielded such charisma in the business world that during his later years, Apple's stock would actually rise or fall according concomitant with his physical health. He represents the quintessential seeker entrepreneur that came through the counterculture determined to bring his spirituality to the workplace, and in the process imparted this aura of sacrality to Apple's public image.

Even though Jobs might be the most prominent example of how the world of high-tech and seeker spirituality share cultural space, he was not the first. Long before either the counterculture or the personal computer, Silicon Valley was a place where spiritual seeking and information technology went hand in hand.

Les Kaye: Zen and work

Kannon Do Zen Meditation Center sits on the north side of Mountain View, California near the southern tip of San Francisco Bay. Today, Mountain View and a cluster of other small affluent communities situated between San Francisco and San Jose comprise the areas popularly dubbed "Silicon Valley." The center operates under the guidance of long-time area resident and ordained Zen priest Les Kaye.

Kaye, the leader of Kannon Do since 1983, offers highly Americanized form of Zen particularly suited to spiritual seeking. Unlike typical Japanese zazen, women may participate fully in all aspects of practice and levels of leadership. In addition, while Zen remains a monastic tradition held under the autocratic authority of the roshi (leader) in Japan, practice at Kannon Do is lay oriented and lay driven. As he explained to one interviewer, "when Zen hit this country, it wasn't the priests who ran out to do it, it was us. We don't have very many monastic training sessions. People aren't interested. People want to practice Zen in their lives."[28] Kaye teaches Zen befitting the democratic and egalitarian sensibilities of American norms. In addition, it allows spiritual seekers the authority to direct and construct their own privatized versions of Zen.

Responsibilities at Kannon Do consume Kaye's professional priorities today, but for nearly three decades prior to 1983, he worked as an engineer for IBM. While being an avid Zen practitioner and hardware engineer might seem like an odd combination, Kaye perceives no conflict between his spiritual practice and his professional life. In fact, he credits IBM as the place where he learned to practice and cultivate Zen. Over the years, Kaye has written and spoken prolifically on the relationship between work and spirituality, and even helped companies like Apple establish meditation centers. If any single individual illustrates how interest in spirituality was present in Silicon Valley from its earliest days, Les Kaye could accept this mantle.

When he moved to San Jose to work for IBM in 1956, the high-tech culture of Northern California differed markedly from the established conservative corporate environment in New York. Barriers to entry remained thin, generating an atmosphere favorable to smaller ventures. Proximity to Stanford, where Willis Harman was turning to consciousness research, encouraged collaboration with the university as well as among firms. Moreover, because projects often held tight deadlines and dealt with some of the most advanced applied technologies, companies tended to exhibit a decentralized structure in order to allow for greater autonomy.

These traits carried over the IBM's new facility in San Jose. Kaye recalls that "the feeling of this new IBM location was like a small start-up company rather than a vast, forty-year-old corporation. High expectations for the innovative product were almost palpable. I could taste the ozone of excitement in the air. Career prospects seemed unlimited."[29] Although the work remained highly stressful and demanding, the more informal context nonetheless empowered engineers to direct their own work, much like the form of Zen he would later come to embrace.

According to Kaye, he first encountered Zen one evening at the house of an associate in 1961. Carousing through a bookshelf, he picked up Alan Watts's *The Way of Zen*.[30] "I was fascinated to discover a dimension of living, attitude of about life, that I had not known before," he recalls.[31] "When I closed the book, I knew my technically oriented, mainstream life was incomplete, that it alone could not provide the balance I was seeking."[32] By 1966, Kaye had joined a local group of like-minded enthusiasts under the tutelage of Shunryu-Suzuki, famed author of *Zen Mind, Beginners Mind* and heavyweight in American Zen. The group consisted largely of middle- to upper-middle class Caucasians who, like

himself, were committed to exploring alternatives to the Western religious traditions from their youth.[33] As the counterculture exploded in subsequent years,
established groups such as these set an example for the youth who were search-
ing for alternative forms of spiritual seeking.

Because his work encompassed such a large amount of time and energy, it
makes sense that his workplace became the context in which he could "practice
Zen in his life." Over the years, he claims, Zen transformed the way he viewed
work. Instead of focusing on his career as a means to an end, or a path to wealth,
Kaye now emphasized work as an intrinsically valuable activity. "I became less
concerned about personal 'success' and the intricacies of business politics,
becoming more interested in treating work as part of spiritual practice: focusing on the value, usefulness, and quality of my activities, creating mutually sup-
portive personal relationships, and maintaining high professional and ethical
standards."[34] Work had become the primary opportunity through which Kaye
could conduct his spirituality.

Moreover, he felt that the "qualities in Zen were no different from the character traits that IBM encouraged in its people: integrity, morality, a capacity for
work, self-discipline, willingness to learn, attention to detail, responsibility, and
perseverance."[35] By interpreting the company's culture through the language of
Zen, Kaye indicates that not only is work a spiritual practice, but this spirituality
is echoed IBM's culture.

Although the workplace functioned as Kaye's "practice place," he avoided
announcing this to his coworkers. Even though a few employees knew of his
interest in Zen, Kaye speculates that they "probably did not see a connection
between spiritual practice and working in a high tech, business environment."[36]
Zen, therefore, was strictly a private discipline, centered on the self, and aimed
at personal moral and spiritual improvement.

This supports Robert Wuthnow's assertion that at the heart of seeker spirituality lies "a renewed interest in the inner self as a way of relating to the sacred."[37]
Consequently, Wuthnow argues, by positioning the self at the center of one's
spirituality, the self simultaneously becomes both the source of all suffering as
well as the locus of happiness. "Ultimately, all that exists is what one is able to
experience."[38] In other words, this type of inward focus, on the self, privileges
individual perception over external reality, cultivating a radical subjectivity.

In his book *Zen at Work*, Kaye conveys a number of stories in which he uses
Zen practice to realign his perception and overcome suffering in the workplace.
For example, when a coworker took credit for work that Kaye had actually per-
formed, he saw himself as the source of his anger. "When I looked closely at what

was really hurt, the only bruise that I could find was to my ego…If I was suffering, it was because I was allowing myself to be captive to my ego's precious image of self."[39] The problem, then, was not that a trusted friend had exploited him, but rather he had allowed his ego to obstruct his perception of the situation. "Zazen practice," he concludes, "enabled my mind to flexible and open enough to accept a new way of seeing the situation."[40]

By the same token, having this flexible, malleable self also enabled Kaye to cope with problems of authority on the job. During one such encounter, an executive known for his short temper fiercely castigated him for writing a poorly crafted memo sometime earlier:

> I was in a rage for hours afterward. Early the next morning in zazen, the incident played again and again in my mind. As if watching a movie while sitting on my cushion, I repeatedly saw how quickly I had lost my composure, how instinctively my emotions had taken over.[41]

Again, Kaye reflects the blame for his suffering back onto himself. The problem within. He continues:

> Weeks later, when my boss confronted me again with his arrogance, I noticed something that had escaped me before. I realized that his irrational anger—demonstrated by his wide eyes, distorted mouth, and tone of voice—was an expression of fear.

In one stroke, Kaye adjusts his perception in order to reclaim a sense of authority. He reformulates contempt for the hot-headed executive into pity for a fragile human being hiding behind a surly ego.

Each of these anecdotes reveals how this radical subjectivity, focused solely on individual perception, can simultaneously recognize the self as continuous source of suffering and empower it. Because the self is mutable, pain and joy simply reflect two choices, and, therefore, Zen merely invests the practitioner with an awareness that an individual always holds the power to choose either.

Over the years, and now in his role as a full-time Zen priest, Les Kaye has been an outspoken voice for work as a form of spiritual practice. He encourages firms to make space for meditation space and yoga facilities, and frequently gives lectures on the spiritual dimension of work. His story exemplifies how seeker spirituality is not opposed to business, but instead has grown up with and is particularly suited to the world of information technology.

Both Les Kaye and Steve Jobs practiced forms of seeker spirituality anchored in an Americanized Zen Buddhism that shaped their professional lives. For each of them, work constituted a forum in which to express their spirituality. Their respective styles of Zen, like other forms of spiritual seeking, were utterly private, locating the sacred within the inner self. Their practice produced a radical form of subjectivity in which subjective experience of the individual remained paramount, and, consequently, celebrated the autonomous individual, embraced egalitarianism, and fomented suspicion of hierarchical authority. The self and its perception of external reality required constant maintenance, leading to a more malleable sense of self.

This looser self serviced each in remarkably different ways through their careers. In his role as entrepreneur, Steve Jobs, through Zen, acquired intense focus and the ability to "bend others to his will" to meet tight deadlines and achieve unthinkable feats of engineering. If reality can be reduced to perception, then having the will to believe brings can manifest that vision in reality.

Les Kaye learned as an employee in the world of high-tech to use zazen not to influence others, but to bend his own perspective to cope with the stresses in the workplace. His practice bolstered his sense of empowerment *in spite of* forces beyond his control. Like Jobs, however, Kaye was committed to the notion that reality was subjective and that perception ultimately shaped how one experienced daily life.

Cultural theorist Sam Binkley acknowledges how this looser form of selfhood is related to aspirations of individual liberty:

> Loosening invoked the idea of a more authentic, innocent, and original source of the self and promised a way of living that was more primary and immediate but also more active and creative. Loose, hip people were empowered to make choices over aspects of their lives that squares, unreflective and constrained by habit, took only for granted.[42]

Binkley characterizes the emergence of this looser self as a response to the rapid social change and political turmoil that occurred during the 1960s. The struggle for civil rights, the unpopular war in Vietnam, and a general discontent toward all forms of bureaucracy facilitated feelings of uncertainty, and anxiety about individual freedom.

As the public struggles of the late 1960s transitioned to the lifestyle revolution of the 1970s, Binkley argues, the loose self "provided a set of living techniques centered on a thematically unified philosophy of life."[43] The fact that youth culture had lost its political edge when Jobs attended Reed College seems to support this claim. Spiritual seeking, for Jobs and his friends, represented an alternative way of living, of experiencing life, of self-improvement rather than social reform.

Still, as much as this new looser form of selfhood was a response to social upheaval, this looser form of selfhood, indicative of seeker spirituality, also was a part of other deeper changes occurring in the social structure of the economy. The high-tech firms of Silicon Valley appearing on the scene beginning in the 1950s displayed a novel organizational structure. First, firms in older, more mature industries were organized bureaucratically, with a pyramidal power structure that emphasized central control. The emerging high-tech industry, on the other hand, developed a flatter, more decentralized form that maximized the autonomy of employees. Given the nature of their work, engineers benefitted from the loosely structured environment, which gave them the latitude to apply their high level of expertise. Under this structure, workplace culture extolled pliability, egalitarianism, and liberality.

The Zen tradition that Les Kaye encountered cultivated these same virtues within the practitioner. It offered him an ethos and a worldview that could overcome the anxieties stemming from this workplace structure. The flow of work in high-tech was anything but unpredictable, and workers constantly moved from project to project in small teams with ever-shifting members. Such dynamic conditions threatened the sense of autonomy required for effective performance. Through Zen, Kaye adopted a looser self that could bolster a sense of autonomy in the midst of ambiguity. All in all, seeker spirituality complemented the experience of high-tech work because it provided individuals a practical means of embodying the virtues necessary for the organizational structure.

Second, as the high-tech industry expanded, so too did its organizational form. Sociologist Arthur Stinchecombe asserts that "organizational forms and types have a history," and "this determines some aspects of the present structure or organizations of that type."[44] In other words, as the prestige and influence of Silicon Valley proliferated, it exported this decentralized, flexible form of production to other firms in the industry. It comes as no surprise, then, that when Steve Jobs cofounded Apple with Steve Wozniak in his parents' garage, he too would adopt this same organizational structure. Furthermore, this form has become one of the standard ways of organizing a business.

In addition, the social context in which a particular organizational structure emerges remains particularly relevant. By the late 1950s, interest in Eastern religion was already a well-established aspect of the local culture. Alan Watts joined the faculty at the American Academy of Asian Studies in 1951, and Shunryu-Suzuki opened the San Francisco Zen Center just eight years later. To live in the Bay Area, especially as a professional, implied likely contact with these communities. Thus, from its early years, the culture of Silicon Valley developed alongside and in relation to a discourse of spiritual seeking. For a company like Google to offer a course on meditation, then, only confirms the cultural history of the industry.

The fact that in the twentieth-first century, workplaces like Google embody the ideal workplace for Americans illustrates a more significant point. "Postindustrial society," as Daniel Bell argues, defines a society that has shifted away from manufacturing toward information technology and service-oriented forms of work, and certainly Silicon Valley has played a historic role in this transition since the late twentieth century. Its enormous success bestows prestige and cultural authority, and invites imitation.

The shift to a post-industrial society, as others have argued, constitutes not merely a change in the mode of production but also a change in the norms, expectations, and, indeed, the moral resources of American society.[45] As such, the industries leading this change, consequently, function as mentors for the larger society. Indeed, businesses of all shades aspire to emulate the decentralized, flexible organizational structure of high-tech firms, and American workers desire places of work that emphasize individual empowerment. As such, the moral discourses tied to Silicon Valley naturally appeal to American society more generally. The kind of spiritual seeking Les Kaye and Steve Jobs found useful for their working lives now embodies a general orientation for American culture. Post-industrial society requires a post-industrial ethic, which reaches beyond the experience of work or the designs of entrepreneurs and into the realm of politics.

5

Conscious Capitalism: Looser Selves,
Freer Markets

In January of 2013, the Harvard Business Review Press published *Conscious Capitalism: Liberating the Heroic Spirit of Business*, coauthored by John Mackey, CEO and cofounder of Whole Foods Market, and Raj Sisodia, author to the best-selling *Firms of Endearment: How World Class Companies Profit from Passion and Purpose* (2007). The book ambitiously argues that "business leaders can liberate the extraordinary power of business and capitalism to create a better world in which people live lives full of purpose, love, and creativity—a world of compassion, freedom, and prosperity."[1] The authors prescribe four basic tenets to guide these "Conscious" businesses: higher purpose, stakeholder integration, conscious leadership, and conscious culture.[2]

On its surface, *Conscious Capitalism* resembles the countless, perhaps even overabundant collection of business books, each claiming to hold the exclusive formula for success within their pages. Yet, this new book received an unusual amount of media attention upon its release, due in no small part to the controversial reputation of Mackey. As the leading organic grocer in the United States, Whole Foods Market, located primarily in urban settings, attracts an ecologically health minded clientele who, at least in the popular imagination, mostly side with the political left. Mackey, however, identifies, occasionally somewhat vocally, with libertarianism, an ideology often considered at odds with the countercultural sensibilities of the organic foods industry. He invited the ire of liberal activists and Democratic politicians when he spoke out against President Obama's proposed healthcare reform bill in an editorial for the Wall Street Journal in 2009.[3] Mackey again waded into rough waters on his 2013 book tour, characterizing "Obama Care" as a form of Fascism.[4]

The negative press, if anything, has simply increased the visibility of the movement Mackey has helped to build. Since the mid-2000s, Conscious Capitalism has blossomed into an influential organization comprised of like- minded business leaders, self-help gurus, and intellectuals seeking to reform society through free enterprise. Each year, Conscious Capitalism hosts an annual conference in a different city, where entrepreneurs and thinkers come together in order to refine their ideas and strategies.

Beyond its focus on how business can improve society, Conscious Capitalism also remains closely bound to and informed by perspectives and practices associated with "seeker spirituality," to borrow Robert Wuthnow's term.[5] The testimony of an attendee at the 2013 annual conference in an article for *Huffington Post* reads as follows:

> Casey Sheahan, CEO of Patagonia, took the stage and said, "I'm going to do something somewhat risky," and then led the entire group in a guided meditation in which we envisioned and then expressed gratitude to our community, our family, and each other. The room was literally vibrating.[6]

Held in a Masonic Center on California Street in the San Francisco, the Conscious Capitalism Conference offered two days of workshops featuring themes like "Storytelling," "Search inside yourself," and "Higher Purpose," where participants could discuss and cultivate new practices aimed at organizational and individual transformation.

Although Conscious Capitalism may appear similar to and share an affinity with "workplace spirituality," only on rare occasions will a minority of its advocates explicitly reference religious or spiritual rhetoric to describe their activities or underlying aims. Conscious Capitalism more overtly resembles other trends in business world like Corporate Social Responsibility (CSR), various forms of consumer and shareholder activism that draw attention to the moral dimensions of market exchange, or social entrepreneurship and so-called B-corporations which incorporate altruistic aims in their business objectives. Yet, as a genealogy of "Conscious Capitalism" reveals, it has matured alongside and in relation to various spirituality movements of the late twentieth century. In this chapter, I explore how Conscious Capitalism evolved in relation to spiritual lives of three key individuals. The term first appeared during the 1990s in the teachings of Philadelphia-area investment counselor David Schwerin, who argued that capitalism and business leaders could benefit from "ageless spiritual wisdom." Second, in the first years of the twenty-first century, bestselling author and futures researcher Patricia Aburdene brought the idea of Conscious Capitalism to a broader audience in her popular book titled *Megatrends 2010: The Dawn of Conscious Capitalism*. Third, within a few years of Aburdene's book, John Mackey of Whole Foods adopted the term to describe his program of business and marketplace reform, and in the process, transformed Conscious Capitalism from an abstract idea into an active social movement within the American business community. While I do not want to suggest that Conscious Capitalism is either inherently or originally "spiritual," the two nonetheless have share and continue to share a comfortable, overlapping conceptual space. More importantly, an analysis of Conscious Capitalism offers a glimpse into how the language of spirituality has shaped and been shaped in the context of global capitalism, particularly in and through the lives of three business elites. Conscious Capitalism, like workplace spirituality, mystifies processes like globalization and economic liberalization, laments the invasive power of the welfare state, and exalts the rugged entrepreneur as the most heroic figure of contemporary society. Thus, Conscious Capitalism, both in its relationship with the private spiritual beliefs of its advocates and in its broader social formation, is simultaneously a business reform movement as well as a neoliberal political project to advance the structural position of business.

David Schwerin and the genesis of Conscious Capitalism

The idea of Conscious Capitalism appears to originate from a little-known book published in 1998 and written by Philadelphia-area investment counselor David Schwerin. *Conscious Capitalism: Principles for Prosperity* lays out an ambitious moral vision for the increasingly globalized society of the twenty-first century. Schwerin contends that the utilitarian, self-interested rationality of Western-style capitalism inadequately addresses the most pressing contemporary social issues, and "that a complete reversal of many long held values and beliefs is a prerequisite for attaining the peace and contentment that is earnestly sought by citizens throughout the world."[7]

The book illustrates how, by the late 1990s, the eclectic spiritual seeking of the baby boomers was reshaping more than simply the privatized practices of individual Americans but also the way in which these perspectives were merging with and transforming prevailing attitudes toward capitalist society. In the midst of the Internet boom and in the wake of the downfall of the Soviet bloc, American business leaders like Schwerin discerned these trends as evidence of a shift toward greater individual freedom, the moral superiority of global capitalism and the obligation of business to serve as the catalyst of human progress. Schwerin and others who would eventually take on the message of Conscious

Capitalism exemplify how the highly individualistic forms of spirituality comprised an essential ingredient in these trends.

Schwerin's notion of Conscious Capitalism developed out of the entanglement between his advocacy in shareholder activism and his interest in esoteric philosophies. In 1968, after earning an MBA in Finance and starting work for an investment firm in his native Philadelphia, he was already drawn into the burgeoning spiritual experimentation emanating from countercultural movements on the West Coast. Largely irreverent of what he describes as the moderate religiosity of his parents, he quickly became involved in a "mystery school," which offered a regimen of practices grounded in the esoteric traditions of Hermeticism and cosmology.

Mystery schools, such as the one in which Schwerin participated, although they claim direct descent from the mystery cults of the ancient Mediterranean, particularly Egypt, are of more modern origin. Closely affiliated with the late-nineteenth-century theosophical movement, mystery schools often combine a mixture of Western and non-Western esoteric practices and beliefs aimed at the inwardly focused, personal transformation of participants. The website for the "Modern Mystery School," for instance, epitomizes the privatized quality of this movement:

Why do mystery schools exist?

1. The main reason mystery schools exist is because life produces so many mysteries (life and death, who and what is God, how does this universe work, etc.) and humans have always craved knowledge about the deeper workings of this existence.

2. One of the deepest mysteries is the mystery of the self; therefore, the ancient decree of these schools has always been "Know Thyself."

3. The deeper teachings of the mystery schools help each individual answer questions such as:
   - Who am I?
   - What am I?
   - Where do I come from?
   - Where am I going?
   - What is my purpose?

4. The shamanic societies understood and taught this knowledge, but as we developed into modern culture, we lost the true understanding of the answers to these mysteries, and the Keepers of this knowledge went underground. Since that time, these teachings have been referred to as "hidden

knowledge." The mystery schools help bring that "hidden knowledge" back
to light.[8]

In addition to teaching the Delphic maxim to "Know Thyself," these schools
offer an implicit critique of modernity, as having lost or forgotten something
once widely sunderstood in the past, a view which Schwerin shares.

Initially, these spiritual interests remained something distinct from his professional life as an investment banker. However, over time, these two began
to overlap when, according to Schwerin, he became acquainted with the concept of *socially conscious investing* that had gained popularity during the late
1970s largely through the efforts of Leon H. Sullivan (1922–2001). An African-
American Baptist minister who had long been an outspoken and respected
advocate for improving the economic prospects of African-Americans, Sullivan
joined the Board of Directors at General Motors (GM) in 1971 where his soon
turned his activism toward the firm's activities. As a civil rights leader, Sullivan
became concerned about GM's business practices overseas in South Africa,
where the firm at the time was the largest single employer of Blacks. Using
his position of influence on the board, he eventually published a declaration
against apartheid that would become known as the "Sullivan Principles," which
laid much of the groundwork for the idea of CSR. The principles stated that
companies were morally obliged to strive for equal rights in all their activities, internally through employment practices and externally in choosing with
whom to engage in commerce.[9] In the United States and eventually worldwide,
the Sullivan Principles motivated widespread divestment in South African businesses that played an important role in eventually undermining the legitimacy
of the apartheid regime.[10]

By 1978 when the Sullivan Principles were garnering attention, David had
left the investment firm and was operating his own small business as an investment counselor, and one of his earliest clients made a request that would alter
his approach to doing business. She was strongly opposed to apartheid and
requested that her money not be invested in any company doing business in
South Africa. He worried that "pressure from those with similar feelings would
result in unintended consequences such as hurting employment opportunities
for the impoverished black S. African population."[11] Schwerin faced a moral
dilemma over competing and seemingly incompatible ethical systems. On one
hand, he was obliged to provide advice aimed at maximizing the return on investment for each client. On the other hand, Schwerin empathized with her convictions to not support firms doing business in a nation supporting Apartheid as

well as with the struggles of disenfranchised South Africans. From his spiritual practices, he had acquired the sense that all humans are interconnected globally, but more importantly, he understood the moral dimension of every private and personal action.

Because conventional economic rationality emphasized only the immediate financial self-interest of the investor, it failed to account for how seemingly rational decisions might shape, for better or worse, the circumstances of other stakeholders. In the years after this event, Schwerin claims that his private moral principles began to play a more prominent role in his investment decisions. He avoided firms whose products damaged the environment or failed to support the larger communities in which the conducted business.[12] This new stakeholder model allowed Schwerin to continue helping others earn a profit while simultaneously accommodating his private moral sensibilities. In fact, he came to believe that the laws of the market actually favored morally conscientious actions.[13]

Schwerin refined this approach into a coherent set of principles based on the practical spiritual lessons acquired at the International Pathwork Foundation, the mystery school of which he was a member. Founded on the lectures of the spiritual medium Eva Pierrakos, Pathwork guides practitioners through "a body of practical spiritual wisdom" to facilitate a profound personal transformation.[14] Through intensive individual and group work, participants inculcate Pierrakos' declaration that "you have the right and ability to mold and create substance with you mind."[15] Schwerin incorporated this principle into his views on business behavior: the correct moral perspective leads to correct moral acts, which in turn, transforms the world.

By the early 1990s, Schwerin states that he began to think seriously about committing his thoughts on business and spirituality to writing. Over the next several years, he refined his ideas for a more humane form of free enterprise, eventually dubbed Conscious Capitalism. In a book of the same name, Schwerin argues that humanity is becoming "conscious" of two universal truths. First, inner, spiritual experience is superior to material, external existence. "The universe," he writes, "seems to be presenting us with the opportunity to devote less time to external sense and security issues and direct more of our energy toward becoming receptive to internal experiences and influences."[16] Drawing on Maslow's hierarchy of needs, Schwerin argues that humans ultimately aspire to self-actualize, to experience their authentic, inner selves.

The external world remains inferior, even epiphenomenal to the inner, subjective reality. "For thousands of years," he declares, "revered spiritual leaders have told us that only one thing exists (spirit, the animating force) and it is mental in nature."[17] Here, Schwerin links the "ageless wisdom" of the mystery schools to the metaphysical model of human evolution developed by Willis Harman, whom he cited routinely. Perception determines and shapes the external reality we experience. Second, in addition to this emerging radical subjectivity, people are becoming more "conscious" of the interconnectness of everyone and everything. Again, rehearsing the ideas of Willis Harman, he stresses that "we are not only superficially connected, but, in fact, an integral part of an infinite, eternal consciousness."[18]

As business leaders apply these fundamental principles to their activities, Schwerin ultimately foresees the unfolding of an entirely new social reality.

> Capitalism is the system that seems best able to reflect the free flowing, multidimensional nature of life and is, therefore, capable of facilitating flexible and expeditious solutions to the problems of a dynamic, growing economy...Conscious Capitalism, reflecting the higher aspects of human nature and honoring the interdependence of life, is based on the understanding that harmonious relationships are essential to everyone's sense of fulfillment and well-being.[19]

Schwerin views capitalism as a close approximation of the natural order, and, Conscious Capitalism simply elevates market society, and therefore human nature, to its highest potential.

Despite such lofty aspirations, when *Conscious Capitalism: Principles for Prosperity* was published in 1998, it sold only modestly in the United States. Although he continues to occasionally lecture at various events around the country, Schwerin has experienced his most marked success in China, where his ideas have proven astonishingly appealing to many leading figures in the emerging market economy. He has written books on spirituality exclusively for Chinese audiences and has even facilitated workshops at the Communist Party School.

Even though Schwerin's direct influence has taken place across the Pacific, his philosophy of Conscious Capitalism would gestate for the next several years in various corners of business thought. Within a few short years of its publication, other, more influential voices would adopt Conscious Capitalism as their banner for social change.

Megatrends: A spiritual vision of business

As David Schwerin found a receptive audience in East Asia for his ideas, another thinker would breathe fresh life into Conscious Capitalism and bring it to the mainstream American business community. In 2005, bestselling author and lecturer Patricia Aburdene published *Megatrends 2010: The Dawn of Conscious Capitalism*, which established Conscious Capitalism as a legitimate path for social reform among business leaders. Set against the backdrop of the dot-com crash and the corporate scandals in firms like Enron and WorldComm, *Megatrends* declared that global capitalism was experiencing a shift in its fundamental values that would reshape free enterprise for the good of all peoples around the world. She attributes this transformation to a rising awareness of "spirit" throughout the world. In doing so, Aburdene recasts labor, business, and the free market as components in this spiritual unfolding for the ears of a business community eager to reconsider its most basic principles.

Megatrends 2010 represents merely the latest installment in the "Megatrends" series, which Aburdene began with her former husband and futurist John Naisbitt in 1982.[20] The book identified a number of "megatrends" that would affect society over the coming decade, in particular the decline of manufacturing and the rise of an "information economy." Naisbitt lent his considerable authority to the book, having served as the assistant to the Commissioner of Education for President Kennedy and special assistant in the Johnson administration, and it subsequently became a New York Times bestseller.[21]

Over the next two decades, the pair produced an entire series of works based on the megatrends concept, typically approaching large-scale changes with remarkable optimism and establishing the ideological foundation for Aburdene's version of Conscious Capitalism. In *Megatrends 2000* (1990), Aburdene and Naisbitt characterize the late twentieth century as the victory of individuals over collective institutions. "As we globalize," they argue, "individuals, paradoxically, become more important, more powerful."[22] The demise of Communism, the privatization of the welfare state, and even the popularity of "experiential" religion bear witness that institutional power is an inadequate arrangement for human prosperity:

> The 1990s are characterized by a new respect for the individual as the foundation of society and the basic unit of change. "Mass" movements are a misnomer. The environmental movement, the women's movement, the antinuclear movement were built one consciousness at a time by an individual persuaded of the possibility of a new reality.[23]

The authors trumpet the familiar maxim among futures researcher like Willis Harman that the correct "consciousness," read perception, constitutes the basic building block of human progress and further that organizations, institutions, and societies are not, in fact, more than the sum of their individual constituents.

The *Megatrends* series propelled Aburdene from the role of Naisbitt's research assistant into the public eye, becoming a respected celebrant of the emerging global economy. After divorcing Naisbitt, she aspired to continue the series on her own, but *Megatrends 2010* breaks with the earlier works, as she explicitly acknowledges the growing importance of spirituality in business.

In the preface, Aburdene identifies herself as "a capitalist and a spiritual seeker," two labels that she views as entirely compatible despite popular perceptions to the contrary.[24] Immediately, she describes how these two competing roles work seamlessly together in her personal life:

> Every weekday, I dwell in each of these very different worlds. Early in the morning I light a candle and journal with my favorite fountain pen. Then I usually meditate. Before settling down at the iMac, I observe one final ritual, switching on the business-oriented cable station, CNBC.[25]

This passage represents one of the few instances where Aburdene publically discusses her private spiritual activities, but it nonetheless illustrates that seeker spirituality holds for her, at least, some significance.

The central argument of the book remains twofold: one descriptive, and the other, prescriptive. First, she maintains that "conscious capitalism is the dynamic matrix of social, economic—and spiritual—trends transforming free enterprise."[26] Second, Aburdene simultaneously provides instructions for carrying on this transformation. Both dimensions, however, rely necessarily on language and concepts associated with spiritual seeking. In the end, Aburdene offers a spiritual account of capitalism broadly and of business practice specifically.

As a spiritual seeker, Aburdene distinguishes private "spirituality" from organized "religion," although many people identify as both. However, she determines that "spiritual transformation, triggered at the individual level, is spilling over from the personal to the institutional."[27] On one hand, Aburdene merely repeats her argument in *Megatrends 2000* that change originates within the individual, and that collectively each person reshapes the world. On the other hand, she simultaneously is refining this claim by restating it through the language of spirituality.

Aburdene cites numerous examples of how these "consciousness" practices are particularly relevant for businesses. Meditation lowers stress; fire-walking encourages risk-taking and bolsters self-confidence; and "HeartMath has created technology that enables a personal computer to measure heart rhythms, then actually allows people to observe how stress and negative thoughts or emotions clamp down on heart rhythms to produce a choppy, turbulent graph."[28] Each of these practices reworks the subject according to the values of the post-industrial workplace. They equip the self with tools to deal with uncertain conditions, to expect constant flux, and that risk-taking is a fundamental ingredient for success.

These same virtues play a vital role in Aburdene's "spiritual" portrait of capitalism. The free enterprise system, itself, stand beyond her critique.

> Capitalism is, or at least should be, synonymous with economic democracy, because free enterprise, when it works well, disperses economic opportunity to everyone! The spiritual value of Justice and the spiritual flow of Abundance are the red-hot ingredients in the secret sauce of free enterprise.[29]

Capitalism's failings, the corruption scandals, the widening wealth gap, stem not from any inherent flaws to the structures of capitalism but from the moral flaws of individuals. Greed, she writes, differs from self-interest.

> When corporations endorse rewards that are exclusively monetary in nature, they attract exactly what they deserve: self-serving leaders, who design corporate cultures where despicable behavior and greed are encouraged and honored. That is the path of corporate self-destruction, and shareholders had better beware.[30]

Aburdene attributes the crisis of capitalism to a pervasive culture of greed, to a lack of "spiritual awareness" within corporate leadership.

Of the few instances where Aburdene criticizes institutional structure, however, she remains committed to laissez-faire principles. For example, she denounces the legal imperative for corporations to maximize profit as an obligation for companies "to engage in a destructive form of capitalism" that overlooks broader social harm.[31] Yet, instead of calling for new laws that would require firms to consider the environmental and socioeconomic consequences of their actions, Aburdene suggests creating a new class of corporation, the socially responsible firm, to compete alongside the traditional corporation. This allows "conscious" investors to *voluntarily* move their holdings to firms committed explicitly toward the common good, without unduly coercing existing traditional corporations. In other words, the forces of the free market, rather than the state, will coerce profit-maximizers to adopt this "conscious" model.

Conscious Capitalism, subsequently, accounts for the ebbs and flows of the free, unrestricted marketplace. Aburdene appeals to the language of spirituality to properly explain the Internet boom of the 1990s and the subsequent recession after the dotcom bubble.

> At the spiritual level, the boom, bust and scandals revealed the dark corners of capitalism that must grow conscious and get *healed* before we can move on to what's next: greater spiritual (inner) and technological (external) progress—on a much firmer moral and economic footing.[32]

In a grand dialectic, the market evolves, and parallels the spiritual progress of humanity, "from elitism to economic democracy, from the fundamental doctrine of 'profit at any cost,' to the conscious ideology that espouses both money *and* morals."[33]

Megatrends 2010, with its practical spiritual vision of Conscious Capitalism, gained a wide audience in business circles. In 2005, the *International Association for Spirit at Work* (now Judi Neal's *Edgewalkers International*) gave it high praise, naming it "Best Book of the Year" for 2005. Aburdene has tirelessly promoted the idea of Conscious Capitalism, lecturing around the country, including a televised workshop on CSPAN. Through her efforts, Aburdene has taken the idea of Conscious Capitalism from the relative obscurity of David Schwerin's singular voice and prepared it for what would become the passion of several highly visible corporate leaders in the years since its publication.

Libertarian spirituality

Within just a few short years of the publication of *Megatrends 2010*, capitalism lay in crisis once again. The financial crisis of 2007–9 that accompanied the collapse of the housing market stoked fears of another Great Depression, as established investment houses like Lehman Brothers and Bear Stearns vanished seemingly overnight. Such tumultuous developments temporarily appeared to undermine the boldest of Aburdene's notions about the future of capitalism. Even the most rigorous defenders of free markets, including former Federal Reserve Chairman Alan Greenspan, recanted their unwavering devotion to economic liberalism, and Conscious Capitalists remained certain that capitalism was the answer to a prosperous global future.[34]

The uncertainty, however, proved fleeting. In fact, for advocates of socially responsible business practices, the collapse only confirmed their conviction that free markets worked best when grounded in correct moral imperatives rather than greater regulation by the state. Since 2008, a group of progressively minded business thinkers, led by Whole Foods founder and CEO John Mackey, have established a well-organized and highly visible nonprofit organization, Conscious Capitalism, committed to the healing power of free markets. They propose to accomplish this "through transformative thinking, programs, events, and communities of inquiry designed to support the elevation of humanity."[35] While this version of Conscious Capitalism shares an affinity with the ideas of Schwerin and Aburdene, it nonetheless bears the mark of Mackey's distinctive mode of spiritual seeking. Over the course of his career, Mackey has cultivated a particularly libertarian worldview and refined a set of spiritual disciplines that accommodate his politics. In other words, Mackey has erected a kind of *libertarian spirituality*, rooted in his countercultural youth and perfected during his years as an entrepreneur. This section traces the spiritual and political evolution of John Mackey, from a rebellious youth in Austin, Texas to the leader of a growing reform movement in American business called Conscious Capitalism.

John Mackey, like Steve Jobs, came of age during the early 1970s in the waning years of the counterculture. Born in Houston, Texas to Bill and Margaret Mackey, he moved to Austin after high school in order to attend the University of Texas. Austin, at the time, represented the regional epicenter for youth rebellion; it was the Lone Star State's variant of San Francisco, replete with a burgeoning rock and alternative country music scene, hippie communes, and spiritual seekers.

Despite these similarities, San Francisco and Austin remained worlds apart. For one thing, each thrived on quite distinct forms of industry. If Northern California symbolized cutting-edge technology and the sophistication of Napa Valley, Texas prospered from the land, quite literally. First, for the first half of the twentieth century, it provided the lion's share of the industrial world's most desired product, petroleum. Despite diminishing returns by the mid-twentieth century, it nonetheless continued to serve as the hub for the American oil industry.

Long before the internal combustion engine made oil the highest traded commodity around the globe, however, Texas was known for its other major export to the rest of the country: beef. Indeed, it is anchored to local identities as well a part of broader American popular culture. The "cowboy," rugged and armed with a six-shooter, yet virtuous and self-reliant, driving herds across the great empty spaces of western country, has become a prominent member of the America's mythological pantheon. Still, however *Giant* James Dean or Rock Hudson might appear to captivated audiences, cattle ranching, like oil, was big business and, thus, became an object of scorn and an embodiment of "the system" for the countercultural stirrings in Texas, and in particular Austin. When John Mackey came to the capital as a youth, therefore, he encountered a countercultural discourse with a distinct regional flavor, which emphasized a loose mode of living and spiritual seeking, but especially new methods of food production that could undermine the power of the cattle juggernaut.

Mackey never graduated college, but these initial years proved to be formative for his adult character. First, he embraced an intuitive, flexible approach to life, relying less on rationality and more on "feelings." "In my early twenties," he recalls, "I made what has proven to have been a wise decision: a lifelong commitment to follow my heart wherever it led me—which has been a wonderful journey of adventure, purpose, creativity, growth, and love."[36] This loose style permitted Mackey to pursue living as a kind of smorgasbord of potential experiences upon which he could draw, depending primarily on his mood or appetite.

His brief stint in college reflects this relaxed mode of living. Unconcerned with planning for the future, Mackey indulged in those courses that peaked his interests in the moment. He states "I only took classes I was interested in, and if a class bored me, I quickly dropped it."[37] While this approach might have hindered his progress toward a college degree, Mackey nonetheless sees this as an advantage. Never enrolling in a single business class, according to him, meant that he "had nothing to unlearn and new possibilities for innovation."[38]

Instead, he spent his early adulthood chasing broad philosophical concerns, as he says, "trying to discover the meaning and purpose of my life."[39] He digested a number of courses in religion, began experimenting with various forms of spiritual practice, such as yoga and meditation, and developed an interest in alternative diets. He became a vegetarian and, at one point, spent two years living in a cooperative community where, he writes, "I grew my hair and beard long."[40] For Mackey, the search for meaning manifested at a place where concerned for healthy food and seeker spirituality converged.

Like many of his peers at the time in the New Left, Mackey was critical of bureaucratic juggernaut of postwar American society with its seemingly blatant disregard for the ecological and socioeconomic consequences of mass production. He agreed with the agendas of groups like Students for a Democratic Society, who were wary of expanded governmental powers as well as the exploitative practices of bloated corporations. By the late 1970s, he eagerly had joined a cooperative in order to help raise the awareness of alternative foods in Austin. However, the experience quickly became a source of discontent. Mackey found the democratic principles of the co-op extremely cumbersome, stifling the innovation and organizational growth, which he believed necessary to influence the larger society.[41]

Armed with a modest amount of capital investment, therefore, Mackey and his wife finally left the cooperative to start a privately owned organic grocery, comically named SaferWay (a twist on the national grocery chain SafeWay). Although the store would expand and evolve into Whole Foods Market, the first years of business proved challenging. In spite of their meager earnings, Mackey and his wife found themselves the targets of criticism from his anti-business voices who accused him of exploiting workers and customers. "Despite my good intentions, I had somehow become a selfish and greedy businessman."[42]

His experience as a struggling entrepreneur contradicted Mackey's assumptions about the exploitative nature of capitalism. He found solace in a source quite unusual for a socially conscious youth at the time: the defenders of classical economic liberalism. Vociferously devouring the works of Ludwig von Mises, Ayn Rand, and Milton Friedman, Mackey experienced a revolution in his thinking. These thinkers offered Mackey a philosophy of human freedom that accounted for his experiences as a social reformer and an entrepreneur. In a free marketplace, Rand states that "all human relationships are *voluntary*. Men are free to cooperate or not, to deal with one another or not, as their own individual judgments, convictions, and interests dictate."[43] Capitalism, unlike any other social order, expressed individual freedom and could foster the kind of social change Mackey was seeking.

Through a renewed committed to the power of free markets, Mackey located common ground between the aspirations of the New Left and the assertions of neoclassical economic philosophers. Both ideologies maintained that centralized, bureaucratic power of any form diminished the freedom of individuals. Moreover, each shared the ultimate goal of liberating the individual from the constraints imposed upon her by the prevailing social order in postwar America. What Mackey found among the characters of *Atlas Shrugged* and the warnings of Hayek's *Road to Serfdom* were an unfamiliar and refreshing set of ideas with which he could retool his own experiment in countercultural entrepreneurialism.

Mackey jettisoned the anti-capitalist rhetoric of the New Left and constructed a new ethos that injected economic liberalism with a dose of the "consciousness transforming" sentiments of the counterculture.

What I love most about the freedom movement, another name for the Libertarian platform, are the ideas of voluntary cooperation and spontaneous

order that when channeled through free markets lead to the continuous evolution and progress of humanity. I believe that individual freedom in free markets
when combined with property rights and the rule of law and ethical democratic
government results in societies that maximize prosperity and establish conditions that promote human happiness and wellbeing.[44]

Mackey reworks markets as utterly anti-institutional, based on "cooperation"
and "spontaneous order," as the logical outgrowth of voluntary human action.
Furthermore, free markets establish the necessary conditions for "continuous
evolution," leading not merely to the pursuit of profit but to ultimate goals of
"human happiness and wellbeing."

The transition that Mackey experienced as a young entrepreneur went
beyond a change of political and ideological orientation. The shift was equally
practical and moral, intimately associated with the various spiritual activities
he cultivated. When Mackey claims that "business can be a wonderful vehicle
for both personal and organizational growth," he casts the entrepreneur and the
firm as vertically integrated spaces for moral activity, who, in dialogue with one
another, facilitate a mode of spiritual seeking.[45] In fact, Mackey's political and
professional identity as a libertarian entrepreneur is inseparable from his spiritual quest. Through these practices, Mackey engendered libertarian sensibilities
and formed habits of perception that were radically subjective.

Mackey acquired a penchant for eclectic privatized spiritual seeking during
college, exploring the contours of Eastern philosophy and religion. While he
and his wife continue to perform a variety of activities, Mackey draws his primary spiritual regimen from *A Course in Miracles*. As a regular practitioner of
A Course in Miracles, he cultivates a radically subjective worldview premised on
the notion that correct perception shapes reality.

Mackey understands spiritual disciplines like *A Course in Miracles* in terms
that conform to the libertarian principles of noncoercive voluntary exchange.
He describes to one interviewer what he appreciates about *A Course*:

My real spiritual path is *A Course in Miracles*, and I've been following that for
15 years, and that's a hard path of forgiveness and love, and mind training. How
that plays out, I suppose, in my work life is I don't push that philosophy on any-
body. Of course, one thing I love about it is it's this self-paced path, as opposed
to a guru type of path. And in interacting with people, I try to see everyone that
I encounter as a spiritual being and my brother/sister and try to deal with them
respectfully and with love.[46]

Spirituality, for him, remains a voluntary activity, not to "pushed" on anyone else. Other spiritual paths that assume a more formal organizational structure or require submission to an external authority violate this principle. Furthermore, he values *A Course* based on its practical usefulness rather than its universal Truth claims. What matters for Mackey is how *A Course* shifts his consciousness, and subsequently, his relationship with others.

The teachings found within *A Course in Miracles* complement Mackey's privatized spiritual style. First published in 1976, the book's author, or more precisely, its "transcriber," Helen Schucman, declared *A Course* to be her effort to capture the words of an "inner voice" that she identified as Jesus. While *A Course in Miracles* espouses a Christian foundation, Catherine Albanese designates the text as part of the New Age movement, a main trait of which is the subjective nature of reality. "New Agers," she notes, "evoke the energetic basis of their spirituality when they tell each other that they create their own reality, affirming the pliancy of matter and its plasticity before the moving of the spirit."[47]

A Course teaches generally that suffering, sin, and evil do not refer to objective conditions in the world but instead result from the misperception of individual experience. Albanese states that "sickness, for *A Course in Miracles*, is a defense against truth, in other words, a blockage and point of fixity."[48] The student who works through the exercises outlined in *A Course*, then, habituates a worldview where the individual is solely responsible for her reality, where the world persists just as it should, and where any unwanted experiences can be mitigated through adjusting her perceptive lens. As the text states, "Nothing real can be threatened. Nothing unreal exists. Herein lies the piece of God."[49]

A Course in Miracles reshapes the self through a series of self-guided, daily reflections, or "lessons," which over time can effectively radicalize the subjectivity of the practitioner. As the text explains, "the purpose of the workbook is to train your mind in a systematic way to a different perception of everyone and everything in the world."[50] In gradual succession, each lesson builds upon the preceding one to habituate within the practitioner a new, radically subjective worldview which, by Lesson 32, becomes "*I have invented the world I see.*"[51]

Through *A Course*, Mackey acquired a spiritual perspective that could agree with his libertarian sentiments. Statements like "*I am not the victim of the world I see*" teach the reader to assume total responsibility for her condition and, subsequently, to reject notions of systemic social injustice as illusory.[52] Indeed, these attitudes, instead, represent the source of the problem and, hence, only a change in perception rids one of this burden. In addition, some lessons prove even more explicitly libertarian, such as Lesson 76, which enjoins the practitioner to envisage that *"I am under no laws but God's."*[53] The lesson explains that man-made laws, because they deny the true relationship between the mind and the body, are inevitably futile attempts to achieve "salvation." "Think," it states, "of the freedom in the recognition that you are not bound by all the strange and twisted laws you have set up to save you."[54] Again, the text advises the reader to rely solely on himself (as a component of the divine) and to realize that involving the state can only hinder his progress.

Through *A Course in Miracles*, Mackey accepted reality as pliable, as a matter of deliberate choice, grounded in a looser, but empowered form of selfhood. "This particular reality that we're in is not the only reality that exists," he told the *New Yorker* in 2010. "In fact, there are an infinite number of realities."[55] The informed individual may freely choose the particular version of events most appropriate for attaining happiness. In the end, h *A Course in Miracles* confirms the libertarian maxim that in a liberal society, the free, autonomous individual holds sole responsibility for the outcome of her life.

Mackey shaped the formal organization and guided the informal culture of Whole Foods according to the principles of his private spiritual practices. Since the turn of the century, subsequently, these spiritual and political commitments have led him to a more vocal public posture. In late 2003, Mackey befriended Michael Strong, a libertarian-leaning headmaster of a New Mexico charter school, and began to discuss the possibility of starting a movement based on their shared views. "After a great deal of brainstorming," Mackey recalls, "we decided to create an organization that would serve as a beacon of liberty, human potential, and making the world a better place."[56] They named their new organization FLOW, an acronym for "Freedom Lights Our World" that also acknowledges the influential work of psychologist Mihaly Csikszentmihalyi.[57]

The concept of "flow" accords neatly with Mackey's radically subjective spirituality, libertarian politics, and respect for entrepreneurship. According to Csikszentmihalyi, "flow" delineates a "state in which people are so involved in an activity nothing else seems to matter; the experience itself is so enjoyable that people will do it even at great cost, for the sheer sake of doing it."[58] Drawing on ideas from humanistic psychology, he argues that human flourishing most fully occurs through creative action, that man, as producer, experiences true happiness. The individual who cultivates the proper mindset of "flow" will inevitably realize her highest potential.

As FLOW took shape, Mackey and Strong articulated three initiatives that would encompass the organization: "Peace through Commerce," "Accelerating Women Entrepreneurs," and last but not least, "Conscious Capitalism." These programs would be explored through various local chapters around the United States known as "FLOW Activation Centers."[59] By 2006, activation centers existed in New York, Austin, and San Francisco Bay.

These groups began to forge a network of like-minded business leaders and thinkers whom Michael Strong eventually brought together as contributors for a collection of essays published in 2009 entitled *Be the Solution: How Entrepreneurs and Conscious Capitalists Can Solve All the World's Problems.*[60] Mackey, who composed the foreword to the work, and the other authors each articulated how a new, more ethical, and spiritually grounded form of capitalism was emerging. True to Mackey's libertarianism, they argued that business represents the best hope for achieving a prosperous global future. The essays bear titles such as "The Entrepreneur as Hero," "Arete and the Entrepreneur," and "Liberating the Spirit for Entrepreneurial Good," in which the authors weave moral and spiritual language into a broad discussion of business strategy. Prominent business leaders and scholars praised the work. As one professor expressed on the book's jacket, "at last, a book about the heart of capitalism as a force for creating good in the world for solving many of our tough social problems. I hope our political leaders read it."[61]

In the few years since the publication of *Be the Solution*, FLOW has ceased to exist while Conscious Capitalism as evolved into an independent organization. Leading executives and business thinkers from a number of industries have signed on to the movement. Its Board of Directors feature individuals such as Doug Rauch, former president of Trader Joe's and Kip Tindell, founder of The Container Store. The organization hosts an annual conference where, over two days, business owners, executives, and thinkers participate in workshops and panel sessions dedicated to free markets, spiritually driven business, and facilitating the spread of "consciousness" around the globe.

Mapping a neoliberal habitus

Thus far, this chapter has traced how three key individuals contributed to the rise of a new social movement namely Conscious Capitalism, within specific areas of the American business community. All of them baby boomers, they emerged from the social strife of the 1960s and 1970s with a penchant for highly individualized forms of spiritual practice which would become entangled with their professional lives. Conscious Capitalism, though lacking an explicit self-identity as "spiritual," was nonetheless nurtured in these practical entanglements. Alongside workplace spirituality, however, it is business reform movement, stressing more effective moral leadership while offering a defense of economic and political libertarianism, both of which advance the interests of global business in perpetuating neoliberalization.

Indeed, the three individuals highlighted in this chapter are business elites working in precisely those industries that have thrived in the context of neoliberalization: finance, information, and the service sector. It is no coincidence that Conscious Capitalism did not emerge from the leaders of the textile industry, from oil barons, or from heavy manufacturing, where hierarchical control of rationally organized production yields the greatest efficiency. For the investment counselor, the futures researcher, and the organic foods entrepreneur, work is a highly fluid, interpersonal, and an abstract creative process that demands alternative practical wisdom.

Schwerin, Aburdene, and Mackey espouse spiritual practices and beliefs that reflect and respond effectively to rhythms of post-industrial life. Conscious Capitalism, for each of them, takes for granted the normative potential of free markets to alleviate injustice; they aspire to an ideal world reduced to autonomous individuals where voluntary action expresses the highest form of morality. The coercive power of the state, in this vision, constitutes a constraint on the maxim of free, voluntary association. In this sense, Conscious Capitalism reifies the so-called neoliberal political program to establish global "free trade," domestic deregulation of business activities, and the rollback of the welfare state.

John Mackey's most recently published treatise entitled *Conscious Capitalism: Liberating the Heroic Spirit of Business* most explicitly reveals this neoliberal platform. "Business does not exist," he writes, "to be a servant or tool of social activists or the government. Some people would like business to act like a dog on a leash and do whatever the government wants them to do. That's been tried; it's called corporatism or fascism. It is about dominating and controlling business to make it serve the goals of political rulers."[62] Here, Mackey asserts the superiority of the voluntary principle as the moral imperative. Coercive institutions, like the State, violate this maxim and therefore diminish human freedom. According to this logic, diminishing the power of the state presumably facilitates the greater good. For instance, Mackey argues that "if business taxes were lower, all other stakeholders would have more—lower prices for consumers, higher wages and benefits for team members, and higher profits for investors, and the amount of money we could give to support the nonprofit sector would also be proportionately greater."[63]

The voluntary principle applies equally to organizational structure of the Conscious business. "Increasingly in the world of business today, individual creativity and innovation must be combined in with a shared sense of harmony and purposeful creation. A decentralized and empowered organization does not perform a symphony; it engages in a kind of improvisational jazz."[64] Conscious Capitalism requires a new workplace structure, comprised of empowered, autonomous, self-regulating teams, which mirrors with remarkable accuracy much of the corporate downsizing and restructuring that has occurred in since the 1970s.

Mackey imagines business as "ultimate source of all taxes and donations," as the origin of all value.[65] He views organized labor as a coercive form of power that constrains progress. "Unions," Mackey asserts, "compete with the company for the hearts and minds of team members. Our belief is that if a company does an outstanding job caring for its team members, creating value for them, and respecting them as key stakeholders, it can successfully avoid unionization."[66] Unions, from this perspective, produce value of their own, and emerge only out of the moral failure of the company's leaders. The Conscious Capitalist is pro-worker and only indirectly anti-union.

Finally, Conscious Capitalism endorses the neoliberal project to foster privatization on a global scale. Admitting that "we want to make Conscious Capitalism the dominant economic and business paradigm in the world to spread human flourishing," Mackey outlines how Whole Foods, through the Whole Planet Foundation, "works to end poverty around the world by making microcredit working-capital loans to millions of impoverished people to help them create and improve their businesses."[67] Here again, Mackey implicitly attacks nonmarket forms of social welfare as inadequate. Conscious Capitalism supports a world where problems are confronted through market solutions and every individual is the CEO of her personal firm.

On one hand, Conscious Capitalism supports the typical union-busting, anti-regulatory, privatized neoliberal worldview. Yet, on the other hand, it also provides Mackey with a moral vocabulary that allows him to move beyond the conventional neoliberal arguments. Quoting Marc Gafni, director of the Center for World Spirituality, he writes:

> The world of business is becoming one of the great cathedrals of spirit. Businesses are becoming places in which meaning can be created, in which mutuality begins to happen. Business is the force in the world that is fulfilling every major value of the great spiritual traditions: intimacy, trust, a shared vision, cooperation, collaboration, friendship, and ultimately love.[68]

At the center of these twenty-first century cathedrals sit the enlightened corporate gurus. "Conscious Companies are led by emotionally and spiritually mature leaders...They embody Mahatma Gandhi's dictum 'We must be the change we wish to see in the world.'"[69] These post-industrial heroes must embody these spiritual principles and master the prescribed spiritual practices in order to bring this new order to fruition.

The spiritual practices and beliefs offered by Schwerin, Aburdene, and Mackey bind the individual practitioner to the larger post-industrial social structure. Mindfulness meditation assuages the uncertainty of laissez-faire, while corporate sponsored fire-walking enhances risk-taking amidst the cut-throat conditions of a globally competitive market. Moreover, a cultivated sense that perception determines reality allows one to readily shift perspective in the face of unpredictable events. In other words, the looser, radically empowered *sense* of self, instilled through these post-industrial spiritual practices, mimics and even reproduces the deregulated, privatized social order of neoliberal society. Bourdieu describes the social agent as "a collective individual or a collective individuated by the fact of embodying social structures...The habitus is socialized subjectivity, a historic transcendental, whose schemes or perception and appreciation are the product of collective and individual history."[70] Put succinctly, what I am beginning to describe here is how this rhetorical, cultural, and practical entanglement of spirituality and work illuminates the underlying neoliberal *habitus* dominating contemporary American society and from which global business elites benefit most. Schwerin's advocacy of socially conscious investing, for instance, reflects more than a program to reform business; it indicates a deeply held assumption about human subjectivity and social relations: individual behavior is motivated by internally generated beliefs, and therefore the failure of even the most mundane of our actions in the marketplace to align with our chosen moral principles constitutes a failure to achieve full personhood. Such a perspective mutes the impact of objective social conditions on individual agency; it ignores the historical situated-ness of all human practice. On the other hand, it *does* take for granted the essential autonomy of the individual as well as the inevitability of the capitalist marketplace. We simply persist within, but without being a part of the marketplace. Both the autonomous individual and reality of the capitalist marketplace remain beyond criticism. More precisely, to use Bourdieu's terminology, Conscious Capitalism reinforces an existing neoliberal *doxa* in which we misrecognize the historically constructed social world as eternal and natural. Conscious Capitalism, and the spiritual perspective(s) discusses herein, only makes sense for a social order where both individuals and markets are unfettered, where business constitutes the highest form of authority, and in which the state exists to maximize the opportunities for business to pursue the benevolent aims of their leaders. In the final section of this book, we take a closer look at how the entanglement of spirituality, corporate culture, and business reproduces this neoliberal habitus in specific, localized contexts.

Part Three

Formations of Spiritual Labor

6

Not the Usual Suspects: Real Estate Rabbis, Monastic Managers, and Spiritual Salesmen in the Big Apple

Up to this point, I have focused on the emergence of a moral language of spirituality as it has emerged over time in management discourse and how it has been entangled with various institutional trends and movement in the business world. The rhetoric of spirituality emerged as a form of criticism against the postwar welfare state. It transformed the language of management, the way entrepreneurs shaped their businesses, and provided the conceptual language for business reform movements like Conscious Capitalism. Academic societies, peer-reviewed journals, and research organizations, which concentrate on "spirituality in the workplace" or "Conscious Capitalism," had risen to prominence. Advocates of spirituality at work venerate scientists like Willis Harman, humanistic psychologists like Abraham Maslow, and businessmen like Robert Greenleaf as pioneers, each of whom stressed the importance of subjective experience, intuitive knowledge, and the "spiritual." They privilege notions of spirituality as utterly private and apolitical and yet as a vital part of the social fabric and the means to a prosperous future. These popular and intellectual movements matured during a period of intense socioeconomic change in which the welfare state was in retreat and post-industrial forms of work began to dominate middle-class careers. It was in and through these processes that spirituality entered the public discussion of work, and it is in light of these broad forces that it must be grasped as a distinct, coherent aspect of post-industrial American culture.

Yet, to describe these developments as a discrete "religious" or social movement, as others have done, would prove myopic.[1] Rather, they are widely scattered groups that often lack an awareness of one another. Some, like the Management, Spirituality, and Religion interest group in the Academy of Management, apply a scholarly lens to workplace spirituality. Others, like Conscious Capitalism, appear more as political action organizations, seeking to not only upend the mindset of business leadership but also to promote a kind of spiritual libertarianism. These groups might be formally organized, featuring well-known spiritual or business leaders, or merely informal networks of individuals who share a desire to incorporate spirituality into their working lives, who use tools like social media to stay connected.

Rather than a movement, what I am describing is an extended family of formal and informal groups, bound together culturally, who engage in a shared discourse about work, business organizations, and capitalism anchored in the conceptual orbit of "spirituality." While others, including myself, have written extensively on prominent examples like Whole Foods or Steve Jobs, little effort has been made to examine the less visible members of this family, those moment. The next two chapters will look at two localized contexts where the language of spirituality comes together with work. In the current chapter, I closely examine a loosely structured network of business elites, who meet intermittently in Manhattan to discuss the intersection of spirituality, religion, and work. While the previous chapters deal primarily with how the entanglement of business and spirituality has unfolded in relation to broad socioeconomic changes over time, the final section takes a closer look at how individuals in their localized settings navigate spirituality and work. Specifically, how, in each case, do the particularities of location in the social structure, personal history, and the available cultural repertoire of spiritual ideas and practices interact to reproduce the status quo? How is individual practice implicated in the perpetuation of a neoliberal social order? Like the more publically visible examples explored in the first two sections of this book, these individuals participate in this movement because it provides tools for overcoming the anxieties wrought by globalization and post-industrial life. The rhetoric of spirituality enables them to make sense of a world governed by neoliberalism. In essence, these are localized moments in the reproduction of global capitalism.

The New York groups

On a muggy June evening, I attended a lecture at Intersections International in midtown Manhattan entitled "The Spirit of Work," part of Intersections' "Power and Values" seminar series. Associated with the Collegiate Church of New York, founded in 1628 and reportedly the oldest continuous congregation in North America, Intersections International is an ecumenical organization "dedicated to building respectful relationships among diverse individuals and communities to forge common ground and develop strategies that promote justice, reconciliation, and peace."[2]

Fred Johnson, artistic director for Intersections, convened the meeting at dusk with the sound of bongos, over which he improvised melodic lyrics welcoming those in attendance and introduced the speakers. People like Alan Lurie and Kenny Moore, two of the facilitators, brought a range of experiences and perspectives on the spiritual aspects of work. Prior to a successful career in human resources for a large energy company, Kenny "the Monk" Moore spent fifteen years in a monastic community and found through religious discipline life lessons remarkably applicable to corporate life. Alan Lurie is an ordained Rabbi and author of *Five Minutes on Mondays: Finding Unexpected Purpose, Peace, and Fulfillment at Work* (2009), who had developed a unique program in the New York real estate firm of which he was managing director. At the beginning of each workweek, Lurie gathers with his coworkers and shares a parable, often drawn from his extensive knowledge of Jewish and other religious teachings, as a way to attend the spiritual needs of his staff.

Intersections International is not alone in its commitment to exploring the relationship between spirituality and work. In fact, this meeting represents only one example of countless formal and informal organized groups that meet regularly in New York City to discuss the topic. Unsurprisingly, these events often draw a regular cast of upwardly mobile business professionals who, for a variety of reasons, wish to take part in this movement. Some working people, like Marc Miller for example, an executive in corporate real estate, use these groups as opportunities to bring their private religious commitments into their professional lives. Others, such as Peter Roche, see spirituality as the foundation upon which thriving, socially conscientious companies might be built. These groups come together not only in churches, but in corporate boardrooms, as well as exclusive societies such as the Princeton Club of New York, where I had seen many of these same faces a few weeks earlier to hear Alan Lurie speak about "Work as a Spiritual Gymnasium." These usual suspects, through a shared interest in spirituality of work, have forged disparate voices into a loosely structured network of business leaders, religious thinkers, and spiritual seekers.

While the aims of its members differ, this community generally envisages spirituality as a means to cope with the stresses of the fast-paced, highly competitive business environment of New York City. Because the prevailing culture of business precludes transcendent principles, they maintain, it inadequately addresses the spiritual needs of individuals and society alike. In particular, they have turned to spiritual language to explain the economic crisis of 2007–8 that wrought havoc in many of the industries in which they operate and undermined many of their assumptions about the promise of hard work. While careers are less secure, and plans for the future uncertain, these communities orient participants toward an alternative narrative of global capitalism that celebrates uncertainty as opportunity and dangles the hope that through inner transformation comes global reform.

Competing aims

Many of the participants in this loosely structured movement understand work, itself, as a kind of spiritual practice. Such views, of course, are not new, and reflect deeply entrenched Western, particularly Protestant, notions of work as a "religious" act. The modern conception of work remains tied historically to reformers like Martin Luther and John Calvin, who broadened the traditional idea of "calling," to include not only the work of the ordained or the cloistered, but also secular pursuits.[3] Despite such historical antecedents, the notion of work as "spiritual" as it is used in these groups represents something quite distinct from earlier ideas of work as a "calling." Whereas Luther sees one's "calling" as a worldly activity conducted in service to God, these new groups prefer a more eclectic, less dogmatically confined idea of work as "spiritual." Authority rests not in God and his commandments, but in the choices of the individual to explore, refine, and express her "spirit" through work.

Real Estate executive Alan Lurie, for example, appears regularly as a lecturer in settings throughout the New York area to talk about the spiritual aspects of work. He began his foray into this movement in a corporate real estate firm where he would bring employees together every Monday morning and deliver a brief inspirational message. In short order, Lurie became an important figure among local business circles in the city and was being invited to speak in a variety of professional contexts. In 2009, he emerged on the national stage as a prominent advocate for workplace spirituality when he authored *Five Minutes on Mondays: Finding Unexpected Purpose, Peace, and Fulfillment at Work*, a collection of the parables that he was sharing with his staff. He blogs regularly for the *Huffington Post* and in 2011, at the International Conference for Faith and Spirituality in the Workplace at the University of Arkansas, Lurie was awarded the *Willis Harman Spirit at Work Award*.

Known popularly as the "Real Estate Rabbi" (a term he personally resists) because of his formal rabbinic training, he claims that "work, in fact, presents the most powerful environment for spiritual development."[4] The workplace confronts individuals with "very real dilemmas and interactions," which, like weights in a gym, serve as tools, when used properly, and can build "spiritual" strength.[5] "Weight-lifting," he explains, "is about resistance. That's what work is, because I'm getting pulled down by the gravity of ego and I have to push against that."[6] Work, then, is not an obligation to God, but an activity through which one struggles deliberately to achieve a more spiritual (less ego-driven) disposition.

Lurie draws inspiration from his formal education as a Rabbi to describe this "spiritual gymnasium." The Hebrew term for work, *avodah*, also means "prayer," and thus, according to him, Jewish teachings have always perceived work and spiritual action as coterminous with one another. "When business is approached with the same spirit as prayer—with positive intention, honesty, and humility—a deeper and lasting success will naturally emerge."[7] Again, while this might closely resemble the Reformed notion of "calling" as an obligation to God, Lurie points out that the ultimate aim of any spiritual practice, including work, is primarily the connection it creates between individuals. "Within Judaism, the point of vertical connection (to God), which one gets through meditation and prayer, is like an extension cord to draw energy into you to allow you to be effective horizontally (with other people). So in Judaism, the idea of spending your whole time doing vertical work, misses the whole point. We are embodied to be of service horizontally."[8]

Although committed to his faith, Alan, like many of his peers in the movement, draws on teachings outside of Jewish tradition. Religion, for him, represents merely a "repository of spiritual teachings from people who had spiritual insights." Spirituality, the true essence of what religion preserves, is something more ineffable and deeply private, "those things which help you identify your true nature, which is spirit. Something is spiritual," he claims, "when it is an experience of a transformative connection."[9] Lurie sees each religion as containing identical spiritual truths, interpreted differently by individuals in different places and times.[10]

Yet, Lurie locates spirituality not only in other religious traditions, but also in ideas normally identified as secular. Like so much of popular discourse on spirituality and work, humanistic psychology informs his ideas. Alan can move, in the course of a few seconds, from discussion about "ego," through Pastor Rick Warren's *Purpose-Driven Life*, to Maslow's hierarchy of needs. Lurie's ideas blur the boundaries between the religious, the spiritual, and the secular. Indeed, because he defines spirituality as utterly transformational, authentic spiritual experiences demand change in all areas of life, not merely during well-defined religious practices. "If it only changes you when you're sitting on the meditation cushion, or at synagogue, and then you go back to the same way you were, that's an experience but it's not transformative; it wasn't the 'real deal.'"[11] All experiences and activities, including work, get redescribed as opportunities for spiritual expression.

While individuals like Alan Lurie view work as a form of spiritual self-development, others are interested in using their religious faith as a moral guide for their careers. Marc Miller, an executive in commercial office leasing, can be found regularly attending many of the various lectures and workshops in New York which focus on this relationship between spirituality and work. Although an acquaintance of Lurie's, he participates in these groups not because he sees work as inherently spiritual, but rather because he is seeking to enhance the ethical foundation that his Jewish faith already brings to his professional life. Religion serves as the interpretive lens through which Miller makes daily decisions, and deals with tough situations in an industry that he describes as "very cut-throat" and particularly prone to unethical behavior.[12]

Miller, the youngest of three brothers, hails from a conservative Jewish family in the borough of Queens; his family engaged in what he calls "stringent" religious practice in the home. Of his two siblings, Miller alone attended a Jewish Day School where he learned Hebrew and studied the texts and traditions of his religious community. Although he later drifted from his religious devotion during college, Miller continued to maintain a strong ethnic identity as a Jew, remaining staunchly pro-Israel and supporting a robust United States-Israeli relationship. In his twenties and thirties, as a young professional living in the city, however, Marc began to reconnect with his religious upbringing. He started attending Bible classes, admittedly for social reasons, "to meet girls," but quickly become immersed in the material.[13]

Now fifty-two, working in commercial leasing, he works primarily on commission, and although competition can be overwhelming, the financial rewards are staggering. With such high stakes, the industry attracts many to whom Marc refers as "bad apples," individuals willing to cut corners and engage in dishonest behaviors to reap significant profits. His religious practice has proven vital in negotiating these turbulent conditions. "Spirituality," Miller contends, "has helped me to deal with that, because if I wasn't a religiously spiritual person, I could've been driven to violence."[14] Recalling an incident when a colleague took credit and commission for a deal that Miller had initiated, he admits to seriously considering physically harming the gentleman. "We invest our heart and soul, with our time and talents that God gave us. Thankfully, for my faith, I didn't kill him or hurt him."[15] Drawing on his faith, Marc left the firm soon thereafter and opened his own business. "In my tradition," he explains, "when you're around bad people, you have to move away from them. Believing in God gave me the faith to realize that this person who did this to me would get his comeuppance on God's time, when He wants it to happen."

The decision to become an entrepreneur proved only to bolster the connection he was forging between work and his Jewish faith. Raising three children leaves Miller with little time for personal religious practice at home, and as a business owner, he now takes a few minutes each day during the workweek for prayer or Bible study. In addition, he regularly attends a Torah class, which meets every Tuesday at Google's New York office and participates in workshops devoted to workplace spirituality around the city. All of these activities illustrate how Marc's professional life serves as a central locale for his religious practice and identity.[16]

All in all, Miller regards conventional business ethics with skepticism and believes religion and spirituality can more effectively guide business behavior. "If a company just has a mission statement or five words that they call values, is that really going to effect their recruiting, their hiring, or how they're going to discipline? I don't think so."[17] People in the world of business, according to Miller, require something more robust, the kind of total worldview that only religious belief can provide. His previous employers espoused ethical values, but because they neither appealed to spiritual concepts nor grounded their principles in religious belief, they failed to effect the daily decisions of staff members. As an entrepreneur, Miller finds the "latitude to spend time during the day, here or there, studying, and just being freer to make ethical decisions."

Marc Miller regards religion and spirituality as distinct, yet relevant to work, unlike Lurie, who regards work, itself, as a spiritual activity. Yet others, like seventy-three-year-old Peter Roche have turned their interest in spirituality into a business opportunity. Roche, through his firm known as the London Roche Perret Group (LRPG), helps other companies "reinvent" their organizational cultures by altering "the ways of working, the interactions, and what people bring to their enterprise, in particular commitment, passion, and engagement," according to their website.[18] While Peter steers away from any formal use of "spirituality" in his firm, he nonetheless characterizes his efforts to change the way people work as a spiritual undertaking.[19]

Peter founded LRPG in 1985 with his wife after moving to the United States from his native Britain, but his interest in religion, spirituality, and organizational change began many years earlier. As young man reared in a Catholic home, Roche entered the seminary, aspiring to serve as a missionary priest. Unfortunately, his superiors thought him a "prankster and practical joker" and encouraged Peter to consider another vocational path. Acquiescing to their request, he landed, by convenience rather than design, in the world of business as an employee in his father's advertising firm. Peter, however, did not remain there for long, and his ambition fueled him to change jobs often in order to take on increasingly prestigious positions. "I took on a lot of jobs I wasn't qualified for, learned how to do it from the inside. No sooner had I mastered one job when I was taking on another job that I wasn't qualified for," he remembers.[20] Eventually, Peter attained a managing director position of a British public company.

Despite his success as a businessman, Roche never relinquished the enthusiasm from his days as a missionary seminarian. He wanted to help others in some way and began to consider how he might introduce these desires into his professional life. In the meantime, Roche had relocated to the United States to be with his wife, a professor of business at Naval Postgraduate School in Monterey, where he became involved in number of what he calls "transformational" self-help programs. Soon thereafter, he started toying with the idea of applying this "transformational approach" to organizations, of rethinking the entire model of business. Within a few years, he and his wife opened a consulting firm dedicated to this premise. LRPG would challenge companies (for a modest fee) "to take on something bold and audacious that they couldn't take on without rethinking the way they manage, the way they be, work, and collaborate."[21]

This "reinvention" process that LRPG offers to its clients is based on the notion that certain fundamental, unconscious values shape the behavior of individuals as well as organizations. "I try to get people to bring these values to the surface," Roche explains, "and start noticing what I must have as a set of values that cause me to behave like this."[22] Exposing these values purportedly allows members of an organization to more clearly discern their individual and collective goals and intentions, rendering work more fulfilling, conflict less likely, and the business more successful.

LRPG avoids using terms like "spiritual" to describe their services, but Roche admits that this kind of work, for him, remains utterly tied to his beliefs about spirituality. Instead, when faced with clients who might react negatively to such language, Roche employs an alternative rhetoric of "values." "My access to talking about things that are spiritual," he states, "without using the word, is to ask people what their fundamental values are, and I pick and choose my language depending on who I'm talking to."[23] For Peter, specific language is less important than the basic truths to which they point. Such language, he feels, are merely superficial labels, and that "what's behind the screen gets obscured by what's in front of the screen." Appealing to religious or spiritual concepts, then, might actually hinder the "reinvention" process for individuals who are resistant to such language.

Despite avoiding "spiritual" language, Roche nonetheless remains actively involved in local groups and international organizations that openly discuss spirituality and work. It was at one such group that gathered every Wednesday in Manhattan where he befriended Alan Lurie, and has since continued to regularly attend his lectures. In addition, Peter maintains ongoing professional relationships with some of the leading voices of the movement, like Judi Neal, whom he met through her organization, the International Association for Spirit at Work.

All in all, this deeper examination into some of the participants of these groups reveals a remarkable degree of heterogeneity in this movement. Individuals come to these meetings for many reasons. Some, like Marc Miller, find these groups as useful ways to embolden the connection between their privately held religious beliefs and professional life, while Alan Lurie and others perceive work as a spiritual activity. Finally, there are those like Peter Roche, who prefer altogether to avoid the rhetoric of "spirituality," but continue to place significance on the need to change the culture of business.

Class power, the Great Recession, and neoliberalism

Among members of these groups, concepts like "spirituality," "values," or "culture" elude stable meanings. Whereas Alan Lurie defines spirituality rather ambiguously as the "experience of a transformative connection," Peter Roche clearly implies something much more private when he equates spirituality with one's "fundamental organizing principles." Moreover, from our conversations, Marc Miller seems to suggest that spiritual and religious represent the same idea. It would be wrong, therefore, to characterize this movement as an ideological monolith by any means. Instead, it might best be considered as a loose formulation of localized groups, on the one hand comprised of a diverse spectrum of peoples, and larger formal organizations, such as the Conscious Capitalism or the interest groups in the Academy of Management one the other hand, all of which relying on various forms of media to continually reconstitute a collective identity. Concepts like "spirit at work" anchor the individuals to a wider social formation, but to what these terms actually refer remains of secondary importance. Rather, to this movement, these constituents bring their competing concepts, motivations, and aims, producing a common discourse and shared sense of identity.

In spite of such wide-ranging differences, however, when we acknowledge that this shared discourse occurs within a larger social and historical context, an extraordinarily consistent set of assumptions becomes clear. Because my ethnographic research occurred between 2011 and 2012, in the wake of the Great Recession, the economic crisis inevitably constituted a considerable amount of discussion among those with whom I spoke. From these conversations, a consistent pattern emerges.

First, it is vital to note the class dimensions of this movement. While the professional backgrounds of these individuals vary, they clearly represent a relatively affluent stratum of American society. Participants in these groups, lectures, and presentations appear to be largely white-collar professionals and business owners. The Intersections International meeting, which I attended, on the "Spirit of Work" illustrates this point. First, each of the four guest speakers represented positions of privilege. As I have already noted, Alan Lurie works in corporate real estate, and he was accompanied that evening by Kenny Moore, a former monk turned business executive currently employed as the director of Human Resources for Keyspan, a Fortune 500 energy company. Joining Moore and Lurie was Carol Folks Prescott, a self-employed performance coach whose clients, according to her website, include business leaders, clergy, doctors, and educators.[24] And Joshua Greene, the fourth guest speaker, spent thirteen years in an ashram before embarking on a thriving career in television.[25]

This gathering exhibited obvious class dimensions, as most of the attendees hailed from upwardly mobile circumstances. In addition to Marc Miller and Peter Roche, both of whom were in attendance that evening, investment bankers, HR managers, and business owners filled the room. The venue failed to attract an obvious working class contingent. There were no cab drivers or employees of the Metropolitan Transportation Authority in attendance (MTA). Rather, this workshop clearly aimed at the affluent, the educated, and the entrepreneurial. In a manner of speaking, the group embodied Maslow's hierarchy of needs; these individuals had already achieved their basic survival needs and were looking for self-actualization. After all, it is these kinds of professions that afford a sufficient level of autonomy and financial security that enable these individuals to even ask the question: is it possible to find meaning and purpose on the job? The professional class, the privileged, are driving force of this movement, at least among these groups in Manhattan.

Second, participants continually diagnose the collapse of the financial markets in 2007–8 in strictly private moral terms. During a presentation at the Princeton Club in New York, Alan Lurie remarked that "the collapse of the financial system was primarily due to individuals in the financial industry holding onto a 'bad faith statement.'" A faith statement, he explains, represents a basic principle through which a person interprets her experience. Using an advertisement from a prominent global bank, Lurie demonstrates how different "faith statements" produce very different experiences of the same event.[26] Superimposed on three identical pictures of a wallet lying in the street are three different words: "misfortune," "obligation," and "temptation." Each of these terms mediates between the audience and the image to produce competing interpretations. The viewer might see the "misfortune" of a lost wallet, the "obligation" to find its rightful owner, or even the "temptation" to take possession of its contents. Lurie proposes that human beings construct meaning in a similar manner. Individuals take in objective data and erect a story around this information using various "faith statements," which they hold about themselves and the world. This interpretation, subsequently, determines how one should next behave.

Superficially, his claims appear akin to Roland Barthes's analysis of popular culture (1957).[27] Like Barthes, Lurie maintains that our interpretive frames determine what we believe and how we act. Yet, for Barthes, the interaction of signifiers, out of which meaning arises gets imposed on the audience *from outside*, whereas Lurie situates the "faith statement," and therefore meaning, as *wholly interior* to the viewer. Lurie's *radical subjectivism*, then, inverts Barthes's strict structural analysis in that the social structure merely persists as is, and meaning (i.e., behavior in the world) arises exclusively from the individual's inner "faith statement." Equipped with this notion of the "faith statement," Lurie is able to effectively reduce the causes of the Great Recession to a collection of individual moral failures. Individual bankers held a bad faith statement, he claims, that declares, "I'm here to make money."[28]

Although we did not discuss the economic crisis specifically, my conversations with Marc Miller reveal similar views about the fundamental role of private morality in business. According to Miller, a morality grounded in religion or spirituality is the essential ingredient for a thriving capitalist society. Again, he understands this as a tempering factor, mitigating an unrestrained and self-indulgent pursuit of wealth. "America was built on the Protestant Ethic and historically, the Jewish people have always been very industrious, and when you look at worldwide competition, and you look at China for instance, their drive for money gives them the ability to do virtually anything to their own people."[29] In other words, without religion and spirituality (e.g., Communist China), business descends into exploitation.

Exploitation and growing inequality are great concerns for Peter Roche as well, and he likewise sees these trends as evidence of a moral crisis. While Alan Lurie denotes this as a "bad faith statement," Roche instead appeals to his language about "values." Individuals "unconsciously acting inconsistently with their values" cause institutions and societies to falter. "The first thing I want people to recognize is that they have a choice, that they can look after their selfish interests and to hell with you, or they can find a way to satisfy what they want, not at your expense," Roche opines.[30]

If the current economic woes stem from a collective moral failure, then its solutions lie not in structural reform, but in the moral transformation of humanity, beginning at the individual level. By adopting a new faith statement, Lurie suggests that our behaviors, and then the world, will change. One should substitute "greed," which characterizes wealth as an end, with "abundance," a faith statement that "recognizes the richness and diversity of creation" and sees "wealth as a tool and a gift," he claims.[31] Peter Roche echoes these sentiments. He hopes that helping individuals to align their behaviors with their core values will ultimately "escalate all the way up through human society."[32] In sum, global reform begins with the interior change of each individual.

This assumption that in human consciousness lies the root of all human potential is one of the most common dimensions of this social movement going back to the early days of the 1970s, when Maslow and Willis Harman declared that perception shapes reality. Judi Neal's Edgewalkers and the Conscious Capitalism Institute reiterate this fundamental principle. It constitutes one of the central tenets that bind this social formation together, and this tells a story about its underlying imaginaries. According to this view, conscious thought, be it under the guise of core values, faith statements, or peak experiences, wholly dictates behavior to the exclusion of all else. Individuals react not their external environment but rather to their *interpretation* of that environment, a reasonable claim in and of itself, but yet this principle goes further and fails to acknowledge (1) that our behavior changes that environment and (2) that the environment, in return, frames the possibilities of perception, and therefore how one might behave. In short, this view posits the individual as essentially autonomous from all social constraints. In a state of nature, she possesses total liberty, and the "myth" of social constraints (institutions, power, etc.) diminishes this freedom.

Lasting structural reform, then, proceeds only from a transformation of consciousness, a point reaffirming the affinity this movement shares with neoliberal ideologies. Alan Lurie writes in the *Huffington Post*, "as much as we can attempt to legislate good behavior in business and enforce consequences, lasting and meaningful change can come only from within the individual. And we will see greed and corruption finally disappear only when those involved begin to see their work in a radically different way."[33] State-imposed rules, according to this perspective, merely treat symptoms, whereas curing the disease, the root cause, requires a voluntary shift in perception. This shift, for Lurie, is a spiritual turn, wherein an individual takes responsibility for her faith statements, and therefore, her behavior.

In valorizing personal responsibility, Lurie translates a key virtue of economic liberalism into the rhetoric of "spirituality."

To a large extent, Lurie is using the idea of work as a "spiritual gymnasium" here, and in his broader project, to explicitly make an argument against the state regulation of business and the economy. His book *Five Minutes on Mondays* can be read as a veritable primer on neoliberal economic ideology. In one chapter, he acknowledges "the devastating results of an unrestricted selfish focus on short-term monetary gain," but reduces this to "bad bankers doing bad things."[34] Lurie celebrates the ebbs and flows of the global market as "a river rapid whose twists, turns, and accelerations obscure our view," and challenges individuals to embrace uncertainty and to take risks.[35] He declares that business leadership in these turbulent conditions must become a "spiritual" practice, "an inward journey, with the conscious intent of personal growth."[36] Lurie's new individual essentially reemerges as the quintessential capitalistic agent. She cultivates a sense of self that can adapt and respond to the ever-changing circumstances of the marketplace, not merely to survive, but, in keeping with the logic of the free market, to *grow*. Spiritual practices, like meditation and prayer, serve dual purposes here. While they facilitate this transformation, regular contemplative practice, as he says, leads to "reduced levels of anxiety," guarding against some of most acute effects of life under this dynamic global marketplace.

Because what counts for Lurie is cultivating the inner change, enforced redistributive policies associated with the welfare state prove wholly dysfunctional; in other words, for him, these policies miss the real point here. Alan openly identifies as an "economic conservative," which in the American political context more accurately means he champions economic liberty with free markets, which he justifies through his spiritual rhetoric. "Religion," he says, "tells us that we chose our situation…Every soul has its own journey, and we have to be responsible. On the other hand, we need to help. So I'm more a fan of private charity than of government mandated charity."[37] Private acts of charity are voluntary, not coerced, and therefore reflect something of the individual's inner character. State-sponsored welfare initiatives, even if they are beneficial, generate resentments because they undermine this principle of voluntarism.

Yet, his appeal to religion here justifies neoliberalism in a second way. If human beings choose their situation and choose their "journey," then each individual remains solely responsible for the conditions of their life. Essentially, suffering is redescribed as a self-imposed opportunity for personal growth. No one else can be responsible for alleviating one's suffering, because ultimately, the individual voluntarily selects the life to be lived prior to birth. This represents a powerful endorsement of the liberal economic model: if you are poor, you have only yourself to blame.

While Alan Lure explicitly supports economic liberalism, others in the movement see things differently. Peter Roche, for instance, describes the increasing concentration of wealth as "unconscionable" and rejects the idea that regulation is essentially harmful. When posed a question about his feelings toward John Mackey's Conscious Capitalism, he responded:

> I would subscribe to that view (libertarianism), if, in fact, human beings were transformed and they didn't have this alter ego of greed and selfishness. But that's not the case, we're going to have to be regulated. For instance, I love to drive fast, and were it not for a penalty of speeding, I would drive 123mph. Come on! There's a lot of things I would do, that are part of my self-expression, that I won't do because of regulation. If we don't deny that side of our humanity, we will want to regulate ourselves and be regulated by others to make sure that we don't do that.[38]

On one hand, Roche's response is surprising, because in the course of conducting this ethnography, he is the only business leader who expressed to me support for state regulation. On the other hand, this statement is not a wholesale rejection of economic liberty. First, using the example of penalties for speeding, he seems to equate "regulation" with "law" and libertarianism with a form of anarchy. However, even prominent economic liberals like Milton Friedman, a hero of Mackey, readily admit that the role of the government is "to provide a means whereby we can modify the rules, to mediate differences among us on the meaning of the rules, and to enforce compliance with the rules on the part of those few who would otherwise not play the game."[39] Ironically, Roche's remarks about regulation accord quite closely to Friedman's characterization of appropriate limited government. Because some individuals are greedy or selfish and refuse to "play along," governments enforce compliance.

Second, Roche rejects libertarianism not because it is wholly incorrect, but that it is unrealistic. In fact, he acknowledges that he would "subscribe to that view" were people no longer prone to greed or selfishness. And yet, ridding individuals of these vices, however, is precisely the aim of his business activities through LRPG. Roche remains devoted to the idea that individual transformations might "escalate all the way up through human society," at which point, he seems to suggest, rules and perhaps regulations would no longer be necessary. So, his views differ from Mackey's libertarianism according to means rather than ends. Mackey believes that in a free market inherently good people rise to positions of power and that rules obstruct this natural process. Roche, conversely, maintains that societies require regulation until a time when sufficient numbers of people are transformed. Both seek a world without regulation and both see "values" as the tool for ultimate reform.

In light of this, both perspectives conform to Bourdieu's definition of globalization as a heterogeneous political project that employs neoliberal ideologies to constitute the economy beyond the confines of nation-states.[40] The various spiritual rhetorics described in this chapter and employed by individuals like Alan Lurie, Peter Roche, and Marc Miller rely on assumptions about individuals and society that, implicitly or explicitly, advance the marginalization of the state and the imposition of "the absolute rule of free exchange."[41] They use spirituality to depict individuals as radically autonomous subjects, wholly capable and responsible for their circumstances, who must *voluntarily* cultivate the proper interiority to overcome suffering.

The Great Recession, then, becomes an opportunity, not for structural or legal reform, but further evidence of a moral crisis at the individual level. Greed and selfishness, rather than dysfunctional political economy, represent the culprits. What is needed is a spiritual resolution rather than a political one. As Alan Lurie suggests, the state, because it relies on coercion, only hinders this progress and should simply step aside.

This rhetoric renders the state as a relic, no longer sufficient for meeting the challenges of the inevitable march of global capitalism. Kenny "the Monk"

Moore described this ideology most concisely when he spoke at Intersections International on the "spirit of work:"

> Traditionally, churches were always the largest buildings in a city. The skyscrapers of today, however, belong to private companies. In the past, if you wanted power, you had to join religion. Later, in the 1800s, you became a statesman, a politician. Today, power is located in business. This is how we make a difference today.[42]

Moore's simple historical narrative suggests that power, in all things temporal and spiritual, has moved from the Church (presumably the Catholic Church of the High Middle Ages) through the nation, and now resides in business. Similarly, democratic deliberation has been superseded by the logic of the global marketplace. Business represents the setting for meaningful action in the twenty-first century, and it is one's participation in these institutions (i.e., work) where one experiences spiritual fulfillment. However accurate or inaccurate, Moore presents this historical move of authority away from the church to business as inevitable, rendering it immune from criticism and leaving as the only option a passive acceptance of its reality. In this way, Moore mythifies globalization and its concomitant neoliberalism as fundamental truths about the world today.

All in all, these networks of small groups, workshops, and lectures that focus on the relationship between spirituality and work represent localized moments in the production of neoliberal globalization. On one level, the movement exhibits a great deal of heterogeneity. Individuals like Alan Lurie, Marc Miller, and Peter Roche participate for a number of reasons, and they often disagree on any precise definition for terms like "spirituality," "religion," or even "work." Nonetheless, these concepts provide cohesion for the movement, serving as the anchors for a shared discourse and a common sense of community.

Again, at a more fundamental level, however, this shared discourse relies on certain *doxa*. Doxa, the experience of the "natural and social world as self-evident;"[43] it is, for him, a misrecognition of politically and historically constructed assumptions as objective reality. In this case, the shared discourse facilitates a misrecognition of libertarian sentiments and a narrative of globalization as established facts. It is libertarian in so far as individuals are assumed to be autonomous agents who act out of internally generated value systems, and it presents globalization as the natural progress of a sui generis marketplace. This misrecognition obscures the possibility that objective conditions might actually shape individual subjectivities, that they are, in fact, not entirely autonomous and self-sustaining.

In addition, presenting globalization as inevitable masks the political and social interests that the phenomenon benefits as well as harms. The rhetoric of spirituality and work, consequently, serves to merely reproduce these two dimensions as doxa in these moments. Simultaneously, it offers an individual the means (meditation, cultivating compassion, etc.) to overcome anxieties stemming from a social structure that it continuously reauthorizes. Through their participation in this movement, individuals acquire the skills to function (and perhaps to thrive) in spite of rising uncertainty and insecurity characteristic of individual life in a neoliberal social order.

7

Sacred Commerce: Neoliberal Spiritualities in a West-Coast Coffee Chain

Walking along Mission Street in the heart of San Francisco, I absorbed the eclectic cultural milieu that lay before me. A group of young white men stood in the doorway of a residence, clandestinely (although the aroma was not so subtle) sharing a joint, as a mixture of urban professionals, homeless, and local Latino residents populated the streets. The store fronts proved equally diverse, ranging from posh eateries and cramped bodegas, to seedy massage parlors and palm readers. I was looking for *Gracias Madre*, a restaurant featuring organic foods that serves as the flagship location for a West-Coast chain of coffee shops called *Café Gratitude*. Amidst the bustle of the street, I experienced some difficulty locating the address, and was worried that I would be late for my meeting with "Erin," the general manager of Gracias Madre.

Cafe Gratitude exhibits a distinct organizational culture, which owners Matthew and Terces Engelhart call "Sacred Commerce," a unique philosophy founded on the view that business can be a "path to spiritual awakening."[1] Whereas many management scholars and business gurus are merely talking about the spiritual dimensions of work, the Engelharts are putting this into practice, shaping the entirety of their business around their exclusive brand of spirituality. They understand Sacred Commerce as a way of life and encourage their employees to enact its principles both inside and outside the workplace. For some, the impact can be profound, as the rhetoric of spirituality becomes the basic fabric out which they make sense of their lives. Sacred Commerce teaches that suffering is a state of mind, and with practice, one can learn to choose to experience life as abundant and fulfilling, regardless of the objective conditions. Like many of the other voices we have examined throughout this book, the Engelharts's most earnest desire is that, in transforming individual conscience, their spiritual program will reform humanity.

As in the broader discourse on spirituality and work, this spiritual rhetoric belies an underlying political dimension thoroughly sympathetic with neoliberal reasoning. Sacred Commerce imagines free markets, unencumbered by government regulations, as the optimal path to social progress. Moreover, it characterizes entrepreneurship as the highest form of freedom and subsequently privileges the authority of business owners over that of workers. Finally, Sacred Commerce shares with neoliberalism a devotion to individual responsibility.

However, unlike the individuals profiled in much of this book, the participants in "Sacred Commerce" work as employees in an organization where this language of spirituality comprises part of the formal culture of the workplace. The subjects of this chapter differ from the business elites and professionals who meet to discuss spirituality in their work; rather they are the employees, managers, and owners of single firm and are therefore bound to and shaped through structures of power unique to workplaces. This case study therefore sheds light on how employees in one setting adopt and adapt this spiritual discourse to craft personal identities, and how owners and managers mobilize the spiritual philosophy to facilitate the goals of production. Specifically, practices couched in the rhetoric of spirituality teach employees at Café Gratitude to perceive human suffering as a symptom of conflict internal to the individual and not the consequence of external factors. Through daily practice, participants accomplish more than new ways of thinking; they cultivate distinct norms, habits, and dispositions that enable them to negotiate the contours of their daily lives. Specifically, they engender and reinforce subjectivities capable of coping with the prevailing anxieties of life in a society governed by the norms of global capitalism.

Café Gratitude and Sacred Commerce

Matthew and Terces Engelhart founded Café Gratitude in 2004, opening their first location in the heart of San Francisco's Mission District, the area of the city where the Spanish first settled the Mission San Francisco de Asis in 1776. Although it continues as an epicenter for the Latino community, the Mission has been in the midst of rapid gentrification as increasing numbers of young, affluent, White Americans call the neighborhood "home." In the years since its founding, the company quickly spread throughout the Bay Area, with new locations opening in Santa Cruz and Berkeley. According to Matthew and Terces, the cafes offer more than healthy, vegan food options; Café Gratitude use a unique practical philosophy called "Sacred Commerce," a set of beliefs and practices that views the workplace as "a sacred container" that teaches employees and customers to experience "prosperity and abundance" in their daily lives.[2] The workspace is a training ground that promises a better way of life, on and off the job. Fighting against what they see as an old paradigm of industrial work, which leaves employees feeling alienated from their labors, the Engelharts claim that, because of their approach to business, their staffs are "actually happy, not pretending to be."[3]

The organizational culture at Café Gratitude reinforces this spiritual perspective for their workers and their customers. The all-organic and vegan menu options are presented in the form of "affirmations" rather than more conventional titles. For example, the Berkeley store offers a black bean burger called "I am magical" or, instead of a strawberry milkshake, customers will order an "I am eternally blessed." These affirmations are meant to disrupt the daily, presumably negative, internal dialogues, which normally shape experience, and redirect individuals to the "great qualities in themselves."[4] In addition to these uncanny menu items, customers can play a game called *The Abounding River*, while they relax with their refreshments. The game asks players to take turns drawing cards that contain introspective activities such as holding hands with another participant and staring into their eyes, or sharing with each other what they are grateful for. Intended to "introduce people to an unfamiliar view or BEING ABUNDANCE," *Abounding River* "encompasses both training people in a day to day practices as well as discovering a Spiritual foundation that opens up a whole new way of looking at money and resources," according to the product description.[5]

Like the customers, employees too engage in specific practices aimed at reinforcing positive self-reflection. At the beginning or every day, workers perform a ritual called a "clearing" before starting work. In their book, *Sacred Commerce: Business as a Path to Spiritual Awakening* (2008), the Engelharts describe the clearing as "a basic technique for distinguishing how the past is impacting the present and then presenting an opportunity to create something new and shift one's attention to something more empowering."[6] The clearing process enables employees to express their private anxieties and to be redirected toward a more positive self-image. Described in detail later in this chapter, the clearing represents the central practice of Café Gratitude's unique workplace culture.

In addition to these daily practices, Matthew and Terces also offer an array of intense workshops, open to employees and the general public (for a fee), which outline in greater depth their ideas about money and spirituality. Their *Sacred*

Commerce Workshop, for instance, invites business owners and managers "to embark on a path to creating a more productive, fulfilling, and profitable life for all."[7] Another course, in which I was able to take part, *The Abounding River Workshop*, give attendees a chance to reform their attitudes toward wealth, to "experience themselves as being the source of unlimited supply."[8] The company also strongly encourages its employees to take part in self-development programs outside the company. Employees, for instance, receive a subsidy if they enroll in seminars held by the Landmark Forum, a self-transformational program that is the successor to Werner Erhard's EST, which was popular during the mid-1970s.

Fundamental to Sacred Commerce is the idea of shifting awareness away from one's more primitive instincts and living a more intentional, socially conscious life. Matthew says, "it's really a shift in priorities from the individual, from survival, from getting ahead, to community and resources."[9] By "putting our attention" on the right perspective, the world can be transformed. Still, even with such lofty goals, Café Gratitude is a company, a workplace where actual people, replete with their own complex biographies, aspirations, and personal struggles, come each day to labor and interact.

Spiritual rhetoric at Café Gratitude

Sacred Commerce provides employees with rhetorical equipment from which they formulate personal narratives that align individual and organizational identities. Because Sacred Commerce avoids any references to specific religious traditions, employees from various backgrounds are easily able to incorporate its lexicon into their own private belief systems. Yet, this conceptual ambiguity also implies that even mundane aspects of life can come to be understood as "spiritual." Activities like cooking, listening to music, or exercising acquire "spiritual" significance. Employees are inclined to redescribe their entire sense of identity in terms of Sacred Commerce, and therefore work becomes a focal point around which other areas of life revolve.

When store manager "Erin" first came to Café Gratitude nearly seven years ago, she was a year from finishing a dual degree in Spanish and Latin American studies, without any expectation of pursuing a career in restaurant management. Erin initially took a part-time job with the company primarily as a means of support while she completed her education. However, she quickly became enmeshed in the culture and was offered a promotion. Still, she insisted on finishing college before assuming any larger responsibilities with Café Gratitude.

Although Erin mentions her initial hesitation to become a manager only in passing, it indicates that how her own narrative might have changed while working for the company. On one hand, she says of her first experience as a customer at Café Gratitude, "the energy and consciousness that was around in Gratitude was so line with my own personal path, that I knew I was going to work there." Yet, after starting her job, she chose to wait nearly a year before moving into a full-time position. Erin had worked in a number of restaurants prior to Café Gratitude, but primarily because those jobs afforded the flexibility and the income she required as a working student. Until her time at Gratitude, she had expected to work for the nonprofit sector, doing "socially conscious" work that improved the lives of others. Indeed, the jobs that had been most rewarding to Erin were the occasional translation duties she would perform for various "outreach initiatives," whereas her ongoing work in restaurants was strictly for instrumental purposes. What Café Gratitude offered Erin was a particular spiritual rhetoric through which she could understand restaurant management as "socially conscious" work that contributes as much as any nonprofit to the wider world.

Erin describes herself as "a completely different person" after seven years at Café Gratitude. While her long-term career goals have certainly changed, such radical claims of total transformation obscure important continuities. She continues to identify religiously as Jewish; she continues to work in restaurants as she had before; and she has not lost her desire for a socially conscious career. Making the claim that she is "a completely different person" anchors Erin's personal narrative to the culture of Café Gratitude. Whether or not she has changed is irrelevant (even assuming such a claim could be accurately measured). Rather, it is a way for Erin to reiterate the connection between her personal narrative and the organization. Her narrative has become organized around the spiritual rhetoric present in Café Gratitude's culture.

When she admits that she experienced a "spiritual awakening" at the age of twenty, for example, she does this because it is a way to include Café Gratitude as a part of this ongoing spiritual journey. Similarly, spiritual rhetoric imbues her job with such profound personal significance that it aligns with her desire for socially conscious work. The changes that Erin has experienced have been predominately affective. "I know myself to be a leader now; I trust myself and am just a lot happier and better adjusted; I know how to navigate my personal and emotional landscape with a lot more ease," she states. These are qualities directly tied to her responsibilities as a manager, and the spiritual rhetoric enfolds these virtues into a comprehensive narrative about her life.

Personal narratives can become completely reorganized around this spiritual rhetoric. "Laura," another manager, recalls an incident that occurred while vacationing in Peru directly prior to seeking a job at Café Gratitude:

> As I sat on the beach, thinking about how I don't want a job just to make money, what's more important to me is finding a place where I feel good, and comfortable. I wanted a place where I can say what I feel, and feel support for managers. When I returned to San Francisco, this is really what I started to put my attention on.

Laura describes this realization as "my first spiritual manifestation of where I saw myself in the workplace." Here, the phrasing that she uses indicates that Laura is interpreting this incident only in light of later experiences. Not only does she refer to this epiphany as a "spiritual manifestation" about work, but she deliberately chooses the phrase "to put my attention on," an idiom directly associated with Sacred Commerce. The company's website states, for example, that "we train our staff to practices *putting their attention on* the outcome they want to create for themselves."[10] This is one of the central practices of Sacred Commerce: to construct a positive vision, to put one's attention on the goal, in order to manifest it in the physical world. Laura has internalized this rhetoric to such a degree that she not only envisages the future in this way but also her past. It places her current expectations about work (as about more than money, a place to feel good, say what she wants, and feel supported) into past, as aspirations that ultimately have been fulfilled at Café Gratitude. The company gave Laura the workplace that she had always been desired, even if she never knew this until she found it.

Spiritual rhetoric also eases workplace conflict. Whenever disputes arise in the workplace, employees know that they are expected to take responsibility for "getting clear" or "being complete," as Laura states. Gossip and backtalk, she says, are merely outward symptoms of inner turmoil which "have no substance, but there's always something rooted behind that, which we want to get at." And in the rare instance that employees are unable to "be complete," a manager will step in to arbitrate the process.

All in all, spirituality functions as a conceptual repository that maintains social relations and upholds existing power structures in the workplace. At times, it upholds power by obscuring it. For example, Café Gratitude does not require employees to attend any of the extracurricular workshops such *Sacred Commerce* or *Abounding River*. Although Erin estimates that, on average, most staff members will complete one or more of these courses during their first months, occasionally an employee will opt out of this altogether. She admits that "the people really go through the training process (meaning the extracurricular workshops) are the ones who really get involved with the culture. The others don't usually end up moving up in the company or even sticking around." Of course, this would make sense to someone like Erin who is devoted to the entire spiritual program at Café Gratitude, but it also sheds light on how an individual's willingness to accept the spiritual components of the job is directly linked to one's future prospects in the company. Informally, employees who opt out of the broader spiritual itinerary essentially segregate themselves from coworkers, who might be more engaged. Potentially, then, failure to "get involved with the culture" could serve as a justification for disciplinary action from management, from being passed over for a promotion to being terminated.

In other ways, too, spiritual rhetoric gets deployed to preserve the interests of the business owners and to undercut the authority of employees. When one manager at Café Gratitude purchased a vacation to Hawaii before asking for the time off from work, the Engelharts "supported her in seeing that she not only diminished her experience of being supported and celebrated by her management team, but she diminished their experience of being people who would of course want her life to be great and would alter their schedules to make her trip happen."[11] They treated the manager's transgression as a spiritual ailment rather than a violation of company policy. This pushes responsibility onto the manager and conceals the control they are exerting over the lives of the staff.

Similarly, this same logic excuses lower pay for workers. It is not wages that are actually insufficient, but rather the employee who has failed to understand that she is "creating being so justified in [her] feeling underpaid and overworked right now."[12] Each person bears "responsibility for your own experience." Wages are only "low," working hour only "long, and workload only "demanding" if one chooses to see them as such. Compensation levels remain intrinsically neutral, according to what the market dictates for the business to succeed.

Matthew moreover uses his spirituality to oppose fringe benefits, as they create an unwarranted relationship of dependence between employer and employee. "When [Café Gratitude] San Francisco offered benefits," he states, "people stayed, but for the wrong reasons. That's where things went bad. The business wasn't created to make wage slaves. People were supposed to move up and out into the world."[13] Matthew understands Café Gratitude as a "revolving door, as a school," equipping individuals with the tools they need to succeed for themselves and to proliferate their spiritual views throughout society. Benefits that encourage long-term tenure merely hinder this mission.

All in all, the practice of Sacred Commerce, on its surface, promises employees greater self-esteem, more rewarding work, and a strong sense of community. Yet, this rhetoric of empowerment equally renders employees complicit in the means of their own subordination to the interests of the employer. Acquiring the *sense* of authority or possessing the ability to *express* frustrations is something quite different from *exercising* authority or *addressing* grievances. The latter remain exclusively within the purview of Matthew and Terces Engelhart, and spiritual rhetoric conceals this fact.

Embodying neoliberalism

While the rhetoric of spirituality impacts the individual identity of employees and upholds the formal power structures in the organization, Sacred Commerce remains deeply bound up with the Engelharts's political orientation. Although he describes himself as "not very political," Matthew Engelharts supports what he calls "compassionate deregulation," a twofold process that seeks to remove government oversight of the economic activity while transforming the prevailing business norms and values. "We have become so litigious and distrustful," he remarks, "and this prevents the entrepreneur from starting a business." Sacred Commerce envisages a society where business, liberated from state constraints, is free to pursue activities that contribute to human progress, and where the workplace serves as the locus of spiritual authority. Managers are the "stewards of consciousness" that "steer the community towards the sacred."[14] Engelhart sees businesses as a new kind of church, a training ground for the interconnected world of the twenty-first century.

Sacred Commerce, therefore, shares similar aims with neoliberal ideologies that seek to empower capital and free trade at the expense of organized labor and the State. The spiritual program engenders attitudes and dispositions amendable to neoliberalism. Sacred Commerce is not only "workplace spirituality," it is also a set of practices and beliefs that reproduce the conditions of global capitalism with its participants. Through daily practices like "the clearing" and in workshops like *Abounding River*, employees continuously reformulate themselves as neoliberal subjects.

Daily "clearings"

The most visible aspect of Sacred Commerce can be found in the daily practice known as "clearing." Each day before beginning work, an employee will sit with a manager or coworker and take a few moments to "get clear." The Engelharts meticulously outline this process in their book *Sacred Commerce* (2008). "It is a basic technique" they write, "for distinguishing how the past is impacting the present and then presenting an opportunity to create something new and shift one's attention to something more empowering."[15]

The process entails four steps: first, the employee is asked to discuss her current struggles, or "wounds." Depending on how the "spirit moves" the clearer, this question differs from day to day, ranging from "what's your biggest fear?" to "what failure has you stopped in your life?"[16] Next, the clearer listens and repeats the employee's words verbatim, an act called "recreation." A second question, intended as "an opportunity to shift one's attention to something new," follows, such as "what are you grateful for?" or "what is blessed about your life?" Finally, the employee responds and the clearer acknowledges "the divine qualities" in her. The clearer, according to Engelharts, resembles a "shaman, a bridge between the visible and invisible worlds," and the clearing draws out this hidden spiritual realm.[17]

The clearing represents an embodied act that presumably fosters "happier, healthier, more productive employees."[18] It commits the employee to a novel set of behavioral norms that mark off the workplace as exceptional. At Café Gratitude, intimate physical contact, emotional vulnerability, and psychological healing are celebrated, and the clearing reasserts these expectations with each performance. Over time, this rhetoric of the wounded self, in need of an antidote, can profoundly alter the individual's sense of self. "When getting cleared daily," the Engelharts claim that "we begin to understand that one's consciousness is the source of experience, that we are making it all up." However, I suggest that these localized practices do more than change individual attitudes toward their jobs. These daily rituals also engender a certain neoliberal "common sense" about the broader social world.

This reinforcement of neoliberal subjectivity becomes visible when we more closely examine a clearing ritual through which store manager Erin led me. As we sit on a picnic-style bench on the front patio of Gracias Madre, she begins with a bit of role playing, pretending as if I am one of her employees, who is coming into work for the day. Erin asks, "Are you committed to being cleared today?" I respond enthusiastically, "Absolutely!" Once the clearing commences, she immediately establishes a new set of rules to govern our interaction. Her voice softens, and she makes a deliberate effort at unwavering eye contact, while I do my best to reciprocate. Then she reaches out and gently clasps my hands from across the table for the duration of the exercise.

The clearing lasts only a few brief moments, and consists of two basic components. First, Erin inquires, "Dennis, what's something you are afraid of being judged for?" While I might have continued to "play" the role of employee, I decide to confide in her my genuine fears of succeeding as a scholar, the anxiety and desire to measure up to my peers and mentors. At this point, Eva performs what the Engelharts refer to as *recreating*. She repeats verbatim what I have just said, and proceeds to ask, "what do you think is underneath the anxiety? What are some other emotions you might see?" After giving me a few clues, Erin explains how my experience of being judged is rooted in a single emotion: *fear*.

> Now just take a few minutes and be there with that, that's a creation right? When I'm putting my attention on being afraid of being judged for not being smart enough, what am I?…See that!? And now when you're ready, tell me, what do your friends or people you know love about you?

After a moment of reflection, I disclose that close friends appreciate my ability to listen, my sincerity, and my honesty. Erin, again, mirrors my words and completes the clearing with a few of her own:

> I want to acknowledge you today for being a really courageous person, for being someone who takes action and makes movement even when you're afraid. I really want to acknowledge you for that. I want to acknowledge you for being committed to making a difference in the world, for impacting the quality of life on this planet through your work, and I also want to acknowledge you for being an amazing friend and for really caring about the people in your life.

Although the clearing takes but a few minutes, I admit to her that I do feel more at ease, having shared deeply personal feelings with a person whom I have just met. Erin explains that

> the clearing is not a conversation. It's actually an alchemical experience where the person getting cleared is getting to see. Where we put our attention is our experience. That's the basis of all this. We're responsible for it. So when you're putting your attention on how you're being judged, you feel all these emotions like fear, anxiety, etc. So you get to see that when you do that, you're creating an experience of fear and anxiety for yourself. And then concerning the second question: I didn't fix you; you get to shift your attention to what people love

about you. We didn't fix you; we didn't give you coaching, but you shifted your own attention to what people love about you, to something that inspires you. Then, you have this new experience. Your experience has changed, not because we fixed the circumstances, but because you shifted your attention, which is like the magic trick of life. A lot of people are dominated by their circumstances, and there's no power in that. If you can understand that it's not the circumstances, but it's who I'm being or what I tell myself about that, then I have all the freedom.

She depicts the clearing as a kind of therapeutic healing: a "shifting of one's attention" away from self-criticism toward a more positive, confident view of the self. Yet, its rhetoric requires me to begin from an assumption that the self is flawed. Only from this point am I prepared accept the need to be healed. Anthropologist Susan Harding observes similar characteristics in the practice of "witnessing" among Baptist fundamentalist communities. "Conversion," she claims, "is the process of acquiring a new religious language," and the foundation of this new language includes, for the potential convert, a perception of one's self as a "sinner."[19] Whether or not the individual "under conviction" actually perceives this prior to the moment of conversion remains irrelevant, as the ritual structure of witnessing essentially reframes the self as the inheritor of original sin. Similarly, the clearing relies a notion of the self as "wounded," not physically but spiritually, necessitating a "shifting of attention."

By doing this, I enact the basic principle of Sacred Commerce: that experience is entirely subjective, the result of free choices. The clearing empowers the individual to take responsibility for her actions. In my case, my fears of failing as a scholar stem from an interior wound that I have incorrectly associated with external factors. Healing, consequently, comes not through outward success, but through the realization that I have chosen fear as a response to my circumstances. As Erin suggests, change occurs "not because we fixed the circumstances, but because you shifted your attention." When individuals can "understand that it's not the circumstances," they achieve "all the freedom." The clearing, therefore, secures a sense of autonomy and omnipotence because it abandons any hint of social determinism.

Because outward conditions are fixed, the clearing process cultivates a malleable, flexible self, which can cope in an unpredictable world. In other words, the self becomes an ongoing project, a canvas on which the artist must create the perfect blend of pigments. Such rhetoric embraces a kind of subjectivity that Nikolas Rose refers to as "the enterprising self," indicative of neoliberal virtues. "The enterprising self," he argues, "will make a venture of its life, project a future and seek to shape itself in order to become that which it wishes to be."[20] The individual must become an entrepreneur in all things and accept personal responsibility for successes or failures, as well as joy or suffering. Furthermore, the enterprising self experiences "freedom" not as a consequence of a just social order but as an internal condition: "a freedom to realize our potential and our dreams through reshaping the style in which we conduct our secular existence."[21] At the center of the clearing is this same perception of life as an opportunity for self-actualization, and the "good life" is nothing more than series of subjective adjustments to overcome harmful interpretive habits.

Rose's depiction of the "entrepreneurial" self clarifies how the clearing ritual exhibits this neoliberal habitus. Bourdieu characterizes the habitus as "a collective individual or a collective individuated by the fact of embodying objective structures."[22] Individual subjectivity and social structure reproduce one another, and the clearing exposes this entanglement. Global capitalism posits the autonomous, rational individual as the fundamental social agent and the marketplace as the perfectly neutral arbiter of all social relations. The clearing, likewise, (re) imprints this same schema within the practitioner. When global market forces render life uncertain and insecure, the individual remains free to "shift attention," perceiving suffering or injustice as opportunity. Practiced daily, the clearing simulates the disposition required to navigate the contours of this social structure.

Abounding River Workshop

While the daily clearing imprints the virtues of neoliberalism on employees at Café Gratitude, the *Abounding River Workshop* redescribes the logic of global capitalism through the spiritual rhetoric of Sacred Commerce. The two-day workshop hails money as a "sacrament" and recognizes "spending" as the supreme moral act. Moreover, like the clearing, it too emphasizes "shifting attention" to deal with suffering, but even more explicitly associates this practices with some of the most enduring consequences of economic liberalization: income inequality, economic uncertainty, and homelessness. Through a series of vignettes and carefully executed activities, I and the other participants confronted these harsh realities and learned to shift our attention in order to see them in a different, more positive light.

Upon entering the classroom, I was asked politely to remove my shoes before entering any further. In the corner behind me, I glimpsed a sizable pile of footwear on the floor where I proceeded to leave my boots. Already, the room was nearly at capacity, with people young and old. While some dressed in khakis and collared shirts, formal blouses, others wore less formal attire: shorts and t-shirts, a few displaying various forms of body art. Across from where I entered, a ring of metal folding-chairs outlined the workshop space, and the Engelharts relaxed casually on a couch at the head of the class. As we slowly found our seats, Matthew and Terces greeted us, engaging in idle chat to make us more comfortable. Each participant had been given a book (for an additional fee), *The Abounding River Logbook*, to which we were to refer as the workshop commenced and, subsequently, to be used as a personal record of our daily practices for the next forty days. Although I will draw primarily on observations made during my ethnographic research of this workshop, the logbook serves as supplemental data for analysis.

At 10:00a.m., we promptly began as Terces offered a few announcements. She thanked Marta MacBeth, the "Vision Coordinator" for Café Gratitude and briefly celebrated the recent opening of a Café Gratitude location in Kansas City, Missouri during the previous month. The Engelharts explained that this workshop had evolved from the *Abounding River Board Game*, which together they had developed thirteen years ago and served as the impetus for Café Gratitude as space where people could "practice its teachings at work." The teachings of the workshop, Terces noted, were "not some ultimate truth, but our view of life." "Take what works for you from this workshop, and personalize it," she exhorted, emphasizing the private, personal nature of these practices and establishing each individual as the locus of final authority. Over the next two days, the class would explore the Engelharts's conviction that "abundance" is a state of mind, "a quality of spirit, of the divine, a flavor" of the human experience. Through a combination of lecture, open discussion, and activities, the workshop challenged participants to assess their personal relationship with money and to begin to transform this relationship in order to experience fulfillment. As the logbook states, "being abundance" requires "living in the assurance of being supplied as a mindful practice to connect to Spirit in everything."[23]

The Engelharts aimed to expose and upend the prevailing assumptions and norms that Americans associate with money by depicting "money" as a conscious actor in our lives, imbuing it with a kind of intentional agency. What is your relationship with money? Do you love or hate it? How would you expect a loved one to react if you treated them the way you treat money? Through these questions, the Engelharts proposed that neither our actions nor the actions of others, but one's attitude toward money and "supply" actually dictates whether we will experience abundance or scarcity.

"Scarcity" represents for the Engelharts a survival from primitive existence and, more importantly, the spurious foundation upon which modern society has been built. The fiction that "I am a body all alone and can die" motivates us to seek security, which today takes the form of seeking possessions and wealth. To this, Matthew implores, "stop thinking that the world's dysfunction can be buffered by us." The truth, he claims, is to realize "our consciousness as the source of our experience of fulfillment and of being supplied with the resources that our physical existence."[24] Over the two, ten-hour sessions, the class would be asked repeatedly to reflect on how prevailing norms of American consumer culture had led them to incorrectly believe that abundance is essentially material rather than psychological.

According to Matthew and Terces, American culture declares that the "outward shapes the inside," whereas in actuality the inner disposition determines what happens "out there." To correct this delusion, they propose an *ethic of spending*, urging individuals to "begin noticing who you are being the moment money passes your hands."[25] Money becomes the ultimate sacrament, "a body fluid linking us all together," but moreover, it is "an expression of Spirit and Abundance flowing through us, connecting us all."[26] This is not the capitalist ethic of Max Weber which elevates thrift and the accumulation of wealth as principal virtues, but nor is it a hedonistic ethic of consumption that values the insatiable desire for commodities. Rather, the Engelharts are promoting spending as an end and a good in of itself, the rewards of which are immaterial and spiritual.

While this spending ethic counters conventional materialistic attitudes toward consumption and Weber's Protestant Ethic, it nonetheless thoroughly supports a capitalist worldview. Instead, *Abounding River* essentially offers a novel set of virtues compatible with the global capitalism of the twenty-first century. Of paramount importance in our finance-driven world is not acquisition or the accumulation of wealth, but the acceleration of exchange itself. Matthew and Terces valorize the global free market as the space in which human beings work together for mutual benefit rather than some myopic self-interest. Furthermore, global capital, like "abundance," depends primarily on perception to function properly. "The stock market and economy," they claim in the *Abounding River Logbook*, "are a vivid demonstration of this principle. The 'value' of the nation's businesses is beholden to our moment-by-moment consumer and investor confidence."[27] The shape of the global marketplace mirrors the basic contours of the individual, and in this way the *Abounding River* relies on a world organized around the principles of the free market.

While capitalism represents the ultimate social expression of the Engelhart's spiritual program, it is a particularly neoliberal form of the free market that remains suspicious of state interference into the economy and celebrates private enterprise as the highest form of virtue. Matthew and Terces repeatedly expressed dismay over the way rules and regulations mostly hinder rather than enable people to do good. In fact, they diagnose law as another symptom of the "scarcity" illusion, arising from our mutual distrust and fear of one another. From this perspective, the see the string of lawsuits threatening the sustainability of Café Gratitude as obstacles to their mission. In their view, the government prevents good people from acting, interrupts the free flow of money, thereby working against the natural currents of abundance.

Several of the anecdotes in the *Abounding River Logbook* reveal how neoliberal ideology informs their teachings. Matthew uses stories about his trips to the former Soviet Union to demonstrate how the managed economies of the Eastern bloc sapped the spiritual vitality of its people. He describes Lithuania in 1992 as a "kingdom of resignation, void of light and smiles and fifty years behind the times," the apparent and unfortunate result of a centrally planned economy.[28] In contrast, he explains how immigrants from the former Communist bloc experienced the wonder of capitalist plenty, but Matthew is actually making a further point here, from which we can understand how his spiritual message of abundance intersects with a neoliberal perspective.[29] Even though he is emphasizing the positive effects of Western-style capitalism on the lives of former Soviets, the story is intended to expose the ease with which people can slip back into an attitude defined by "scarcity." The wide array of foods, goods, and services introduced at the end of the Cold War no longer captivate people; "yesterday's abundance is today's not enough," he states.[30] His points here remain somewhat inconsistent; on one hand, state intervention into the economy produces real material suffering, but on the other hand, it is ultimately up to the individual to choose an attitude of abundance, regardless of the larger social and political conditions. These two positions, however, can be reconciled from a neoliberal perspective, which advocates freer markets, a diminished role for the state, and an ethical sentiment of personal responsibility. Laissez-faire capitalism demands that individuals assume total responsibility for their happiness as well as their suffering, because the marketplace stands as a neutral structure. Like the more traditional defenses of free markets might explain poverty and injustice as the products of individual moral failings, the Engelharts understand suffering as a character flaw. However, they go even further, stating that real material deprivation is not, in fact, real at all but rather an illusion that one can choose to eliminate through the cultivation of the proper attitude.

The Engelharts brought this into sharp focus during the workshop with one particularly powerful story of a homeless woman. As a way of "stretching" the boundaries of their generosity, Matthew and Terces decided that they needed to do more than simply provide food to local homeless and concluded to find someone to take in to their home for a day, allow them to bathe, eat, and so on:

> The next day we pulled up to a collection of shopping carts and bundles and saw a woman named Jason whom we had previously fed. We asked her if she would like to come to our home for a bath. She said, "I would love to, but not today. How about tomorrow at 3 p.m.?" She explained that her husband had been arrested and that she couldn't leave all their belongings.
>
> We said, "Sure," and drove off, both of us remarking to one another that in our imaginations if we lived on the streets and someone offered us a bath, we would jump at the chance![31]

The story continues with Matthew and Terces repeatedly, but unsuccessfully, attempting to schedule an appointment with Jason, who always seems to be very busy. Finally, once they are able to pick her up, the woman shares the details of her life, that living on the streets had been more a blessing than a curse. On the streets, for instance, "she had lost weight at last, had more time to read, and had a great community of friends who share and look out for one another."[32] Her optimism surprised the Engelharts, who had assumed that the life of a homeless woman like Jason would be encompassed by misery, hardship, and interminable struggle. While helping a seemingly helpless individual, they had learned an important lesson: "Homelessness is just another way of life," Terces declared to us as we sat in the workshop. "It's not worse. It just looks different from my perspective. This woman has healthier than she'd ever been in her entire life."

On one hand, the Engelharts had discovered in their former attitudes a form of imperialism. They had approached the homeless as if they were wholly impotent, void of any aspirations, and dependent on the good will of others. To surmise that the weakness of these people, they felt, was to deny them the dignity of their humanity. Certainly, these individuals living on the streets or in shelters cannot be reduced to statistics or some singular label, the "homeless." Yet, even as Terces emphasizes the agency and subjectivity of the homeless, she simultaneously ignores the structural conditions in society that give rise to homelessness as a historical phenomenon. Moreover, her statement appears to situate home-lessness alongside other lifestyles, as if one freely chooses to identify as homeless in the same way another might choose to be a sports fan, a hipster, or a vegetar-ian. This viewpoint erases the possibility that Jason's weight loss could be due to malnourishment or that her greater free time to read stems from a lack of sus-tainable and secure employment. Instead, the Engelharts employ a consumerist logic to invert cause and effect here; Jason has chosen homelessness, like one might select a particular brand of toothpaste, because of its perceived personal benefits.

Stories like Jason's confirm the six virtues, or "Spirit Currents," the moral foundation of the *Abounding River Workshop*; virtues heavily associated with the Engelharts's libertarian political perspectives. These six principles tend to por-tray life as radically individualistic and shaped according to the logic of global capitalism. The first principle, "Creation-Responsibility," endorses a radically subjective worldview, establishing the individual as the creator of her own expe-rience. Reality, in other words, is defined not by any external circumstances, which are considered neutral, but by the interpretation one has voluntarily cho-sen. Suffering of any kind, therefore, is simply reduced to a feeling, a state of mind indicating that one's ego is refusing to relinquish control.

Being entirely responsible for how one chooses to experience the contours of one's life is of ultimate importance in a world subject to the unpredictable whims of the global marketplace, and the remaining five Spirit Currents aim at justify-ing this particularly neoliberal environment. "Love/Acceptance," for example, teaches that struggle has a purpose: "the circumstances of our lives are the boul-ders in the current of Spirit directing us in the optimum direction...The system is perfect."[33] Throughout history, the Engelharts exclaim, progress has only come on the heels of great injustice. Without the African slave trade, "there would be no Jazz, no Gospel Music;" without religious intolerance in Europe, "there would be no Quakers to birth Pennsylvania, no Irving Berlin or George Gershwin, no Bob Dylan;" and, moreover, only the tyranny of the Roman Empire could make possible the Christmas story, the Reformation, and ultimately the Bill of Rights and the American democracy.[34]

This perfect "system" curiously resembles the ebb and flow of the free market, the notion that capitalism embodies "creative destruction" defined by economist Alfred Schumpeter and embraced by neoliberals. Schumpeter maintains that, in a capitalist system, economic development emerges out of the destruction of a previous order. In short, out of tragedy comes triumph, thereby excusing hardship and suffering entailed in the process of creative destruction. For the

Engelharts, this principle holds true especially even today. Only after "really tasting the gutter" can a drug addict enter recovery; only after Matthew's failed first marriage could he achieve a more authentic love; and as he recalls, when his clothing business was failing during the early 1990s, only by realizing the futility of trying to change circumstances beyond his control could he come to terms with the fact that he could no longer pay his employees.[35] The free market works "perfectly" because it mirrors the natural order of things. Even as it causes suffering, it spurns individuals to act and to take responsibility for improving themselves.

Abounding River offers more than simply listing a set of principles applicable to daily life. In addition, participants are expected to perform these neoliberal virtues throughout the course of the workshop. The Engelharts had designed an embodied pedagogy that worked on our bodies to transform us into subjects who could more successfully navigate the turbulent seas of a world ruled according the logic of global capitalism. These classroom rituals invited us to become entrepreneurs of the self, to take control of our perception, and ultimately demonstrated how these reformed selves should be situated in neoliberal society.

One activity, which I will refer to as the "laughing ritual," brings into stark relief the kind of subjects imagined in the world according to *Abounding River*. The Engelharts asked the entire class to stand up, and, regardless of our current mood, to laugh aloud together for an entire minute. Beginning with a few uncomfortable chuckles, giggles, and sniggers, the sound soon erupted into a cacophony of roaring howls, snorts, and rejoicing. The laughter was contagious, and on the off chance that I experienced any embarrassment, a glance around the room quickly erased any discomfort as the absurdity of the moment eventually produced feelings of happiness. In fact, once time had expired, we found it rather difficult to cease, and I daresay most of us did not wish to stop. Matthew and Terces waited silently and patiently for us to return from our farcical excursion and then explained the point of the exercise. We were learning, they claimed, that our circumstances do not dictate how we feel, what we think, and our actions, but rather our choices to feel, to think, and to act, produce our experience. Our laughter was not a response to some external stimuli; it was a deliberate performance that fostered joy.

The laughing ritual disposes participants to a form of selfhood closely associated with neoliberalism in which personal choice is not only a reference to an act of consumption, but the fundamental ingredient upon which identity gets erected. Anthropologist Carla Freedman characterizes the neoliberal subject as an "entrepreneur of the self—in which the individual is defined as a self-propelled, autonomous economic actor ever-responsive to a dynamic marketplace."[36] She suggests that neoliberal subjectivity involves viewing the self as an individual project in continuous need of reform. The self, therefore, must remain flexible and capable of responding to the constantly changing conditions of a laissez-faire social order. This imperative for an adaptive self places the onus on the individual for "economic viability as the state and private industries are exempt from providing the kinds of social support and welfare they once, in many contexts, were expected to offer."[37]

Similarly, the practice of deliberately laughing aloud endorses this belief, but takes its logic even further. Not only must the individual embrace an entrepreneurial approach to life in general, she also must diagnose suffering as a purely private matter, as the consequence of a failure to intentionally choose happiness. Such a perspective accounts for an apparent contradiction of neoliberal society: that the individual is presumed free and totally responsible for herself, but simultaneously subject to the unpredictable machinations of the global marketplace. The laughing exercise, however, severs the effects of neoliberal society from individual responsibility, reducing the scope to reflexive work on the self. Consequently, despite the uncertainty of life under the free market, the individual can maintain *a sense of* stability, autonomy, and even empowerment. Reality has become, in essence, wholly subjective, and she can choose to laugh, to be experience joy, while underemployed, downsized, and even homeless.

Although the Engelharts do not directly link the laughing exercise to neoliberal capitalism, other activities in the workshop make this connection more explicitly. One such activity, described in my firsthand narrative below, requires the class to simulate the "flow of money" around the world in order to demonstrate how a free market elevates every member of society:

On the first day of Abounding River, as we were sent off to lunch at their restaurant Gracias Madre, in the mission district, the Engelharts instructed us to tip our servers twice the amount we would normally leave. The point, they explained, was to practice the Spirit Current of "gratitude," and to reflect on how this affected us. Upon returning to class, our reactions were varied. One gentleman in attendance, who I will refer as Kevin, was somewhat embarrassed. Currently unemployed and living in a shelter, Kevin expressed shame that not only had he nothing extra to give, but he had to rely on the generosity of his peers to merely afford a meal. On the other end of the spectrum, Mitch, a wildly successful business owner accustomed to meticulously accounting for every dollar spent, was equally hesitant to give up more of his hard-earned money.

Still, nearly everyone in the class agreed that the experience was positive. It not only made the meal more enjoyable, but also encouraged us to be more mindful of our interactions with the beneficiaries of our gratitude: the servers.

I realized later that this exercise in gratuity had prepared the class for another activity centered on the intrinsic value of spending. About an hour into the afternoon session, Matthew asked the class to stand up, dig into our pockets, and take out an amount of money with which we might be comfortable parting. For some of my classmates, like Kevin, this meant no money at all, while others eagerly displayed twenty-dollar bills. As for myself, I was feeling slightly sheepish, as I could only muster a few loose coins, having unexpectedly spent the bulk of my cash on tipping the server at lunch.

Matthew and Terces, next, brought us, money in hand, into a circle at the center of the room, where we stole quick glances at one another in order to clandestinely compare our "worth." The activity, they explained, was simple: for an entire minute, we were to attempt "giving away" all of our money to others in the class. Whenever we find ourselves without any money, Matthew instructed us to hold our hands out, palms up, wait to receive money from another, and finally give it away again, in an endless cycle of giving and receiving. The game quickly descended into chaos and my loose change spilled onto the floor. Like the children's game "hot potato," we laughed and smiled as frantically as we sought to give away what came our way, yet not knowing what we would be asked to do with the money once sixty seconds had expired. Soon, however, we forgot these thoughts, "our internal chatter of the ego" disappears, and "everyone experiences being connected, being part of one whole."[38]

At one minute promptly, the Engelharts stopped us, and we sat in complete silence (with the exception of the sound of one of my coins slipping through the fingers of a fellow classmate). Matthew then whispered that for the following minute, we were too tightly hold on to whatever money with which we had been left. He drew our attention to how the "energy" in the room had become "flat" and how difficult it was for participants even to look at one another. "When we hoard our money," Matthew continued in his soft tone, "we stifle life itself." "Keep the cycle of giving and receiving going—keep things in the flow."

The Engelharts returned us to our seats, with hands still grasping crumpled bills, and asked, "how many of you are givers and have a hard time receiving?" Nearly all of us nodded in agreement. "Ask for what you want, and be grateful for what you get," Terces reiterated as she encouraged us to open our hands to see what we had received. "We all want to take care of each other, but we're afraid to go first," she declared as she glanced at our homeless classmate, Kevin. Then, looking back to the rest of the class, Terces extended a proposition: "Would any of you like to give what you have received to Kevin?" As much as I could have used the twenty-three dollars in my hand, I and, indeed, everyone else knew that our friend from the shelter was experiencing a much greater need. Slowly, each of us walked over to where Kevin was seated on a pillow, and placed our money in front of him. The emotion of the moment was remarkably powerful. Unable to look any of us in the eye, Kevin could only stare blankly at the wall behind the Engelharts, and soon he, a few others began to weep.

This particular exercise left an indelible impression on my memory of *Abounding River*, and equally affected others, I suspect. Together, the thirty-odd participants had scraped together several hundred dollars (and change) for Kevin. Earlier that morning during introductions, Kevin had expressed desperation over his current plight. A middle-class professional and father, he had been a victim of the recent economic crisis, which had begun in 2008. Downsized and unable to find another job, Kevin found himself without a home and picking up temporary work whenever he could manage. I cannot be sure if Matthew and Terces had previously planned to use this activity as an opportunity to help Kevin or if it was a spontaneous decision in moment. In either case, it was a chance for the class to embody the principles about which we had been hearing so much.

While the exercise undoubtedly fostered a genuine act of compassion from the class toward Kevin, it was accomplished in the context of a ritualized simulation of Matthew Engelhart's "compassionate libertarianism." The activity re-presented the functioning of the free market as a fundamental principle of social relations. At its core is the principle that all legitimate action is voluntary: we all began with varying amounts of resources, but we only gave what we had freely chosen to give. Moreover, the activity demonstrated that, in the context of free market exchange, even the most the needy, in this case Kevin, will receive sufficient help, if not through the sheer opportunity to participate in this great exchange, then through the charity and compassion of others.

The marketplace, as depicted in this exercise, is not the classic capitalism of Max Weber, which emphasized thrift and the rational investment of capital. Instead, it was an idealized reproduction of advanced global capitalism, in which the accelerating pace of monetary exchange generates value. Our physical bodies served as the territory for this exercise. We could literally "feel" the vitality of exchange as well as the glum of hoarding. To save is to seek security, which is ultimately motivated by fear, and, according to the Engelharts, the state represents the ultimate social expression of fear. Without explicitly saying it, the exercise was showing us through our bodies that society works best when it maximized free exchange and minimizes fear (i.e., the state).

The Engelharts's interpretation of the activity, however, obscures some significant differences and similarities between itself and the marketplace it presumably represents. First, exchange in the marketplace is transactional, whereas "gifting" more appropriately characterizes our actions. Giving is imprecisely equated with spending, and this ignores the subtler social relations that operate through the exchange of gifts. The giving of gifts sets in motion a series of social relations quite distinct from market exchange. Whereas market transactions occur immediately and imply no further obligations for either party, giving brings forth an asymmetrical relationship between giver and receiver. As we continuously handed over money, the cycle of reciprocity requires us to respond to one another with obligation, gratitude, and even deference. "Giving is also a way of possessing," as Bourdieu suggests, and in one sense, when we handed our money to Kevin, we were taking ownership of him.[39] Our gift to him was a strategic use of our social capital, and his response was gratitude, evident in the tears he shed. Thus, on one hand, the activity identifies spending as a form of giving, which inscribes the power relations of gift exchange onto the market. However, on the other hand, the power relations inherent in our generosity toward Kevin become obscured and characterized as a natural consequence of a neutral marketplace.

In following the precepts of Sacred Commerce, the Engelharts ask employees and workshop participants to embrace the logic of global capitalism. A world ordered according to these principles persists without class distinctions, and suffering, if it ever exists, results from our individual choices to interpret our experiences as beyond our control. Homelessness and deprivation indicate personal preferences rather than systemic conditions stemming from the weakening of public forms of social maintenance. Whatever our material status, we are, each of us, already wealthy in some metaphysical sense. As they claim, "the fact that we don't experience the quality of being rich has no validity because we've allowed circumstance to determine our experience."[40] In the cosmos of a capitalism, social conditions constitute the collective relations of individuals acting in the marketplace, and because an unfettered market operates perfectly, injustice is an abject impossibility.

The Sacred Commerce workshops, the formal teachings of the Engelharts, and the overall organization culture at Café Gratitude illustrate one example of how the entanglement of spirituality with business reinforce

The components of Sacred Commerce—the workshops, the formal teachings of the Engelharts, and the overall organizational culture at Café

Gratitude—analyzed in this chapter demonstrate how participants embody and actively reproduce the norms of neoliberalism. In the workshops, individuals embrace voluntarism and locate the source of suffering (and therefore its resolution) solely within themselves. Consumption and capitalist exchange are ritually reenacted as ethical maxims that bind society together in an organic solidarity of mutual interdependence. Through our willingness to symbolically perform market actions, we not only forge solidarity with other workshop participants but also witnessed the market as the mechanism to address real social deprivation, exemplified in the story of Kevin. *Abounding River* communicates the "common sense" of neoliberal political reasoning that market-based solutions most effectively address social concerns.

Just as *Abounding River* ritually elevates the free market, organizational rituals like the daily "clearings" accommodate employees to neoliberal capitalist relations in the workplace. In habituating the conviction that suffering is alleviated from within, clearings exacerbate an individualism already prevalent in capitalist society by linking it to specific corporate culture. While it obscures external sources of suffering generally, the clearing habitually reminds employees that workplace distress that threatens the flow of production must necessarily be addressed as a matter of self-help, as a correction to an employee's perspective. Clearings merely represent one aspect in the full repertoire of Sacred Commerce at Café Gratitude, but they nonetheless exemplify how spirituality is mobilized in ways that render business interests as identical to employee "spiritual" health.

As the personal biographies of Erin and Laura indicate, employees adopt and adapt the concepts and language of Sacred Commerce to craft their individual identities. In constructing personal narratives through this lens, the line between individual and organization becomes further muted, leaving these employees dependent on their employer for not only material sustenance but also for vital aspects of personhood. This raises the existential risks associated with ending employment, as individual jeopardize more than their financial security but also their psychological wellbeing. Establishing strong ties to organizational identity certainly facilitates workplace concord, employee satisfaction, and therefore productivity, but under the conditions of neoliberal capitalism characterized by increasingly fleeting employment, such bonds could prove all the more harmful to workers. Still, perhaps in teaching employees to accept responsibility for their own suffering, Sacred Commerce readies workers for the rugged conditions of neoliberal society, giving some a fortitude to survive, or under the right circumstances even thrive.

Conclusion

The key to this business is personal relationships. Roll with the punches. Tomorrow is another day…Hey, I don't have all the answers. In life, to be honest, I've failed as much as I've succeeded. But I love my wife. I love my life. And I wish you my kind of success.

—Dicky Fox, Founder, Sports Management International (SMI)[1]

The above quotation represents the final lines of the 1996 Oscar-nominated film *Jerry Maguire*, the tale of a disenchanted sports agent who leaves the corporate world to find a new, better way of life. The words are spoken by Dick Fox (portrayed by Jared Jussim), the deceased mentor of the protagonist (Tom Cruise). Because the first chapter of this book started with a discussion of Arthur Miller's *Death of a Salesman*, it is only fitting that we finish by considering how another, more recent morality tale in which work in central to the plot equally highlight a particular cultural moment. Both stories wrestle with notions of work, individual dignity, success, and failure. Each explores characters who attempt different strategies to find meaning and significance in life through a particular relationship to labor. Loman clings to a naïve hope that he can overcome despair through sheer personal ability alone in his work as a salesman. His son Biff, sensing the futility and the hypocrisy of his father's superficial self-confidence, rejects capitalist definitions of success altogether, preferring to steal instead. However, like his father, Biff, too, relies on a fantasy, of some nostalgic return to nature, finding real happiness out west as a farmhand. Each develops a distinct relationship to capitalist labor through the particular myths to which they subscribe.

The major characters in *Jerry Maguire* also unfold according to the particular relationship they cultivate with their work. The film begins when Jerry, the film's protagonist, experiences a sort of "dark night of the soul" through which he realizes that his career at a large corporate sports agency is utterly devoid of meaning and purpose. "Who had I become?" he asks, "Just another shark in a suit?" Out of this crisis Maguire is inspired to spend one night frantically drafting a "mission statement, a suggestion for the future of our company," in which he will recommend "fewer clients. Less money. More attention. Caring for them, caring for ourselves." When he ultimately presents his bold idea to the firm, his employer naturally fires him, in small way due to the fact that calling for less money and fewer customers represents an utter threat to the logic of business. Maguire resembles a composite of Willy Loman and his son Biff, because even though he wishes to escape the alienation of corporate life, he continues to believe that "personal relationships" will ultimately yield true success.

Maguire's story ends not in individual defeat with suicide but in a triumph of the free individual. As it turns out, Arthur Miller was wrong. We can have our dreams *and* success in the capitalist marketplace, if only we leave behind the indifference of corporate bureaucracy and become entrepreneurs. *Jerry Maguire* celebrates the small business owner as the hero who takes risks and ultimately finds something more valuable than profit; he finds friendship, romance, and family—he discovers happiness. The film will conclude on this positive note, and yet leaves one significant element only partially resolved. Will SMI, the bloated corporate firm, actually suffer in light of Jerry's success? Maguire does pilfer some important clients from his former employer, but it seems reasonable to suspect that the company will likely survive, and perhaps, as Bob Sugar's (Jay Mohr) uninspiring attempt to hug one of his clients near the end of the film hints, SMI might try to adopt some of Maguire's more personal approach. All in all, the film offers two choices, both of which simply reinforce the inevitability of a capitalist social order. One either embraces the corporate workplace or starts one of their own.

Jerry Maguire is story that very much belongs in the last years of the twentieth century, at precisely the time when real-life business leaders and management reformers were beginning to routinely exhibit interest in the relationship between spirituality and work. The film shares the sentiments of Conscious Capitalists that caring for the wellbeing of employees and customers is a better way of doing business. Jerry Maguire, the character, embodies Robert Greenleaf's "servant-leader" and could easily qualify as one of Judi Neal's "Edgewalkers," contemporary shamans of market society who possess a special vision.

If *Jerry Maguire* differs from the individuals, ideas, and institutions discussed in this book, it is the obvious lack of religious or spiritual language. Jerry demonstrates no interest in seeing his journey as spiritual or describing his philosophy as metaphysical, but, I must pose the question—to what degree does the lack of religious rhetoric matter? The shortest and plainest answer is: not all that much. Religion and spirituality represent a few of the strategic tools in the repertoire of American corporate culture. Appeals to religious concepts, teachings, or figures are claims to authority, attempts to resist existing norms, or merely "common sense" perspectives that maintain the status quo. The introduction of practiced deemed religious or spiritual into corporate life perform similar functions; employees and employers alike find them useful because they complement the conditions of production.

The entanglement of religion and business described in this book is not an indication of a new religious movement in the business world, or of some intrinsically "spiritual" dimension to work. In addition, it is not an extension of "religion" out of the church and into the business world, or a lay-driven movement for those who wish to express their "faith at work." It does, however, reveal a story about the growing cultural authority of business, and of the tendency for all aspects of culture—religion being no exception—to be put in the service of neoliberalization.

Corporate interest in spirituality echoes basic changes in the way Americans think and behave toward work. Although Jerry Maguire avoids religious language, he too wants these same intrinsic rewards from work. Moreover, just as advocates for workplace spirituality universalize the experience of business elites as indicative of work more generally, the film presents the privileged as the ordinary. Maguire is already successful and presumably financially secure, but his distress, according to the film, is our distress too. Regardless of our financial circumstances, we all need work that yields meaningful relationships and gives us the chance to serve the greater good.

While the main protagonist sounds remarkably similar to the advocates of spirituality at work, his sole client and friend, Rod Tidwell (Cuba Gooding, Jr.), affirms another important theme of this book. Tidwell is a struggling African-American NFL wide receiver who, against all reason, stays with Jerry after he is fired from SMI. Like Maguire, he is facing a particular work-related dilemma of his own. Tidwell's career has not proven as lucrative as he or his wife (Regina King) expected. Although he initially believes that SMI has underrepresented his interests, Tidwell's realizes over the course of the film that financial success only comes when we excel for its own sake, not for the material rewards. Only when he ceases to view his gameplay as an exchange for wages does Tidwell find happiness.

Tidwell's storyline, of course, asserts that material rewards serve poorly as an incentive. Financial success, instead, is a natural byproduct, a side effect of work done well. One finds happiness in the task at hand, not in the paycheck. In addition to the problematic racialized dimensions with an African-American learning to stop looking for unearned success, the story effectively presents the reality of diminishing incomes resulting from neoliberalization as a consequence of poor individual character. Audiences are told that money comes to those who don't complain and simply do their jobs well. Again, like workplace spirituality, *Jerry Maguire* imparts moral imperatives bent toward the interests of business.

Both *Jerry Maguire* and the moments of historical entanglement described in this book are itineraries that offer us potential schemes according to which we may or may not conform. They are scripts for sense-making that acquaint us with how we are supposed to act and what we should expect from our experiences. *Jerry Maguire*, in the example of Maguire and Tidwell, proposes strategies for surviving and thriving in a social world defined by neoliberalization. Similarly, as much as Conscious Capitalism, MSR (Management, Spirituality, and Religion), or Sacred Commerce may reproduce the conditions of neoliberal, global capitalism, they do provide practical strategies, the practical wisdom by which we order our lives, whether we choose to acknowledge it or not.

This project has attempted to demonstrate how social trends like the "faith and work" movement, corporate mindfulness programs, or any other attempt to integrate religious or spiritual language and practice into the workplace are quite typical and conventional business practices. Neoliberalization has greatly diminished the welfare state, labor power, and has effectively empowered business to influence the global political economy to serve capital under the banner of "globalization," a term that essentially symbolizes increasing inability of states to control markets. This "new economy," driven by high technology, finance, and mass consumption, has introduced new forms and new arrangements of work, many of which depend on interpersonal skills and affective labor. Corporate efforts to promote core values, spiritual or otherwise, or to demonstrate concern with employee wellness, be they through smoking cessation programs or through mindfulness training, are reflections of this new socioeconomic order.

Naturally, this language of spirituality is most evident in those industries that have helped to shape this new economic landscape, for example in high-tech firms like Google or Facebook that provide meditation rooms, or among financial elites in New York City who use spiritual practices to overcome the stress of highly competitive work. In addition, this language can be found in the retail world, in places like Café Gratitude, when managers and staff discuss "Sacred Commerce" and share their personal stories of growth through work.

This observation—that the entanglement of religion and business is an aspect of corporate culture—should not imply that religion, as a socioeconomic phenomenon, exclusively serves the status quo. The individuals featured in this story confound such one-sided portraits because their religious and spiritual lives permeate more than their work. They emerge and evolve in relation to all of social life. It is for this reason the analysis in this book extends beyond work to consider business as an institution, and capitalism as a particular kind of social order. All of these—work, business, and political economy—are implicated in the production of culture and, this book has sought to demonstrate how they collectively matter for the history of religion in the United States.

Of course, a great many aspects of this topic remain to be explored. First, any of the ideas, institutions, or individuals highlighted in this book deserve more careful attention. I have deliberately emphasized those aspects of biographies that proved most directly relevant to tell the larger story of religion and American business, however, many of these individuals led very elaborate religious lives that could further deepen our knowledge and challenge our assumptions about religious history and culture. Second, there is a distinct global dimension to this trend that, for purely arbitrary reasons of disciplinary loyalty, I have left unexplored. Corporate interest in spirituality has followed globalization and has manifested in ways peculiar to the histories and cultural norms of various locales across the world. Moreover, groups like the Management, Spirituality, and Religion interest group in the Academy of Management comprise an international membership with attendees coming from all continents to share ideas and practices. Finally, I have knowingly privileged the voice of religious liberals, so-called New Agers, and generic spiritual eclectics (for lack of better terms) primarily because the contrast between their social liberalism and the implicit affirmation of neoliberalism appears, to me, all the more counterintuitive. However, recent disputes, involving Christian companies like Hobby Lobby or Chic-Fil-A, over the rights of religious business owners to refuse business activities that violate their "deeply held beliefs" show that religious conservatives are a part of this story as well. All in all, American business plays an important role in the history of religion and, to paraphrase JZ Smith, it is a story worthy of the scholar's invention.

Notes

Introduction

1 "Tyson Center for Faith and Spirituality in the Workplace," *Sam M. Walton College of Business*, accessed 20 April 2016, http://tfsw.uark.edu/.

2 This poem can be found in John O'Donohue, *To Bless the Space Between Us: A Book of Blessings* (New York: Random House, 2008).

3 "Walton History," *University of Arkansas*, accessed 10 April 2014, https://waltoncollege.uark.edu/history.asp.

4 Bethany Moreton, *To Serve God and Wal-Mart* (Cambridge: Harvard University Press, 2009), 5.

5 "Definitions," *Institute for Mindful Leadership*, accessed 12 April 2014, http://instituteformindfulleadership.org/definitions.

6 "Clients," *Institute for Mindful Leadership*, accessed 12 April 2014, http://instituteformindfulleadership.org/clients/.

7 "Courses and Workshops," *Institute for Mindful Leadership*, accessed 12 April 2014, http://instituteformindfulleadership.org/course-and-workshops/.

8 Dan Gilgoff, "How Davos Found God," *CNN: Belief Blog*, accessed 28 January, 2011, http://religion.blogs.cnn.com/2011/01/28/how-davos-found-god/.

9 Larry Elliot and Jill Teanor, "And breathe...Goldie Hawn and a Monk Bring Meditation to Davos," *The Guardian*, 23 January 2014.

10 See Chapter 3 for a detailed discussion of these claims.

11 Judi Neal, *Edgewalkers: People and Organizations That Take Risks, Build Bridges, and Break New Ground* (Westport, CT: Praeger Publishers, 2006), 9.

12 Douglas Hicks, *Religion and the Workplace: Pluralism, Spirituality, Leadership* (Cambridge: Cambridge University Press, 2003), 20.

13 David W. Miller, *God at Work: The History and Promise of the Faith at Work Movement* (New York: Oxford University Press, 2007), 7.

14 Jeremy Carrette and Richard King, *Selling Spirituality: The Silent Takeover of Religion* (New York: Routledge, 2005), 134.

15 Ian Mitroff and Elizabeth Denton, *A Spiritual Audit of Corporate America: A Hard Look at Spirituality, Religion, and Values in the Workplace* (San Francisco: Jossey-Bass Publishers, 1999), 14.

16 Lake Lambert III, *Spirituality, Inc.: Religion in the American Workplace* (New York: New York University Press, 2009), 18.

17 Hicks, *Religion and the Workplace*, 118.

18 King and Carrette, *Selling Spirituality*, 7.

19 Talal Asad, *Genealogies of Religion: Discipline and Reasons of Power in Christianity and Islam* (Baltimore: Johns Hopkins University Press, 1993), 29.

20 King and Carrette, *Selling Spirituality*, 3.

21 George J. Gonzalez, *Shape-Shifting Capital: Spiritual Management, Critical Theory, and the Ethnographic Project* (Lanham, MD: Lexington Books, 2015), 11.

22 Courtney Bender, *The New Metaphysicals: Spirituality and the American Religious Imagination* (Chicago: University of Chicago Press, 2010), 6.

23 Joseph E. Stiglitz, *Globalization and Its Discontents* (New York: W.W. Norton, 2003), 9

24 Pierre Bourdieu, *The Social Structures of the Economy. translated by Chris Turner* (London: Polity Press, 2005), 225.

25 David Harvey, *A Brief History of Neoliberalism* (New York: Oxford University Press, 2005), 2.

26 Ibid., 19.

27 Ibid.

28 Ibid.

29 Jamie Peck, *Constructions of Neoliberal Reason* (New York: Oxford University Press, 2013), xiii.

1 The Death and Resurrection of a Craftsman: Toward a New Mythology of Work

1 Brooks Akinson, "At the Theatre," *The New York Times*, 11 February 1949.

2 *Death of Salesman*, 49th edition (New York: Penguin Plays, 1976), 73.

3 William H. Whyte, *The Organization Man*, New ED edition (Philadelphia: University of Pennsylvania Press, 2002), 7.

4 Ibid., 3.

5 C. Wright Mills, *White Collar: The American Middle Classes, 50th Anniversary edition* (New York: Oxford University Press, 2002), xxii.

6 Ibid., 219.

7 Judith Merkle, *Management and Ideology: The Legacy of the International Scientific Management Movement* (Berkeley: University of California Press, 1980), 58–59.

8 Other scholars have documented the contributions of the "industrial relations" school of management, which originated in the extensive study of worker satisfaction by Elton Mayo at the Hawthorne plant. See Lake Lambert, *Spirituality Inc.: Religion in the American Workplace* (New York: NYU Press, 2009) for a detailed discussion of the turn toward industrial psychology.

9 The earliest advanced degrees concerned with business administration appeared in the 1920s, with Harvard introducing an MBA (Masters of Business Administration) in 1921. A few years later, in 1925, the Massachusetts Institute of Technology established the first Master's explicitly dedicated to Management in its Department of Economics and Statistics, which would eventually spawn an independent school of Industrial Management (later renamed the Alfred P. Sloan School of Management) in 1952.

10 Steve Denning, "The Best of Peter Drucker," *Forbes*, 29 July 2014.

11 "Drucker's Childhood and Youth in Vienna," *Drucker Society of Austria*, 2009, accessed 6 February 2016, http://www.druckersociety.at/index.php/peterdruckerhome/biography.

12 For a discussion of the influence of the Austrian school on neoliberal economic philosophies, see Jamie Peck, *Constructions of Neoliberal Reason* (New York: Oxford University Press, 2013, reprint edition).

13 Peter Drucker, *The Practice of Management* (New York: Harper, 1954), 4–5.

14 Ibid., 5.

15 Ibid., 261.

16 Ibid., 266.

17 Ibid., 272.

18 Douglas McGregor, *The Human Side of Enterprise: Annotated Edition* (New York: McGraw-Hill, 2006), 43.

19 Douglas McGregor, "The Human Side of Enterprise," *Leadership and Motivation, Essays of Douglas McGregor*, edited by W. G. Bennis and E. H. Schein (Cambridge, MA: MIT Press, 1966). First published in *Adventure in Thought and Action*, Proceedings of the Fifth Anniversary Convocation of the School of Industrial Management, Massachusetts Institute of Technology, Cambridge, 6 April 1957. Reprinted in *Management Review*, 46: 11, 1957, 22–28.

20 Ibid.

21 McGregor, *The Human Side of Enterprise*, 312.

22 McGregor, "The Human Side of Enterprise," 1957.

23 McGregor, *The Human Side of Enterprise*, 60.

24 McGregor, "The Human Side of Enterprise," 1957.

25 For example, the pharmaceutical firm, Proctor and Gamble reportedly enlisted McGregor to implement his management theory at their production facility in August, GA during the late 1950s. In *Guide to Management Ideas and Gurus* (London: The Economist Newspaper, Ltd., 2008), author Tim Hindle, as a result of McGregor's changes, the Augusta plant achieved productivity levels of 30 percent above any other P&G facility by the mid-1960s.

26 McGregor, "The Human Side of Enterprise," 1957.

27 Quoted from the diaries of Abraham Maslow in Robert Shaw and Karen Colimore, "Humanistic Psychology as Ideology: An Analysis of Maslow's Contradictions," *Journal of Humanistic Psychology*, 28: 3, 1998, 108.

28 Abraham Maslow, *Motivation and Personality* (New York: Harper, 1954), 236.

29 Annie N. L. Ng, Corrine L. Y. Chong, Josiah Y. X. Ching, Jowell H. H. Beh, Patricia P. F. Lim, "A Critical Comparison of the Psychoanalytic and Humanistic Theory," accessed 6 April 2015, https://www.academia.edu/7304762/A_Critical_Comparison_of_the_Psychoanalytic_and_Humanistic_Theory.

30 Abraham Maslow, "A Theory of Human Motivation," *Psychological Review*, 50, 1943, 382.

31 Robert Shaw and Karen Colimore, "Humanistic Psychology as Ideology," 56.

32 Ibid., 57.

33 McGregor, *The Human Side of Enterprise*, 51.

34 Other historians have documented this episode in the life of Maslow in detail. See Richard Donkin, *The History of Work* (New York: Palgrave-Macmillan, 2010), Laura L. Koppes, *Historical Perspectives in Industrial and Organizational Psychology* (New York: Psychology Press, 2007).

35 Maslow, quoted in Edward Hoffman, *The Right to Be Human: A Biography of Abraham Maslow* (Florida: John Wiley and Sons, Inc., 1999), 259.

36 Abraham Maslow, *Maslow on Management* (New York: John Wiley and Sons, Inc., 1998), 8.

37 Ibid., 1.

38 Ibid., 39.

39 Abraham Maslow, *Religions, Values, and Peak-Experiences* (New York: Penguin Compass, 1970), 19.

40 Ibid., 45.

41 Ibid., 68.

42 Eugene Taylor, *Shadow Culture: Psychology and Spirituality in America* (Washington, DC: Counterpoint Press, 1999), 280. See also Jeffrey Kripal, *Esalen: America and the Religion of No Religion* (Chicago and London: University of Chicago Press, 2007) and Jessica Grogan, *Encountering America: Humanistic Psychology, Sixties Culture, and the Shaping of the Modern Self* (New York: Harper Perennial, 2012) for descriptions of the influence of Abraham Maslow on religion and spirituality since the 1960s.

43 McGregor, "The Human Side of Enterprise," 2.

44 Peter Drucker, *The New Realities* (New York and London: Routledge, 1989), 223.

2 A New Business for Business

1 Political scientist Maria Rydahl Ahlgreen, for example, attributes this statement to Milton Friedman's 1970 essay in *The New York Times Magazine* "The Social Responsibility of Business Is to Increase Profit," 13 September 1970, although

Friedman never actually uses these words. See Rydahl Ahlgreen, "When the Business of Business became Everybody's Business," *The Magazine for International Business and Diplomacy*, 2, December 2010, accessed 16 April 2016, http://ibde. org/component/content/article/114-when-the-business-of-business-became-everybodys-business.html. The quote is alternatively associated with Alfred Sloan in a number of publications, sometimes with a citation of 1964. For an example of this, see Tim Hindle, *Guide to Management Ideas and Gurus* (New York: Bloomberg Press, 2008), 307.

2 Friedman, "The Social Responsibility of Business is to Increase Profits."

3 Peter Drucker, "Worker and Work in the Metropolis," *Daedalus*, 97: 4, 1968, 1244.

4 Peter Drucker, *The Age of Discontinuity: Guidelines to Our Changing Society* (New Brunswick and London: Transaction Publishers, 1992), xvix.

5 Ibid., 212.

6 Ibid., 236.

7 Ibid., 43.

8 In 1913, AT&T settled an antitrust suit with the U.S. Attorney General in the so-called Kingsbury Commitment in which the corporation agreed to no longer acquire competitors and to allow the federal government to impose special operating rules on the firm. In exchange, AT&T would be allowed to practically function as the sole provider of long-distance service and to retain proprietary control over its vast empire of Bell Telephone subsidiaries. See Peter Temin and Louis Galambos, *The Fall of the Bell System: A Study in Prices and Politics* (New York: Cambridge University Press, 1989).

9 Peter Drucker, "Foreword," *On Becoming A Servant Leader: The Private Writings of Robert K. Greenleaf* (San Francisco: Jossey-Bass, 1996), xi–xii.

10 Robert K. Greenleaf, "A Forward Look at Management Development," *Transcript of Address to the Bureau of Industrial Relations* (University of Michigan: Ann Arbor, Michigan, March 1958), 19.

11 Ibid., 23.

12 Ibid., 25.

13 Ibid., 23.

14 Robert K. Greenleaf, "The Crisis of Leadership," *On Becoming a Servant Leader: The Private Writings of Robert K. Greenleaf,* edited by Don M. Frick and Larry C. Spears (San Francisco: Jossey-Bass, 1996), 287.

15 Ibid.

16 Ibid., 290.

17 Ibid., 289.

18 Ibid., 297.

19 Ibid., 332. See also Exodus 13: 21–22 NRSV.

20 Ibid.

21 Ibid., 333.

22 Ibid.

23 Ibid., 290.

24 John Woolman, *Considerations on the Keeping of Negroes: Recommended to the Professors of Christianity of Every Denomination*. Originally published in Philadelphia: Tract Association of Friends. Full text available online at archive.org.

25 Greenleaf, *On Becoming a Servant Leader*, 290.

26 Bruce Barton, *The Man Nobody Knows* (Indianapolis: Bobbs-Merrill Company, 1925), vii. Bruce Barton (1886–1967) co-founded in 1919 the advertising agency, Barton, Durstine, and Osborn (later Batten, Barton, Durstine, and Osborn). He also served two terms in the U.S. House of Representatives from 1937–1941 from the state of New York. For a detailed account of how Barton's popular book, *The Man Nobody Knows*, reflected wider patterns of popular Christian readers, see Erin Smith, *What Would Jesus Read? Popular Religious Books and Everyday Life in Twentieth-Century America* (Chapel Hill, NC: University of North Carolina Press, 2016), especially Ch. 4.

27 Russell Conwell, "Acres of Diamonds," *Temple.edu*. Web, retrieved 13 February 2016.

28 Ibid., 313.

29 Ibid., 316.

30 Ibid., 336.

31 Ibid., 324.

32 Ibid., 322.

33 Robert K. Greenleaf, "The Servant as Leader," *Servant Leadership: A Journey Into the Nature of Legitimate Power and Greatness* (New York: Paulist Press, 1977), 13.

34 Robert K. Greenleaf, "The Servant as Leader (original 1970 edition)," *The Servant-Leader Within: A Transformative Path*, edited by Hamilton Beazley, Julie Beggs, and Larry C. Spears (Mahway, NJ: Paulist Press, 2003), 52.

35 Greenleaf, "The Servant as Leader," (1977), 41.

36 Ibid., 53.

37 Greenleaf, "The Servant as Leader," (1970), 70.

38 "About Greenleaf University," *Greenleaf University, Institute for Professional Studies, An American Graduate School*, 2014, http://greenleaf.edu/about.htm.

39 Richard M. Nixon, "Address to the Nation on Labor Day, September 6, 1971," courtesy of *The American Presidency Project*, University of California, Santa Barbara, http://www.presidency.ucsb.edu/ws/?pid=3138.

40 Ibid.

41 Ibid.

42 Ibid.

43 The Bretton Woods system was child of a 1944 conference that took place in Bretton Woods, New Hampshire, in which the Allied Nations agreed to a set of rules governing monetary relations between them. Participant countries agreed to

fixed exchange rates for their currencies, which would be backed by the U.S. dollar and gold.

44 "Gas Fever: Happiness in a Full Tank," *Time Magazine*, 18 February 1974.

45 James O'Toole, Elisabeth Hansot, William Herman, Neal Herrick, Elliot Liebow, Bruce Lusignan, Harold Richman, Harold Sheppard, Ben Stephansky, and James Wright, Work in America: Report of a Special Task Force to the Secretary of Health, Education, and Welfare [the tile should be italicized] (Cambridge and London: The MIT Press, 1973), xv.

46 Ibid., xvi.

47 Ibid., 12.

48 Ibid.

49 Ibid., 27.

50 Ibid., 2, 3.

51 Ibid., 13.

52 Ibid., 47.

53 Ibid., 48.

54 "Port Huron Statement of the Students for a Democratic Society, 1962," accessed 14 November 2015, http://coursesa.matrix.msu.edu/~hst306/documents/huron.html.

55 Ibid., 20.

56 Ibid., 1.

57 Ibid., 2.

58 Ibid.

59 Ibid., xix.

60 Ibid., 23.

61 Ibid.

62 See Willis W. Harman, *Fundamentals of Electronic Motion* (New York: McGraw-Hill, 1953) as an example of his early engineering research at Stanford.

63 Art Kleiner, *The Age of Heretics: A History of Radical Thinkers Who Reinvented Corporate Management* (San Francisco: Jossey-Bass, 2008), 159.

64 Ibid., 13.

65 Taken from a transcript of an interview with Willis Harman on the U.K. television program, "dprogram," accessed 12 April 2015, http://www.dprogram.com/willis_harmanp1.html.

66 Steven M. Gelber and Martin L. Cook, *Saving the Earth: The History of a Middle-Class Millenarian Movement* (Berkeley: University of California Press, 1990), 84.

67 Willis Harman, "Some Aspects of the Psychedelic-Drug Controversy," *Journal of Humanistic Psychology*, 3, 1963, 105.

68 Between 1961 and 1963, Dr. Leary led a study on 32 prisoners at Concord State Prison in Massachusetts. The experiments involved the administration of psilocybin with accompanying psychotherapy sessions. Subsequent research has remained highly critical of these tests, for example, see Rick Doblin, "Dr. Leary's Concord

Prison Experiment: A 34-year Follow-Up Study," *Journal of Psychoactive Drugs*, 30: 4, 1998, 419–426.

69 The "Staggers-Dodd" bill (Public law 90–639), signed into law on October 24, 1968, effectively rendered the possession of LSD illegal.

70 "Corporate History," *SRI International*, accessed 12 April 2015,

71 Willis Harman, "A Utopian Perspective on the Future," *An Evangelical Agenda, 1984 and Beyond: Addresses, Responses, and Scenarios from the "Continuing Consultation on Future Evangelical Concerns"* held in Overland Park, Kansas, December 11–14, 1979 (Pasadena: William Carey Library, 1979), 27.

72 Willis Harman, "The Emerging 'Wholeness' Worldview and Its Probable Impact on Cooperation," *World Futures: The Journal of New Paradigms Research*, 31: 2–4, 1991, 75.

73 Willis W. Harman, "Creating a Sustainable Global Society—The Evolutionary Path," *World Futures: The Journal of New Paradigm Research*, 47: 4, 1996, 283.

74 Harman, "A Utopian Perspective on the Future," 32.

75 Willis Harman, *An Incomplete Guide to the Future* (New York: W.W. Norton and Company, 1979), 123.

76 Willis W. Harman, "Humanistic Capitalism: Another Alternative," *Journal of Humanistic Psychology*, 14: 1, 1974, 7.

77 Harman, *An Incomplete Guide to the Future*, 138.

78 Willis Harman, *Global Mind Change: The New Age Revolution in the Way We Think* (Sausalito, CA: Warner Books, 1988), 121.

79 Harman, *An Incomplete Guide to the Future*, 136.

80 Hendrik Gideonese, quoted in Kleiner, *The Age of Heretics*, 175.

81 "Overview," *Institute for Noetic Sciences*, accessed 3 March 2014, http://noetic.org/about/overview.

82 Edgar Mitchell, quoted in "IONS Leaders," *Institute for Noetic Sciences*, accessed 22 March 2014, http://noetic.org/about/IONS-leaders/.

83 "About," *World Business Academy*, accessed 2 February 2014, http://worldbusiness.org/about.

84 See "Mission Statement," *World Business Academy*, accessed 2 February 2014, http://worldbusiness.org/about/mission-statement.

85 Harman, *Global Mind Change*, 130.

86 Ibid., 131.

87 Ibid.

88 Willis Harman, "A System in Decline or Transformation?" *The New Business of Business: Sharing Responsibility for a Global Future*, edited by Willis Harman and Maya Porter (San Francisco: Berrett-Koehler Publishers, 1997), 34.

3 Management, Spirituality, and Religion: Theology and Spiritual Practice in Neoliberal Society

1 "About MSR," *Management, Spirituality, & Religion Interest Group of the Academy of Management*, accessed 12 January 2016,

2 "Conference 2015," *Management, Spirituality, & Religion Interest Group of the Academy of Management*, accessed 17 May 2016, http://group.aomonline.org/msr/page2.html.

3 "About MSR," accessed 12 January 2016, http://group.aomonline.org/msr/page1.html.

4 In Chapter five of *God At Work: The History and Promise of the Faith and Work Movement* New York: Oxford University Press, 2007), David Miller discusses in detail the so-called Faith and Work Era, which accordingly runs from approximately 1985 to the present.

5 Lake Lambert III, *Spirituality, Inc: Religion in the American Workplace* (New York: NYU Press, 2009), 120.

6 Jerry Biberman and Michael Whitty, "Overview," *Work and Spirit: A Reader of New Spiritual Paradigms for Organizations* (Scranton, PA: University of Scranton Press, 2000), xii.

7 "Facts from EBRI," *Employee Benefit Research Institute*, February 2005, https://www.ebri.org/pdf/publications/facts/0205fact.a.pdf.

8 Thomas Peters and Robert Watermann, *In Search of Excellence: Lessons from America's Best Run Companies* (New York: Harper and Row, 1982), 12.

9 Gerald F. Cavanagh, "Spirituality for Managers: Context and Critique," *Journal of Organizational Change Management*, 12: 3, 1999, 186.

10 Donde P. Ashmos and Dennis Duchon, "Spirituality at Work: A Conceptualization and Measure," *Journal of Management Inquiry*, 9: 2, 2000, 134.

11 Ibid.

12 Judi Neal, "Spirituality in Management Education: A Guide to Resources," *Journal of Management Education*, 21: 1, 1997, 122.

13 Stephen J. Porth, John McCall, and Thomas A. Bausch, "Spiritual themes of the 'Learning Organization'" *Journal of Organizational Change Management*, 12: 3, 1999, 211.

14 Judith A. Neal, Benyamin M. Bergmann Lichtenstein, and David Banner, "Spiritual Perspectives on Individual, Organizational, and Societal Transformation," *Journal of Organizational Change Management*, 12: 3, 1999, 175.

15 Miller, *God at Work*, 70.

16 Ibid.

17 Jay A. Conger and Associates, *Spirit at Work: Discovering the Spirituality in Leadership* (San Francisco: Jossey-Bass Publishers, 1994), 6.

18 Ibid., 3–6.

19 Ibid., 6.

20 Ibid., 7.

21 Miller, *God at Work*, 63.

22 Ibid.

23 Philip H. Mirvis, "'Soul Work' In Organizations," *Organization Science*, 8: 2, 1997, 199.

24 Gilbert W. Fairholm, *Capturing the Heart of Leadership: Spirituality and Community in the New American Workplace* (Westport, CT: Praeger publishing, 1997), 5.

25 Lambert, *Spirituality, Inc.*, 38.

26 Doreen Massey, "Vocabularies of the Economy," *Soundings*, 54, 2013, 9–22.

27 See Parker Palmer, *Let Your Life Speak: Listening for the Voice of Vocation* (San Francisco: Jossey-Bass, 2000) in which Palmer narrates his spiritual struggle to uncover his true calling in life.

28 Parker Palmer, *The Active Life: A Spirituality of Work, Creativity, and Caring* (San Francisco: Jossey-Bass, 1999), 9.

29 Parker Palmer, "Leading from Within: Out of Shadow, into the Light," *Spirit at Work*, edited by Jay Conger (San Francisco: Jossey-Bass, 1994), 27.

30 Ibid., 24.

31 Ibid.

32 Palmer, *A Spirituality of Work*, 60.

33 Ibid., 68.

34 Ibid.

35 Ibid., 156.

36 Ibid.

37 Ian Mitroff and Elizabeth Denton, "A Study of Spirituality in the Workplace," *Sloan Management Review*, Summer, 1999, 85. This article summarizes the results of the study outline in their larger publication, *A Spiritual Audit of Corporate America* (1999).

38 Ibid., 91.

39 Ian Mitroff and Elizabeth Denton, *A Spiritual Audit of Corporate America: Spirituality, Religion, and Values in the Workplace* (San Francisco: Jossey-Bass, 1999), 7.

40 Mitroff and Denton, "A Study of Spirituality in the Workplace," 91.

41 Ibid., 7.

42 Mitroff and Denton, *A Spiritual Audit*, 5.

43 Ibid., 90. The examples of firms in this taxonomy are provided by the authors of the study and do not reflect the position of this book.

44 Ibid., 89. Mitroff and Denton propose a list of the main characteristics of spirituality as a summary of their findings.

45 Ibid., 85–6.

46 See *A Spiritual Audit*, 187–195. Appendix A offers a template of the "Questionnaire on Meaning and Purpose in the Workplace" used in their survey of two thousand Human Resource professionals.

47 Ibid.

48 See, for example, John Millman, Jerry Ferguson, David Trickett, and Bruce Condemi, "Spirit and Community at Southwest: An Investigation of Spiritual Values-Based Model," *Journal of Organizational Change Management*, 12: 3, 1999, 221–233. Although Southwest Airlines avoids using explicitly "spiritual" language to describe its organizational culture, the authors label its emphasis on values, play, and informality as befitting Mitroff and Denton's "values-based" organization and therefore an example of organizational spirituality.

49 Douglas Hicks, *Religion and the Workplace* (Cambridge: Cambridge University Press, 2003), 58.

50 See Lambert, *Spirituality, Inc.*, 121 and Miller, *God at Work* 110. Both authors specifically mention Judi Neal's integral role in the founding of the Management, Spirituality, and Religion Interest Group at the Academy of Management, as well as briefly discuss her activities in other organizations.

51 "Judi Neal Bio," *Judith Neal and Associates*, accessed 25 August 2013, http://www.judineal.com/pages/corporate/nealbio.htm.

52 Neal, *Edgewalkers*, 32.

53 Shakti Gawain, *Creative Visualization: Use the Power of Your Imagination to Create What You Want in Your Life* (Novato, CA: Nataraj Publishing, 2002), 11.

54 Neal, *Edgewalkers*, 33.

55 "Judi Neal Bio," *Judith Neal and Associates*, accessed 27 August 2013, http://www.judineal.com/pages/corporate/nealbio.htm.

56 Neal, "Spirituality in Management Education: A Guide to Resources," 121.

57 Neal, et al., "Spiritual Perspectives, on Individual, Organizational, And Societal Change," 175.

58 Neal, *Edgewalkers*, 11.

59 "About Us," *Edgewalkers International*, accessed 27 August 2013, http://edgewalkers.org/content/about-us.

60 Neal, *Edgewalkers*, 181.

61 Ibid., xv.

62 Ibid., 44.

63 Ibid., 3.

64 Ibid., 12.

65 Ibid.

66 Ibid., 63.

67 Russell McCutcheon, *Critics, Not Caretakers: Redescribing the Public Study of Religion* (New York: SUNY Press, 2001), 25.

4 Zen and the Art of Microprocessing: Liberating the Entrepreneurial Spirit in Silicon Valley

1 http://www.forbes.com/sites/toddessig/2012/4/30/google-teaches-employees-to-search-inside-yourself/.

2 http://www.pcmag.com/article2/0,2817,2414497,00.asp.

3 Walter Isaacson, *Steve Jobs* (New York: Simon and Schuster, 2011), 14–15.

4 Ibid., 15.

5 Ibid.

6 Robert Wuthnow, *After Heaven: Spirituality in America Since the 1950s* (Berkeley: University of California, 1998), 3.

7 Ibid., 7.

8 David Sheff, "Steve Jobs," *Playboy*, February 1985, found at http://www.txtpost.com/playboy-interview-steven-jobs.

9 Isaacson, *Steve Jobs*, 34.

10 Theodore Roszak, who popularized the term, defined the 1960s counterculture as a movement against the prevailing norms of society born, unlike most dissent, of affluence rather than deprivation. See Theodore Roszak, *The Making of a Counter Culture* (Berkeley: University of California Press, 1995).

11 Peter Braunstein and Michael William Doyle, "Historicizing the American Counterculture of the 1960s and 70s," *Imagine Nation: The American Counterculture of the 1960s and 70s*, edited by Peter Braunstein and Michael Doyle (New York: Routledge, 2002), 10.

12 Sheff, "Steve Jobs," *Playboy*, http://www.txtpost.com/playboy-interview-steven-jobs/.

13 "Steve Jobs College Mentor was a Drug Dealer Turned Billionaire Mining Magnate," *Daily Caller*, 24 October 2011, http://dailycaller.com/2011/10/24/steve-jobs-college-mentor-was-a-drug-dealer-turned-billionaire-mining-magnate-aapl/.

14 Isaacson, *Steve Jobs*, 38.

15 Ibid., 37.

16 Ibid.

17 http://dailycaller.com/2011/10/24/steve-jobs-college-mentor-was-a-drug-dealer-turned-billionaire-mining-magnate-aapl/.

18 http://www.txtpost.com/playboy-interview-steven-jobs/.

19 See Thomas J. Peters and Robert H. Waterman, *In Search of Excellence: Lessons from America's Best-Run Companies* (New York: HarperBusiness, 2004).

20 Isaacson, *Steve Jobs*, 48.

21 Ibid.

22 Isaacson, *Steve* Jobs, 51, quoting a friend of Steve Jobs, Elizabeth Holmes.

23 Ibid., 38.

24 Andy Hertzfeld, "Reality Distortion Field," *Folklore.org*, http://folklore.org/
    StoryView.py?story=Reality_Distortion_Field.txt.

25 Isaacson, *Steve Jobs*, 119.

26 Ibid.

27 http://www.txtpost.com/playboy-interview-steven-jobs/.

28 http://www.dharmaweb.org/index.php/Les_Kaye_Roshi_-_Kannon_Do_Zen.

29 Les Kaye, *Zen at Work: A Zen Teacher's 30-year journey in Corporate America*
    (New York: Three Rivers Press, 1996), 2.

30 Alan Watts, *The Way of Zen* (New York, Vintage, 1999).

31 Kaye, *Zen at* Work, 9.

32 Ibid.

33 "History of Kannon Do," *Kannon Do Zen Meditation Center*, accessed 3 May 2012.
    http://www.kannondo.org/about-us/history-of-kannon-do.

34 http://www.cuke.com/Cucumber%20Project/interviews/kaye-z&b.html

35 Kaye, *Zen at* Work, 54.

36 http://www.cuke.com/Cucumber%20Project/interviews/kaye-z&b.html.

37 Wuthnow, *After* Heaven, 142.

38 Kaye, *Zen at Work*, 149.

39 Ibid., 71.

40 Ibid., 73.

41 Ibid., 119.

42 Sam Binkley, *Getting Loose: Lifestyle Consumption in the 1970s* (Durham: Duke
    University, 2007), 3.

43 Ibid., 17.

44 Arthur Stinchecombe, "Social Structure and Organizations," *Handbook of
    Organizations*, edited by James G. March (Chicago: Rand-McNalley, 1965), 153.

45 Richard Sennett discusses how the "New Capitalism," driven in part by information
    technology, encourages "short-term thinking," "flexible labor," and an ethic of
    consumption." See Richard Sennett, *The Culture of the New Capitalism* (New
    Haven: Yale University, 2006).

5 Conscious Capitalism: Looser Selves, Freer Markets

1 John Mackey and Raj Sisodia, *Conscious Capitalism: Liberating the Heroic Spirit of
   Business* (Cambridge: Harvard Business Review Press, 2013), 9.

2 Ibid., 33.

3 John Mackey, "The Whole Foods Alternative to Obama Care," *The Wall Street Journal*, 11 August 2009.

4 April Fulton, "Whole Foods Founder John Mackey on Fascism and 'Conscious Capitalism,'" *National Public Radio Morning Edition*, 16 January 2013.

5 Robert Wuthnow, *After Heaven: Spirituality in America Since the 1950s* (Berkeley: University of California Press, 1998).

6 Schuyler Brown, "Magic at the Conscious Capitalism Conference in San Francisco," *Huffington Post*, 9 April 2013.

7 David A. Schwerin, *Conscious Capitalism: Principles for Prosperity* (Boston: Butterworth-Heinemann, 1998), 5.

8 "Our Vision," *The Modern Mystery School*, accessed 3 August 2013 http://modernmysteryschool.com/our-vision.

9 "The Global Sullivan Principles," *The Leon H. Sullivan Foundation*, accessed 12 August 2013, http://www.thesullivanfoundation.org/about/global_sullivan_principles.

10 Judith F. Posnikoff, "Divestment in South Africa: They Did Well by Doing Good," *Contemporary Economic Policy*, 15: 1, 1997, 76–86.

11 Transcript of a speech delivered at Claremont University on socially responsible business, "Conscious Capitalism: Principles for Prosperity." Provided to the author by David Schwerin.

12 Ibid.

13 Ibid.

14 http://pathwork.org/, accessed 08//04/2013.

15 Eva Pierrakos, "The Power of the Word," *Pathwork Guide Lecture No. 233*, 24 September 1975, http://pathwork.org/lectures/the-power-of-the-word, accessed 08/04/2013.

16 Schwerin, *Conscious Capitalism*, 153.

17 Ibid., 19.

18 Ibid., 69.

19 Ibid., 86.

20 See John Naisbitt, *Megatrends: Ten New Directions Transforming Our Lives* (Warner Book Inc., 1982). Although Aburdene is not given authorial credit in the work, she served as Naisbitt's research partner and would receive recognition as a coauthor of subsequent works in the series.

21 www.naisbitt.com, accessed 7 December 2012–13.

22 John Naisbitt and Patricia Aburdene, *Megatrends 2000: Ten New Directions for the 1990s* (New York: William Morrow and Company, 1990), 299.

23 Ibid., 298.

24 Patricia Aburdene, *Megatrends 2010*, preface.

25 Ibid., preface.

26 Ibid., 45.

27 Ibid., 7.

28 Ibid., 118–126

29 Ibid., 161.

30 Ibid., 165.

31 Ibid., 166.

32 Ibid., 172.

33 Ibid., 176.

34 "Greenspan Admits 'Flaw to Congress, Predicts More Economic Problems," *PBS Newshour*, 23 October 2008, http://www.pbs.org/newshour/bb/business/july-dec08/crisishearing_10-23.html.

35 www.consciouscapitalism.org/aboutus

36 Mackey and Sisodia, *Conscious Capitalism*, 7.

37 Ibid., 1

38 Ibid.

39 Ibid.

40 Ibid.

41 Mackey and Sisodia, *Conscious Capitalism*, 3.

42 Ibid., 4.

43 Ayn Rand, "What Is Capitalism?" *Capitalism: The Unknown Ideal* (New York: Signet Publishing, 1967), 2.

44 John Mackey and Michael Strong, *Be The Solution: How Entrepreneurs and Conscious Capitalists Can Solve All the World's Problem* (Hoboken, NJ: John Wiley and Sons, 2009), xviii–xiv.

45 Mackey and Sisodia, *Conscious Capitalism*, 7.

46 Ibid.

47 Catherine L. Albanese, "The Subtle Energies of Spirit: Explorations in Metaphysical and New Age Spirituality," *Journal of the American Academy of Religion*, 67: 2, June 1999, 312.

48 Ibid.

49 Helen Schucman, *A Course in Miracles: Preface, Text, Workbook for Students, Manual for Teachers, Clarification of Terms*, 2nd Edition (Mill Valley, CA: Foundation for Inner Peace, 1992), 1.

50 *A Course in Miracles, Workbook for Students*, 1.

51 Ibid., 49.

52 Ibid., 48.

53 Ibid., 134.

54 Ibid.

55 http://www.newyorker.com/reporting/2010/01/04/100104fa_fact_paumgarten

56 Mackey and Strong, *Be the Solution*, xv.

57 See Mihaly Csikszentmihalyi, *Flow: The Psychology of Optimal Experience* (New York: HarperCollins, 1990).

58 Csikszentmihalyi, *Flow*, 4.

59 http://www.flowidealism.org/Community/FAC.html

60 John Mackey and Michael Strong, *Be the Solution: How Entrepreneurs and Conscious Capitalists Can Solve All the World's Problems* (Hoboken: Wiley and Sons, 2009).

61 R. Edward Freeman, Olsson Professor of Business Administration, Academic Director, Business Roundtable Institute for Corporate Ethics, University of Virginia, in *Be the Solution*.

62 Mackey and Sisodia, *Conscious Capitalism*, 125.

63 Ibid., 136.

64 Ibid., 237.

65 Ibid., 137.

66 Ibid., 158.

67 Ibid., 64.

68 Ibid., 225.

69 Ibid., 179.

70 Pierre Bourdieu, *The Social Structures of the Economy*, translated by Chris Turner (Cambridge: Polity Press, 2005), 211.

6 Not the Usual Suspects: Real Estate Rabbis, Monastic Managers, and Spiritual Salesmen in the Big Apple

1 Lake Lambert refers to "workplace spirituality" as a new religious movement in the business world, and David Miller traces the history of what he calls the "faith at work movement" during the twentieth century. See Lake Lambert III, *Spirituality Inc: Religion in the American Workplace. (New York*: NYU Press, 2009), and David W. Miller, *God At Work: The History and Promise of the Faith at Work Movement* (New York: Oxford University Press, 2007).

2 "Intersections," *Colleiate Churches of New York*, accessed 14 February 2014, http://www.collegiatechurch.org/?q=content/intersections.

3 Max Weber, *The Protestant Ethic and the Spirit of Capitalism*, translated by Talcott Parsons (New York: Routledge, 2006), 40.

4 Alan Lurie, "Work as a Spiritual Gymnasium," *Huffington Post*, Religion Section, accessed 4 January 2012, http://www.huffingtonpost.com/rabbi-alan-lurie/work-as-a-spiritual-gymnasium_b_1173113.html.

5 Alan Lurie, *Five Minutes on Mondays: Finding Unexpected Purpose, Peace, and Fulfillment at Work* (Upper Saddle River, NJ: FT Press, 2009), xxii.

6 Alan Lurie in discussion with the author, 23 May 2012.

7 Lurie, *Five Minutes on Mondays*, 7.

8 Alan Lurie in discussion with the author, 23 May 2012.

9 Ibid.

10 Alan Lurie, lecture on "The Spirit of Work" at The Princeton Club, May 2012.

11 Alan Lurie in discussion with the author, 23 May 2012.

12 Marc Miller in discussion with the author, 25 May 2012.

13 Ibid.

14 Ibid.

15 Ibid.

16 Ibid.

17 Ibid.

18 "What We Do: Organizational Reinvention," *LPR Group Website*, accessed 12 March 2014, http://www.lprgroup.com/orgreinvention.php.

19 Peter Roche in discussion with the author, 19 June 2012.

20 Ibid.

21 Ibid.

22 Ibid.

23 Ibid.

24 "About Carol," *Carol Fox Prescott*, website, accessed 4 March 2014, http://carolfoxprescott.com/about/.

25 *Joshua M. Greene Official Website*, accessed 7 March 2014, http://www.atma.org/biography/.

26 Alan Lurie used an advertisement from the HSBC Bank's "Different Values" campaign post 2008 financial crisis. To view this advertisement, please see John Swansburg, "HSBC's Bizarre Lumberjack Ad," *Slate.com*, accessed 27 October 2008, http://www.slate.com/articles/business/ad_report_card/2008/10/hsbcs_bizarre_lumberjack_ad.html.

27 Roland Barthes, *Mythologies*, translated by Annette Lavers (New York: HarperCollins, 1957).

28 Alan Lurie, "Work as a Spiritual Gymnasium," 16 May 2012.

29 Marc Miller in discussion with the author, 25 May 2012.

30 Peter Roche in discussion with the author, 19 June 2012.

31 Alan Lurie, "Work as a Spiritual Gymnasium," 16 May 2012.

32 Peter Roche in discussion with the author, 19 June 2012.

33 Ibid.

34 Alan Lurie, *Five Minutes on Mondays*, 243.

35 Ibid., 88.

36 Ibid., 28.

37 Alan Lurie in discussion with the author, 23 May 2012.

38 Peter Roche in discussion with the author, 19 June 2012.

39 Milton Friedman, *Capitalism and Freedom: Fortieth Anniversary Edition* (Chicago: University of Chicago Press, 2002), 25.

40 Pierre Bourdieu, *The Social Structures of the Economy*, translated by Chris Turner (London: Polity Press, 2005), 224.

41 Ibid., 228.

42 Kenny Moore, speaking at "The Spirit of Work," *Intersections International*, New York, NY, 13 June 2012.

43 Pierre Bourdieu, *Outline of a Theory of Practice*, translated by Richard Nice (New York: Cambridge University Press, 1977), 164.

7 Sacred Commerce: Neoliberal Spiritualities in a West-Coast Coffee Chain

1 Matthew Engelhart and Terces Engelhart, *Sacred Commerce: Business as a Path to Spiritual Awakening* (Berkeley: North Atlantic Books, 2008).

2 Engelhart and Engelhart, *Sacred Commerce*, 7.

3 Ibid., 18.

4 "About Our Practice," *Café Gratitude*, accessed 30 March 2014 http://cafegratitude. com/about-our-practice/.

5 "Abounding River Boardgame," *Magical Marketing*, http://www.graphicgirlz.com/ cafe/boardgame.html.

6 Engelhart and Engelhart, *Sacred Commerce*, 25.

7 "Sacred Commerce," accessed 4 April 2014, https://www.facebook.com/events/ 540540045992796/.

8 "Abounding River Workshop," accessed 3 April 2014, http://gracias-madre.com/ 2013/03/03/207/.

9 Interview with Matthew Engelhart.

10 "About Our Practice," *Café Gratitude*, accessed 3 April 2014, http://cafegratitude. com/about-our-practice/.

11 Engelhart and Engelhart, *Sacred Commerce*, 71.

12 Ibid., 96.

13 *Abounding River Workshop*.

14 Engelhart and Engelhart, *Sacred Commerce*, 49.

15 Ibid., 25.

16 Ibid., 29.

17 Ibid., 31.

18 Ibid., 26.

19 Susan Friend Harding, *The Book of Jerry Falwell: Fundamentalist Language and Politics* (Princeton: Princeton University Press, 2000), 57.

20 Nikolas Rose, *Governing the Soul: The Shaping of the Private Self* (Free Association Books, 1999), 146.

21 Ibid., 157

22 Bourdieu, *Social Structures of the Economy*, 211.

23 Matthew Engelhart and Terces Engelhart, *Abounding River Logbook: An Unfamiliar View of Being Abundance* (Berkeley: North Atlantic Books, 2007), 22.

24 Ibid., 2.

25 Ibid., 62.

26 Ibid.

27 Ibid., 22.

28 Ibid., 57.

29 Ibid., 69.

30 Ibid.

31 Ibid., 59.

32 Ibid., 60.

33 Ibid., 48.

34 Ibid., 47.

35 Ibid., 41.

36 Carla Freeman, "Neoliberalism: Embodying and Affecting Neoliberalism," *A Companion to the Anthropology of the Body and Embodiment*, edited by Frances E. Mascia-Lees (Chichester, UK: Blackwell, 2001), 356.

37 Ibid., 356.

38 Engelhart and Engelhart, *Abounding River Logbook*, 64.

39 Bourdieu, *Outline of a Theory of Practice*, 195.

40 Engelhart and Engelhart, *Abounding River Logbook*, 70.

Conclusion

1   All quotes from *Jerry Maguire* were retrieved at *Wikiquote*, accessed 6 June 2016, https://en.wikiquote.org/wiki/Jerry_Maguire.

Selected Bibliography

Akinson, Brooks. "At the Theater." *New York Times*, 11 February 1949.

Albanese, Catherine L. "The Subtle Energies of Spirit: Explorations in Metaphysical and New Age Spirituality." *Journal of the American Academy of Religion* 67: 2 (1999).

An Evaneglical Agenda, 1984 and Beyond: Addresses, Responses, and Scenarios from the "Continuing Consultation on Future Evangelical Concerns" held in Overland Park, Kansas, 11–14 December 1979. Pasadena: William Carey Library, 1979.

Asad, Talal. *Genealogies of Religion: Discipline and Reasons of Power in Christianity and Islam*. Baltimore: Johns Hopkins University Press, 1993.

Ashmos, Donde P. and Duchon, Dennis. "Spirituality at Work: A Conceptualization and Measure." *Journal of Management Inquiry* 9: 2 (1999).

Barthes, Roland. *Mythologies*. Translated by Annette Lavers. New York: HarperCollins, 1957.

Bender, Courtney. *The New Metaphysicals: Spirituality and the American Religious Imagination*. Chicago: University of Chicago Press, 2010.

Biberman, Jerry and Michael Whitty. *Work and Spirit: A Reader of New Paradigms for Organizations*. Scranton, PA: University of Scranton Press, 2000.

Binkley, Sam. *Getting Loose: Lifestyle Consumption in the 1970s*. Durham: Duke University Press, 2007.

Bourdieu, Pierre. *Outline of a Theory of Practice*. Translated by Richard Nice. New York: Cambridge University Press, 1977.

Bourdieu, Pierre. *The Social Structures of the Economy*. Translated by Chris Turner. London: Polity Press, 2005.

Braunstein, Peter and Doyle, Michael William. *Imagine Nation: The American Counterculture of the 1960s and 70s*. New York: Routledge, 2002.

Brown, Schulyer. "Magic at the Conscious Capitalism Conference in San Francisco." *Huffington Post*, 9 April 2013.

Canfield, Jack, Hansen, Mark, Rogerson, Maida, Rutte, Martin, and Clauss, Tim. *Chicken Soup for the Soul at Work*. Deerfield Beach, FL: Health Communications, 1996.

Carrette, Jeremy and King, Richard. *Selling Spirituality: The Silent Takeover of Religion*. New York: Routledge, 2005.

Cavanagh, Gerald F. "Spirituality for Managers: Context and Critique." *Journal of Organizational Change Management* 12: 3 (1999).

Conger, Jay, ed. *Spirit at Work: Discovering the Spirituality in Leadership*. San Francisco: Jossey-Bass Publishers, 1994.

Csikszenmihalyi, Mihaly. *Flow: The Psychology of Optimal Experience*. New York: HarperCollins, 1990.

Denning, Steve. "The Best of Peter Drucker." *Forbes*, 29 July 2014.

Donkin, Richard. *The History of Work*. New York: Palgrave Macmillan, 2010.

Drucker, Peter. *The Age of Discontinuity: Guidelines to Our Changing Society*. New Brunswick and London: Transaction Publishers, 1992.

Drucker, Peter. *The New Realities*. New York and London: Routledge, 1989.

Drucker, Peter. *The Practice of Management*. New York: Harper, 1954.

Drucker, Peter. "Worker and Work in the Metropolis." *Daedalus* 97: 4 (1968).

Elliot, Larry and Teanor, Jill. "And Breathe… Goldie Hawn and a Monk Bring Meditation to Davos." *The Guardian*, 23 January 2014.

Engelhart, Matthew and Engelhart, Terces. *Sacred Commerce: Business as a Path to Spiritual Awakening*. Berkeley: North Atlantic Books, 2008.

Engelhart, Matthew and Engelhart, Terces. *The Abounding River: A Personal Logbook*. Berkeley: North Atlantic Books, 2007.

Essig, Todd. "Google Teaches Employees to 'Search Inside Yourself.'" *Forbes*, 30 April 2012.

Fadiman, James, Harman, Willis, Savage, Charles, and Savage, Ethel. "LSD: Therapeutic Effects of the Psychedelic Experience." *Psychological Reports* 14 (1964): 111–120.

Fairholm, Gilbert. *Capturing the Heart of Leadership: Spirituality and Community in the New American Workplace*. Westport, CT: Praeger Publishing, 1997.

Fischer, Claude S. and Hout, Michael. *Century of Difference: How America Changed in the Last One Hundred Years*. New York: Russell Sage Foundation, 2008.

Freud, Sigmund. *The Future of an Illusion*. New York: W.W. Norton & Co., 1990.

Friedman, Milton. *Capitalism and Freedom: Fortieth Anniversary Edition*. Chicago: University of Chicago Press, 2002.

Friedman, Milton. "The Social Responsibility of Business Is to Increase Profits." *The New York Times Magazine*, 13 September 1970.

Fukuyama, Francis. *The End of History and The Last Man*. New York: Free Press, 2006.

"Gas Fever: Happiness in a Full Tank." *Time Magazine*, 18 February 1974.

Gawain, Shakti. *Creative Visualization: Use the Power of Your Imagination to Create What You Want in Your Life*. Novato, CA: Nataraj Publishing, 2002 [1978].

Gawain, Shakti. *Living in the Light*, 25th Anniversary Edition. Novato, CA: New World Library, 2010 [1985].

Gelber, Steven M. and Martin L. Cook. *Saving the Earth: The History of a Middle-Class Millenarian Movement*. Berkeley: University of California Press, 1990.

Gonzalez, George J. *Shape-Shifting Capital: Spiritual Management, Critical Theory, and the Ethnographic Project*. Lanham, MD: Lexington Books, 2015, 11.

Greenleaf, Robert K. "A Forward Look at Management Development." *Transcript of Address to the Bureau of Industrial Relations*, University of Michigan: Ann Arbor, March 1958.

Greenleaf, Robert K. *On Becoming a Servant Leader: The Private Writings of Robert K. Greenleaf.* Edited by Don M. Frick and Larry C. Spears. San Francisco: Jossey-Bass, 1996.

Greenleaf, Robert K. *Servant Leadership: A Journey Into the Nature of Legitimate Power and Greatness.* New York: Paulist Press, 1977.

Greenleaf, Robert K. *The Servant-Leader Within: A Transformative Path.* Edited by Hamilton Beazley, Julie Braggs, and Larry C. Spears. Mahway, NJ: Paulist Press, 2003.

Grogan, Jessica. *Encountering America: Humanistic Psychology, Sixties Culture, and the Shaping of the Modern Self.* New York: Perennial, 2012.

Harman, Willis W. *An Incomplete Guide to the Future.* New York: W.W. Norton, 1979.

Harman, Willis W. "Creating a Sustainable Global Society—The Evolutionary Path." *World Futures: The Journal of New Paradigms Research* 47: 4 (1996).

Harman, Willis W. *Fundamentals of Electronic Motion.* New York: McGraw-Hill, 1953.

Harman, Willis W. *Global Mind Change: The New Age Revolution in the Way We Think.* New York: Warner Books, 1988.

Harman, Willis W. "Humanistic Capitalism: Another Alternative," *Journal of Humanistic Psychology* 14: 1 (1974).

Harman, Willis W. "Some Aspects of the Psychedelic-Drug Controversy." *Journal of Humanistic Psychology* 3 (1963).

Harman, Willis W. "The Emerging 'Wholeness' Worldview and Its Probable Impact on Cooperation." World Futures: *The Journal of New Paradigms Research* 31: 2 (1991).

Harman, Willis W. "The Voluntary Sector in a Time of Social Transformation." *Non-Profit and Voluntary Sector Quarterly* 2: 2 (1973): 112–115.

Harman, Willis and Maya Porter, eds. *The New Business of Business: Sharing Responsibility for a Global Future.* San Francisco: Berrett-Koehler Publishers, 1997.

Harvey, David. *A Brief History of Neoliberalism.* New York: Oxford University Press, 2005.

Heelas, Paul and Morris, Paul. *The Values of Enterprise Culture: The Moral Debate.* New York: Routledge, 1992.

Hicks, Douglas. *Religion and the Workplace: Pluralism, Spirituality, Leadership.* Cambridge: Cambridge University Press, 2003.

Hoffman, Edward. *The Right to Be Human: A Biography of Abraham Maslow.* Florida: John Wiley and Sons, Inc., 1999.

Isaacson, Walter. *Steve Jobs.* New York: Simon and Schuster, 2011.

Kaye, Les. *Zen at Work: A Zen Teacher's 30-year Journey in Corporate America.* New York: Three Rivers Press, 1996.

Kleiner, Art. *The Age of Heretics: A History of Radical Thinkers Who Reinvented Corporate Management.* San Francisco: Jossey-Bass, 2008.

Koppes, Laura L. *Historical Perspectives in Industrial and Organizational Psychology.* New York: Psychology Press, 2007.

Kripal, Jeffrey. *Esalen: America and the Religion of No Religion*. Chicago and London: University of Chicago Press, 2007.

Lambert III, Lake. *Spirituality Inc.: Religion in the American Workplace*. New York: New York University Press, 2009.

Lot, Stephanie M. "Google Tops Fortune's Best Places to Work (Again)." *PC Magazine*, 18 January 2013.

Lurie, Alan. *Five Minutes on Mondays: Finding Unexpected Purpose, Peace, and Fulfillment at Work*. Upper Saddle River, NJ: FT Press, 2009.

Lurie, Alan. "Work as a Spiritual Gymnasium." *Huffington Post*, 4 January 2012.

Mackey, John. "The Whole Foods Alternative to Obama Care." *The Wall Street Journal*, 11 August 2009.

Mackey, John and Sisodia, Raj. *Conscious Capitalism: Liberating the Heroic Spirit of Business*. Cambridge: Harvard Business Review Press, 2013.

Mackey, John and Strong, Michael. *Be the Solution: How Entrepreneurs and Conscious Capitalists Can Solve All the World's Problems*. Hoboken, NJ: John Wiley and Sons, 2009.

March, James G. *Handbook of Organizations*. Chicago: Rand-McNalley, 1965.

Maslow, Abraham. "A Theory of Human Motivation." *Psychological Review* 50 (1943): 370–396.

Maslow, Abraham. *Maslow on Management*. New York: John Wiley and Sons, Inc., 1998.

Maslow, Abraham. *Motivation and Personality*. New York: Harper, 1954.

Maslow, Abraham. *Religion, Values, and Peak Experiences*. New York: Penguin Compass, 1970.

Massey, Doreen. "Vocabularies of the Economy." *Soundings* 54 (2013).

McCutcheon, Russell. *Critics Not Caretakers: Redescribing the Public Study of Religion*. New York: SUNY Press, 2001.

McGregor, Douglas. *The Human Side of Enterprise: Annotated Edition*. New York: McGraw-Hill, 2006.

McGregor, Douglas. "The Human Side of Enterprise." *Leadership and Motivation, Essays of Douglas McGregor*. Edited by W. G. Bennis and E. H. Schein. Cambridge, MA: MIT Press, 1966.

Melley, Timothy. *Empire of Conspiracy: The Culture of Paranoia in Postwar America*. Ithaca, NY: Cornell University Press, 2000.

Merkle, Judith. *Management and Ideology: The Legacy of the International Scientific Management Movement*. Berkeley and Los Angeles: University of California Press, 1980.

Miller, David W. *God at Work: The History and Promise of the Faith at Work Movement*. New York: Oxford University Press, 2007.

Millman, John, Ferguson, Jerry, Trickett, David, and Condemi, Bruce. "Spirit and Community at Southwest Airlines: An Investigation of a Spiritual Values-based Model." *Journal of Organizational Change Management* 12: 3 (1999): 221–233.

Mills, C. Wright. *White Collar: The American Middle Classes, 50th Anniversary Edition.* New York: Oxford University Press, 2002.

Mirvis, Philip. "Soul Work in Organizations." *Organization Science* 8: 2 (1997): 193–206.

Mitroff, Ian and Denton, Elizabeth. *A Spiritual Audit of Corporate America: A Hard Look at Spirituality, Religion, and Values in the Workplace.* San Francisco: Jossey-Boss, 1999.

Mitroff, Ian and Denton, Elizabeth. "A Study of Spirituality in the Workplace." *Sloan Management Review* (Summer, 1999).

Moreton, Bethany. *To Serve God and Wal-Mart.* Cambridge: Harvard University Press, 2009.

Neal, Judith. *Edwalkers: People and Organizations That Take Risks, Build Bridges, and Break New Ground.* Westport, CT: Praeger Publishers, 2006.

Neal, Judith. "Spirituality in Management Education: A Guide to Resources." *Journal of Management Education* 21 (1997).

Neal, Judith A., Benyamin M. Bergmann Lichtenstein, and David Banner. "Spiritual Perspectives on Individual, Organizational, and Societal Change." *Journal of Organizational Change Management* 12: 3 (1999).

Palmer, Parker. *Let Your Life Speak: Listening for the Voice of Vocation.* San Francisco: Jossey-Bass, 2000.

Palmer, Parker. *The Active Life: A Spirituality of Work, Creativity, and Caring.* San Francisco: Jossey-Bass, 1999.

Paumgarten, Nick. "Does Whole Foods' C.E.O. Know What's Best For You?" *New Yorker*, 4 January 2010.

Peck, Jamie. *Constructions of Neoliberal Reason.* New York: Oxford University Press, 2013, xiii.

Peters, Thomas and Waterman, Robert. *In Search of Excellence: Lessons from America's Best Run Companies.* New York: HarperBusiness, 1982.

Porth, Stephen J., John McCall, and Thomas A. Bausch, "Spiritual Themes of the 'learning organization.'" *Journal of Organizational Change Management* 12: 3 (1999).

Rand, Ayn. *Capitalism: The Unknown Ideal.* New York: Penguin Group, 1967.

Roszak, Theodore. *The Making of A Counter Culture.* Berkeley: University of California Press, 1995.

Schucman, Helen. *A Course in Miracles Combined Volume: Preface, Text, Workbook for Students, Clarification of Terms, Supplements*, 3rd Edition. Mill Valley, CA: Foundation for Inner Peace, 2007.

Sennett, Richard. *The Culture of the New Capitalism.* New Haven: Yale University, 2006.

Shaw, Robert and Colimore, Karen. "Humanistic Psychology as Ideology: An Analysis of Maslow's Contradictions." *Journal of Humanistic Psychology* 28: 3 (1998).

Sheff, David. "Steve Jobs." *Playboy*, February 1985.

Stiglitz, Joseph E. *Globalization and Its Discontents.* New York: W.W. Norton, 2003.

Tapscott, Don. *The Digital Economy: Promise and Peril in the Age of Networked Intelligence.* New York: McGraw-Hill, 1997.

Taylor, Eugene. *Shadow Culture: Psychology and Spirituality in America.* Washington DC: Counterpoint Press, 1999.

Taylor, Frederick Winslow. *Principles of Scientific Management.* Lexington, KY: ReadaClassic.com, 2010.

Tipton, Steven. *Getting Saved From the Sixties: Moral Meaning in Conversion and Cultural Change.* Berkeley: University of California Press, 1984.

Vasquez, Manuel A. and Marquardt, Marie Friedmann. *Globalizing the Sacred: Religion Across the Americas.* New Brunswick: Rutgers University Press, 2003.

Weber, Max. *The Protestant Ethic and the Spirit of Capitalism.* Translated by Talcott Parsons. New York: Routledge, 2006.

Whyte, William H. *The Organization Man, New ED edition.* Philadelphia: University of Pennsylvania Press, 2002.

Woolman, John. *Considerations on the Keeping of Negroes: Recommended to the Professors of Christianity of Every Denomination.* Originally published in Philadelphia: Tract Association of Friends. Full text available at http://www.archive.org.

Work in America: Report of a Special Task Force to the Secretary of Health, Education, and Welfare. Cambridge: MIT Press, 1973.

Wuthnow, Robert. *After Heaven: Spirituality in America Since the 1950s.* Berkeley: University of California Press, 1998.

Internet References

"The Abounding River Boardgame." *Graphicgirlz.* http://www.graphicgirlz.com/cafe/boardgame.html.

"Abounding River Workshop." *Gracias Madre.* http://gracias-madre.com/2013/03/03/207/.

"About Carol." *Carol Fox Prescott.* http://carolfoxprescott.com/about/.

"About Greenleaf University." *Greenleaf University, Institute for Professional Studies, An American Graduate School,* 2014, http://greenleaf.edu/about.htm.

"About Our Practice." *Café Gratitude.* http://cafegratitude.com/about-our-practice/.

"About Us." *Conscious Capitalism.* www.consciouscapitalism.org/aboutus.

"About Willis Harman." *World Business Academy.* http://www.worldbusiness.org/about/about-willis-harman/.

Barrett, Richard. "Spiritual Unfoldment at the World Bank." *Paraview.* 1998. http://www.paraview.com/features/unfolding.htm.

"Biography." *Joshua M. Greene Official Website.* http://www.atma.org/biography/.

Buxton, Dickson and Zweig, David. "Paul N. Temple." *Merchants of Vision.* https://worldbusiness.org/publications/merchants-of-vision-january-19-2006/.

"Clients." *Institute for Mindful Leadership.* http://instituteformindfulleadership.org/clients/.

"Consciousness Matters." Institute for Noetic Sciences. http://noetic.org/about/vision/.

Conwell, Russell. "Acres of Diamonds." *Temple.edu.*

"Courses and Workshops." *Institute for Mindful Leadership.* http:// instituteformindfulleadership.org/course-and-workshops/.

"Definitions." *Institute for Mindful Leadership.* http://instituteformindfulleadership.org/ definitions/.

Doucet, Bradley. "The Life of Ayn Rand." *The Atlas Society: Objectivism in Life and Thought.* http://www.atlassociety.org/life-biography-of-ayn-rand.

"Drucker's Childhood and Youth in Vienna." *Drucker Society of Austria.* http://www. druckersociety.at/index.php/peterdruckerhome/biography.

Dunn, Drew. "Interview with Les Kaye." *Crooked Cucumber.* http://www.cuke.com/ Cucumber%20Project/interviews/kaye-z&b.html.

"Flow Activation Centers." *FLOW: Liberating the Entrepreneurial Spirit for Good.* Accessed 15 June 2013. http://www.flowidealism.org/Community/FAC.html.

Frick, Don M. "Robert Greenleaf: A Short Biography." *Robert Greenleaf Center for Servant Leadership.* https://greenleaf.org/about-us/about-robert-k-greenleaf/.

Gilgoff, Dan. "How Davos Found God." *CNN: Belief Blog.* Accessed 28 January 2011. http://religion.blogs.cnn.com/2011/01/28/how-davos-found-god/.

"Grants and Awards." *World Business Academy.* http://noetic.org/about/grants-and-awards/.

Hertzfeld, Andy. "Reality Distortion Field." *Folklore.org.* http://folklore.org/StoryView. py?story=Reality_Distortion_Field.txt.

"History." *Tyson Center for Faith and Spirituality in the Workplace.* http://tfsw.uark.edu/ history.asp.

"History of Atlas Shrugged." *Ayn Rand Novels.* http://aynrandnovels.org/learning-more/atlas-shrugged/history-of-atlas-shrugged.html.

"History of Kannon Do." *Kannon Do.* http://www.kannondo.org/about-us/ history-of-kannon-do.

"Intersections." *Collegiate Churches of New York.* http://www.collegiatechurch.org/ ?q=content/intersections.

"Interview with Les Kaye." *Dharma Web.* http://www.dharmaweb.org/index.php/Les_ Kaye_Roshi_-_Kannon_Do_Zen.

Management Movement. Berkeley: University of California Press, 1980.

Neal, Judi. "Bio." *Judith Neal and Associates.* http://www.judineal.com/pages/corporate/ nealbio.html.

Ng, Annie N. L, Corrine L. Y. Chong, Josiah Y. X. Ching, Jowell H. H. Beh, Patricia P. F. Lim. "A Critical Comparison of the Psychoanalytic and Humanistic Theory." https:// www.academia.edu/7304762/A_Critical_Comparison_of_the_Psychoanalytic_and_ Humanistic_Theory.

Nixon, Richard M. "Address to the Nation on Labor Day, September 6, 1971," courtesy of *The American Presidency Project*, University of California, Santa Barbara, http:// www.presidency.ucsb.edu/ws/?pid=3138.

"Port Huron Statement of the Students for a Democratic Society, 1962." *Humanities and Social Sciences Online*. http://www.h-net.org/~hst306/documents/huron.html.

"Rev. Sarah Q. Hargrave, Staff Minister." *Golden Gate Center for Spiritual Living*. Accessed 16 April 2014. http://www.ggcsl.org/ministry/rev_hargrave.html.

"Sacred Commerce Workshop." *Café Gratitude Facebook Site*. https://www.facebook.com/events/540540045992796/.

"Spirit At Work: A Continuing Conversation." *San Francisco Chamber of Commerce*. Accessed 14 April 2014. http://members.sfchamber.com/events/Spirit-at- Work-2462/details.

"Steve Jobs' College Mentor was a Drug Dealer Turned Billionaire Mining Magnet." *Daily Caller*. Accessed 24 October 2011. http://dailycaller.com/2011/10/24/steve-jobs-college-mentor-was-a-drug-dealer-turned-billionaire-mining-magnate-aapl/.

Truman, Sarah E. "Samadhi in Space: An Interview with Apollo 14 Astronaut Dr. Edgar Mitchell." *Ascent*, 2007. http://www.ascentmagazine.com/articles.aspx?articleID=195&issueID=30.

Tyson Center for Faith and Spirituality in the Workplace. Accessed 12 April 2014. http://tfsw.uark.edu/.

"Walton History." *University of Arkansas*. Accessed 10 April 2014. https://waltoncollege.uark.edu/history.asp.

"What We Do: Organizational Reinvention." *LPR Group*. Accessed 12 March 2014. http://www.lprgroup.com/orgreinvention.php.

Index

9 781350 081208